Garry Brown's
GREATEST HITS

GARRY BROWN'S GREATEST HITS

Columns & Stories from Sixty-Four Years in Journalism

GARRY BROWN

Levellers Press
AMHERST, MASSACHUSETTS

Published by *Levellers Press*, Amherst, Massachusetts

Printed in the United States of America

ISBN 978-1-937146-96-2

"Keep it short and make it sparkle."

—Advice from my boss, Dutch Robbins, before I wrote my first game story for *The Springfield Union*, July, 1950.

This book is dedicated to:

—*My wife, Mary Bukowski Brown, who always has understood the heart and soul of a newspaperman.*

—*Our children, Melissa, Peter and Paul, who gave their love and writing/editing skills to this volume.*

—*Peter's wife, Meng-Shiou Shieh, who encourages me to keep writing and working.*

—*Our grandchildren, Sonia, Conlan, Kanya and Rayna, who provide the inspiration for many of the columns in this collection.*

Table of Contents

Foreword

by *Paul A. Brown*

I PRACTICALLY GREW UP AT FENWAY PARK. This was one of the perks of having a father whose main beat as a sportswriter involved coverage of the Boston Red Sox for the Springfield Newspapers. For a span of about 35 years – a blink of an eye considering the span of his ongoing association with the Springfield news publications which dates back to 1950 – Dad made the schlep back and forth to Fenway Park. Often his beat would take him on the road for extended excursions to Winter Haven, Florida and later Fort Myers as well as various big league parks in the lower 48 and Canada.

Between time on the road and his obligations as Sports Editor, Dad would spend many a night away from his family. Ever mindful of maintaining quality time with his brood, oftentimes the family would accompany him to Fenway, especially for weekend day games. (He would get complimentary tickets from the Red Sox Media Relations Department) Back in the '70s, the Red Sox were constantly teetering on the edge of breaking the curse (losing the '75 World series to the Cincinnati Reds after a startling Game 6 comeback on Carlton Fisk's 12th-inning homer) but they weren't the powerhouse World Series contenders they have grown to be in this century. Fenway Park of the '70s was more accessible to working-class New Englanders than it is now. Back in those days above the Green Monstah was "nothin' but net" – to steal a line from another sport – and bleacher seats could be had for less than $2.00. Baseball wasn't the money-driven machine that it is today. Games were shorter and length of game was not dictated by a television network's scheduling block. In those days, the Fenway Faithful could sit through a doubleheader in the time it would take to trudge through nine innings today. If we weren't commuting, we would stay overnight. Room 104 at the Fenway Howard Johnson was our home away from home and section 29 underneath the shed in left field was our roost.

Those were magical times. My heroes were always just that far away, playing that amazingly unpredictable game. More amazing to me was the fact that Dad's job enabled him to talk to these men and report back to the general public what we all wanted to know. And he did it with style, ease and grace.

The usual routine was, he did his job, we enjoyed the games and we waited for him to write and file his story. Then we as a family would frequent some of the more touristy spots in Boston for dinner or a movie.

Back in the 1970s, reporting a game story wasn't as easy as hitting a send button. These stories were typed on paper and sometimes read verbatim over the phone to someone on the copydesk back at the sports department who would retype what Dad had written. By 1977, I believe he had access to what Hunter S. Thompson had dubbed "the Mojo wire" – a teletype machine which could transmit a facsimile of his written text over the phone. This sped up the process. But in a game as unpredictable as baseball one lesson I had to learn was patience.

In June of 1977, I had just turned 13. I was already a sci-fi geek and a card-carrying member of the James Doohan Fan Club. (Chief Engineer Montgomery Scott from the Starship Enterprise) I already had been to a Star Trek convention. So when the buzz on the street about a new movie called *Star Wars* hit home, I knew I had to go. It was June 18, 1977. The Sox were playing the New York Yankees at Fenway. The plan was, Dad would cover the game, then we would head to Quincy Market for a quick dinner at Durgin Park, after which we would go to the movie theater near Government Center for the 7 p.m. showing of *Star Wars*.

The game was pretty exciting. Captain Carl Yastrzemski drove in five runs with two homers, Bernie Carbo put two solo shots into the net above Lansdowne St. and George Scott also homered with his 17th of the season. The Red Sox won 10–4, but the real excitement came in the sixth inning when Jim Rice popped a short flyball to right fielder Reggie Jackson. Reggie didn't get to the ball in time and Rice turned it into a double. Yankees manager Billy Martin exploded. He removed Reggie from the game, and confronted him in the dugout for his lack of hustle. Martin had to be physically restrained by Yogi Berra from brawling with Jackson.

After the game, my dad and his buddy, *Boston Globe* columnist Ray Fitzgerald, caught wind that Reggie was going to forgo the usual player's exit and would slip out of Fenway Park through the main ticket office on Jersey Street. They rushed down from the press box and chased after Mr. October in a sudden downpour, trying to get his side of the story. They persisted until Jackson slipped into a cab near the Howard Johnson in Kenmore Square.

Plans changed. Dad would meet us at the theater for the 9 o'clock show since there was no way he would make it for 7. My mom, my brother and I went to Quincy Market where the sights, sounds and smells did not disappoint. There was an organ grinder with a capuchin monkey dressed as a bellhop who would take nickels, dimes and quarters, place them in a pouch about his waist and kindly tip his hat. The monkey was so well-trained, he refused to accept copper. That night we also encountered a sword swallower – a grizzled, tattooed, bare-chested chap who said, "down the hatch without a scratch," as a 19-inch blade slipped past his gullet.

We sauntered back to the theater at a leisurely pace, only to find a large crowd in line being given the news that the 9 p.m. show had sold out.

After covering the Red Sox game, chasing Reggie Jackson in a soaking rain through the streets of Boston, filing both a game story and a side feature story about the incident between Billy Martin and Reggie Jackson, Dad finally joined us at the theater. It had been such a full and exciting day, he easily could have said, "It's been a long day. We're all tired, so let's see the movie another time." But that didn't happen. He bought tickets for the midnight show. We passed the time, him telling us the story about chasing Reggie Jackson around Boston. My mother had pad and pencil in her pocketbook, so we played Hangman as we waited for the movie. Finally, the moment came when the theater emptied and those who were departing were grinning ear to ear. Armed with popcorn and wide-eyed wonderment, we entered the auditorium. The lights dimmed and those magic words appeared:

"A long time ago in a galaxy far, far away."

That was a spectacular day.

A typical day in my life, growing up under the care of Garry Brown usually involved the following situation, which would have one of two outcomes. We'd be in a public place, such as a restaurant or store, when a stranger, to me, would walk up and begin speaking to my father like they were long-lost acquaintances perhaps even close friends who had drifted apart. The person would walk up to my father with a smile, right hand outstretched, and when they connected my father would make eye contact as the person said something like,

"Great column, this morning, Garry!" or "Do you think the Sox are going to let Pedro go as a free agent?" or "How is the Labrador retriever?"

After those meetings I would ask, "Dad, who was that?" His response was usually, accompanied by a humble smile as he shrugged his shoulders and said, "I don't know." Really, being out in public with my father is like being in the presence of a rock star. What awed me was the second outcome of the previous interaction, Where my father would recognize the person who was complimenting him on a column and would say, "I remember you…" He then would go on to recall statistics or a play from a game he covered when the former athlete was in high school decades earlier. The guy could only stand there, flabbergasted.

People often come up to him and comment on his weekly column "Hitting to All Fields." He gets most comments regarding the goings-on of the three generations of Labrador retrievers who have peppered his column with their antics. People who don't necessarily like sports read his column because they can identify with lines like "Honk if you remember Haystacks Calhoun."

His column is a series of one-liners highlighting current events, such as who is hot in various sports and leagues. Sometimes he may include a brief endorsement of a movie, or "Ye Old Handicapper" will appear with his pick for an upcoming horse race. Although, it would be wise not to put money on Garry's picks as Springfield lawyer Ron Kidd pointed out in an email with the subject line, "Only You… " Dad thought the email was going to be about the Platters' hit song, but the content of the email read, "… could take an undefeated horse and turn it into an also ran."

What you will find in this book is a journalistic memoir. It is a collection of Garry's favorite columns, many of which have nothing to do with sports. It will give a glimpse into the world of a man who entered the field of journalism when a brigade of reporters, copy editors, gofers, engravers, linotype operators, fully-staffed composing rooms and shifts of pressmen were necessary to produce three daily newspapers and a Sunday paper. He is still writing, keeping up with the times, filing his stories through email and even blogging when he covered his last live sporting event, a Falcons AHL playoff hockey game at the Springfield Mass Mutual Center.

Garry demonstrates his knack for writing by bringing back to life Indian Orchard, a small town main street where he grew up, with articles about a marbles champion who would later become his sports editor; or his father, the writer/assistant postmaster who gave him his first trip to Fenway Park where he saw his idol, Bobby Doerr play and where his father taught him how to keep a box-score. That story concluded with Garry having the opportunity to meet and interview Bobby Doerr at a Red Sox old-timers day.

The content of this book is vivid, rich and full of textures and emotions which can only come from the mind of a man who has been writing about the subjects he knows and loves, every day, for 66 years and counting.

– Paul A. Brown, *January 2016.*

Introduction

I WAS 18 YEARS OLD, WITH ONE FINAL EXAM TO GO before completion of my freshman year at American International College.

I was at home, 154 Myrtle Street, Indian Orchard, studying for that last exam. It would be a buster, because it would be given by a real taskmaster, U.S. history professor John Mitchell.

The phone rang at around 2 in the afternoon. To my everlasting surprise, the call came from Dutch Robbins, one of the old-timers in *The Springfield Union*'s sports department.

"We have a job opening. Are you interested?" he said.

"Well…yes. Absolutely," I said, stammering all the way.

"Come in today, and we'll give you a trial. Work starts at 4 o'clock," he said. Then he hung up, leaving me in shock.

Dutch knew me because I had been going into the Springfield Newspapers building on Cypress Street since I was 12 years old. My dad, an Indian Orchard Post Office employee, had a part-time job, covering the Orchard for *The Springfield Daily News*. Four or five nights a week, he would drive downtown and we would go up to the second floor of the newspaper office, where he would leave his pile of news items on the desk of Frank Kelly, managing editor of *The Daily News*.

His office was adjacent to the sports department. At that time of night, *The Union*'s sports staff would be on duty. My dad often would stop there to hand them a brief story about an Orchard Twilight League game.

One night, my dad asked me if I wanted to write the baseball story. I loved the idea, and pounded out three paragraphs on his old Underwood typewriter.

We handed my story to Vic Wall, another of *The Union*'s old-timers. In seconds flat, he edited my story, blue-penciling most of it.

"Sit down and take another crack at it," he said.

I did, carefully noting how he had edited the first one.

The next morning, my rewritten story appeared in the sports section. What a thrill.

I kept doing those little stories for my dad, and Dutch and Vic apparently noticed some improvement. That's what led to the phone call.

I took that three-day trial, and was hired full time. I left AIC for a year to concentrate on the job. Then I went back, going to school days and working nights. I graduated at the age of 22, and along the way met my future wife in a world lit class.

Some 59 years later, I retired from my sportswriting job, but I soon resumed writing for *The Springfield Republican* as a free-lancer. I wanted to keep busy in retirement, and writing was the right way for me.

Over all those years, and right into 2016, I have done so many stories and columns, I shudder at what the word count must be. In this volume, I have collected some of my favorite pieces, not all of them sports-related, from my years of writing for *The Springfield Republican* and *Union.* It's a labor of love – and it all began with a phone call I shall never forget.

– Garry Brown, *January, 2016*

Early Train Out of Town

This column was written Sept. 11, 2001, soon after disaster struck New York City.

New York in September. I would be covering a four-game series between the Boston Red Sox and New York Yankees, starting Friday and running through Monday. That meant free time in the mornings Friday and Monday, free time in the evenings Saturday and Sunday.

Hey, we said, let's go down early. Maybe we can get theater tickets.

So it was that my wife, Mary, and I boarded an early train on Thursday, Sept. 6, 2001, bound for The City That Never Sleeps. The main focus on the trip would be baseball writing, of course. Mary understood that only too well after 40-something years of marriage to a newspaperman.

Thursday went beautifully. We walked over to Times Square, and soon had acquired some half-priced tickets to "The Full Monty," playing at the Eugene O'Neill Theater on 49th St. It was a perfect setup, an uproariously good show within walking distance of our hotel.

Friday included a trip through Bloomingdale's to check those New York prices, followed by a visit to the Radio and Television Museum near Rockefeller Center.

After my weekend's work covering afternoon ballgames, the evenings consisted of dinner at neighborhood restaurants and leisurely walks along

Second and Third Avenue.

Come Monday morning (after the Red Sox had dropped three in a row), we set out for a trip to Ellis Island, where Mary's father, Piotr I. Bukowski, twice had come through its immigration station as a teen-age boy from Poland. He first arrived in 1914, but was sent back because he had little money and nobody to meet him and vouch for him (his older brother Frank, who was then living in Three Rivers, Mass., was supposed to take care of that, but missed connections). Piotr soon made another crossing, and that time his brother and other relatives were there to meet him, so he was allowed to stay.

Memories of "Jaju" – our kids' pet name for their beloved grandfather – led us to New York's historic Battery Park on a beautiful morning. We wanted to see The Great Hall through which he passed on his way to a new life. We wanted to look up his record. And there it was, his name on a ship's manifest, steerage class.

As we boarded the ferry for Ellis Island we looked back at a breath-taking sight. Lower Manhattan gleamed in the September sunlight, the twin towers of the World Trade Center dominating our view of America's financial heartland.

After an inspiring tour of the museum on Ellis Island, we ferried back to the Battery. It soon would be time for my final baseball assignment of this trip. We decided to take a cab back to our hotel – it was just too nice a day to go underground. The driver whisked past the World Trade Center, which loomed over us in all its power and glory.

At Yankee Stadium that night, a thunderstorm drenched the field, but Yankee management made every effort to play. I called Mary and told her the game might not start until 9 o'clock. I suggested that we take a later train in the morning, because I might not get through working until well after midnight.

"No," she said, "let's go early, anyway. I don't know what it is, but I just have a feeling that we should leave early. You can sleep on the train. I'll have the bags packed. And let's not hang around for breakfast. You can grab something at the train station."

Anyway, the game finally was rained out, so I had no problem getting up early. At Mary's urging, we easily caught the 7:05 out of Penn Station, though I still wondered why I had to give up breakfast at the hotel, and I still didn't get why Mary kept insisting that we get out of town early.

Shortly after 9 a.m., our daughter Melissa called from Springfield.

"Where are you?" she asked in a voice that sounded panicky.

"We're on the train, just pulling out of Stamford," I said.

"Oh, thank God!" she said. Then she told us the terrible news.

How close we had come. One morning removed from tragedy, two hours removed from being stranded amid the chaos that grips New York.

We sat back quietly and held hands. It was time for prayer.

Where Have You Gone, Superman?

News item: A near-mint condition copy of "Action Comics No. 1," published in June 1938 and featuring the debut of Superman, sells at auction for $2.161 million.

I walked into Mr. Riordan's store on Oak Street, Indian Orchard, with my best friend, Marty Rickson, at my side. We headed straight for the magazine rack – and there it was, "Action Comics No. 1."

We both bought a copy, then raced up Oak Street and across Cottage Hill Park to my front porch. There, rocking in a swing built for two, we devoured "The Adventures of Superman."

It was all new and wonderful, the story of a crime-fighting superhero. He would go on to have his own radio show, which always began with the announcer intoning, "Faster than a speeding bullet, more powerful than a locomotive, able to leap tall buildings in a single bound!"

At the age of 6 going on 7, I didn't really know what a locomotive was, but it sure sounded impressive.

Memories of that special June day in 1938 came rushing back recently as I did my obligatory surfing on the internet. Suddenly, an image of that Action Comics cover flashed on my computer screen. There it was – the very magazine I had in my hands so many years ago. At the time, it cost one thin dime. Now it was worth...$2.161 million?

Eventually, my first edition copy of Action Comics – featuring the one and only "Man of Steel" – wound up in a pile at the back of my bedroom closet. There, it joined Detective Comics, starring Batman and Robin; and DC Comics, featuring Captain Marvel and Wonder Woman. Oh, yes, that closet also contained the exploits of the Green Hornet, Green Lantern, Plastic Man and Captain America, among others.

What happened to all those classic comic books? As I well remember, my dear mother threw them out during one of her spring-cleaning binges. Collectors and auctioneers estimate that only 50 to 100 copies of Action Comics No. 1 remain in existence today – and we all know why.

The $2.161 million copy was found in a Los Angeles storage locker. It gained a 9.0 rating on a scale of 10 by comic-book aficionados because it had been so well preserved while in the middle of a stack of other magazines.

No such stack in my closet, sad to say.

I loved my mother, but she and I differed when it came to certain "collectibles" in my possession. Another case in point – my all-time favorite baseball team, the Boston Red Sox of 1946.

One day, my father saw me pasting Red Sox clippings into a scrapbook, which I had started on Opening Day of '46 and kept throughout that season. In June, he did a fatherly thing – took me to my first game at Fenway. On the way out of the park, he bought me a full set of photographs of Red Sox players, 8 by 10s yet.

I loved those photos so much, I tacked all 25 of them – even those of little-known relievers like Mike Ryba and Mace Brown – to my bedroom wall.

They lasted through the '46 season and the World Series (let's not talk about that), but not much longer. One day, my mother said it was time for them to go. Farewell, Bobby Doerr.

If you lived through that era, you know about other collectibles that eventually made their way to the dump. For instance, I had an Army of lead soldiers which my mother ordered gone – and I can thank her for saving me from lead poisoning.

Many other "collectibles" also disappeared over the years, and not always during spring cleaning. I just can't remember whatever happened to my Springfield Indians games programs from the late 1940s, or my collection of baseball cards, featuring Ted Williams and Joltin' Joe DiMaggio. Also long lost – the flashy little "two-way wrist radio" I had obtained by mail

from Dick Tracy comics. Moving out of our old house probably had something to do with loss of those treasures.

Hey, such loss happens with every generation. My mother-in-law and I were the best of friends, but she did have the bothersome knack of tossing away stuff she deemed to be junk. In most cases, she was right, but our oldest son still longs for a baseball card collection that included Carl Yastrzemski of the Red Sox and his favorite National Leaguer, a little-known New York Mets pitcher named Bill Hepler.

Yes, my friend Jennie took care of that collection one day when she decided that our son's bedroom had just too much clutter. Nothing new there. She had done the same thing with some of my wife's old favorites from her girlhood – like her very own copy of Action Comics No. 1, purchased at Hastings' in downtown Chicopee.

Oh, well, now we see that Superman is back, soaring across movie screens in an outfit that doesn't quite match his original image. No red shorts, and a costume fabric that looks more like leathery lizard skin.

Sorry, but that's just not right. The genuine Superman suit, as designed by Jerry Siegel and Joe Shuster, can be seen on the cover of that unforgettable 1938 comic book.

Wish I had one. Don't we all?

The Greatest Sox

Note: This column was written Oct. 26, 2004, after the Boston Red Sox ended an 86-year wait by winning the World Series.

Boston had its "Miracle Braves" in 1914. Now it has its "Miracle Red Sox," writing a new and glorious page in baseball history.

Those Braves, featuring Springfield's own Rabbit Maranville at shortstop, swept the World Series 90 years ago in a comeback that has marked them for the ages.

Now, though, the Miracle Braves have been topped. Boston and the rest of New England has never seen a team like the 2004 Red Sox – one of the best of all time, playing right before our very eyes, winning a World Series in four straight and finally putting an end to the so-called "Curse of the Bambino."

It happened last night at Busch Stadium in St. Louis. Sweep. A quick path to baseball glory. A new era for Red Sox baseball, guaranteed to give their loyal fans catharsis from too many years of heartbreak.

The Curse of the Bambino is nonsense, of course, New England's masochistic way of flagellating itself for 86 years of Red Sox failure to win the World Series. Babe Ruth – The Bambino – did not curse the Sox after they sold him to the Yankees in 1919, but it was a convenient way for us to blame losing on some-

thing more than the normal course of events in Red Sox history.

Well, no more of that. Take that Curse and stuff it. Instead, take 2004 and substitute it for 1918 – the last year the Red Sox won this thing. No need to hark back to that misty past and wish that the Sox could be now what they were then, winners of five of the first 14 World Series.

No need for any more of that, because this team simply is the greatest. Better than any of those five World Series winners? Absolutely. There simply is no comparison between baseball of the 21st century and baseball of the early 20th. It was so much easier then. Win the pennant and go to the World Series. Simple as that.

Just think how hard it is to win the modern-day World Series. Eight teams qualify for the playoffs, which means that a team must win 11 games – three in the first round, four in the league championship round, four in the World Series – before it can claim the big prize. That's a mini-season of pressure play, packed into three weeks. And all that after playing a longer schedule – 162 games – than those old-time teams had to deal with. They played 154 games, except for that 1918 team, which played a shortened version because of United States involvement in World War I.

Yes, it was easier back then, no matter what the old-timers might say. They didn't play night games. They didn't travel across the country to play Game 4 one night, Game 5 the next afternoon as sometimes happens in 21st century ball.

Boston's sweet sweep of the St. Louis Cardinals leaves a longtime writer (and secret fan) wondering what we all should do now. How, for instance, does New England react to this? What do we have to complain about now? It was easy to moan about the Red Sox and pick on them when they kept letting us down. Now they have shown us the glory of winning a World Series, and it's almost too much to bear.

We can take it, though. Just like New England Patriots fans, we will learn to deal with being champions. It'll just take a little while, maybe after the big parade is over in Boston. Then it will settle in: Boston Red Sox, 2004 World Series winners.

Just think. When spring training comes, everyone will be referring to them as the "defending world champion Red Sox." Can you believe it? Would you have believed it going into the third weekend of October, when they were three down to the New York Yankees and trying to recover from a 19-8 hammering in Game 3 of the American League Championship Series?

Boston's comeback to win that series may be the greatest of all time.

Sure, the Miracle Braves came from last place to win the pennant. Sure, Leo Durocher's 1951 New York Giants erased a 13½-game deficit to catch the Brooklyn Dodgers before beating them on Bobby Thomson's "Shot heard 'round the world" in a National League playoff. Sure, the New York Yankees came from 14 out to break Boston hearts in 1978.

Great comebacks, but is there anything better than this one? One inning away from elimination by the Yankees – remember, the Sox trailed 4-3 going into the ninth of Game 4 – and now this? It just doesn't get any better. Beating the Yankees, whom many Red Sox players refer to as "a great team," was enough to stamp the Bostonians in our memories forever. Yet it was merely the first step to the greater glory they now celebrate with Red Sox fans across the land.

Red Sox pitcher Pedro Martinez said that every game with the Yankees this season "was like a World Series game." The Sox wound up beating the Yankees 15 times from April to October. That should have told us all we needed to know about them. No doubt about it – they are the greatest team in the history of the Red Sox franchise. Better than the first World Series winners of 1903. Better than the Smoky Joe Wood team of 1912. And yes, better than any Boston team of the Babe Ruth era.

We salute them. Now we have to learn how to feel like champions, because that day finally has arrived.

Go Sox.

When the Post 21 Kids Came Home

IT BEGAN WITH A ROUSING SENDOFF at Springfield's Union Station. Fifteen kids in their Sunday best posed for a newspaper photographer, then clambered aboard the waiting train.

Representing Springfield Post 21, they were bound for Gastonia, North Carolina, and a shot at the American Legion junior baseball national championship.

When they arrived, they soon learned all they would ever want to know about the segregated South of 1934.

Instead of being greeted in the style befitting a team that had earned a place in the Eastern semifinals, they were greeted by the ugly face of racism. The presence of a black player on the Springfield team simply would not be tolerated.

Manager Sid Harris was told Ernest "Bunny" Taliaferro could not stay at the tournament headquarters hotel with his 14 white teammates. Later, after a harrowing day on the streets of Gastonia and at the field where the tournament would be played, Harris was told Taliaferro would not be allowed to play.

The situation grew menacing. Threats were made against Taliaferro and his teammates. Harris received a phone call saying that he would be "found in an alley." Bottles and rocks were thrown at the players as they tried to take part in a workout. By the end of the day, Harris and Coach Babe Steere feared for their players' safety.

Off they went to Charlotte, 20 miles south of Gastonia, where they were told accommodations would be available. When they got there, Harris told his players the awful truth: "They say we can play, but Bunny can't."

Then he said, "We can play, or we can go home. What do you want to do?"

Daniel M. Keyes, now a retired Chicopee District Court judge, played on that team as a backup infielder. He remembers the scene vividly, even though it happened 69 years ago. "Somebody said, 'Let's go home.' Then we all said it. Bunny was our best player, but that wasn't the point. We would have voted the same way if they had told us our batboy couldn't be with us. We just knew what we had to do. If he couldn't play, we wouldn't play."

The team, which had been so excited about its first long train ride, now faced another – a sleeper out of Charlotte back to Springfield via New York City.

Harris arranged for his players to see a game at Yankee Stadium before they headed back to Springfield. (One Post 21 player referred to the Yankee game as a "booby prize.")

When they returned to Union Station, an estimated crowd of 1,000 greeted them. They were treated like homecoming heroes, and rightly so.

Their stand against racism – all the more remarkable because of their age – came 14 years before Jackie Robinson broke major league baseball's color line, and 29 years before the Rev. Martin Luther King Jr. delivered his "I have a dream" speech.

Lawyer Linda C. Taliaferro of Harrisburg, Pennsylvania, one of Bunny's six children, said he never talked about the Gastonia trip when they were growing up.

"We learned about it by looking at his scrapbook," she said. "The first thing we noticed was a photograph of my grandparents at the train station, waiting for the team to come back. They looked so anxious, and we finally realized it was because they didn't know if dad would be coming home dead or alive. It was an awful thing, but it turned out to be a real American story of black and white standing together. We're very proud of him and his teammates."

Because of the team's bold statement against racial injustice, it has a unique place in Springfield sports history. And now, thanks to a dedicated committee, the team has a place of honor at Forest

Park, where it played many of its Hampden County games that summer. A memorial listing the players was dedicated August 22, 2003, the anniversary of Post 21's withdrawal from the eastern tournament.

The Post 21 squad drew players from all the Springfield schools. Cathedral was represented by second baseman Tony King, catcher Bobby Triggs, infielder Paul O'Connell and pitcher John Coffey. Shortstop Ray O'Shea, third baseman Joe Kelly and Keyes came from Classical. From Trade came outfielders Elmo "Kaiser" Lombardi and Lou Grondalski, catcher Steve Kogut and pitcher Henry Laczek. Taliaferro came from Tech with first baseman Fran Luce and outfielder Walter Lawler. Commerce was represented by pitcher Elliot Malaguti.

Keyes called the Gastonia experience "a defining time in our lives."

Said King, the team's captain: "I can remember taking a walk by myself while we were waiting to find out about the hotel, and two black gentlemen, probably in their 50s, were walking toward me. When they saw me, they stepped into the gutter and let me pass. I was stunned. I never got over that."

Grondalski, an Indian Orchard boy who went on to receive a Purple Heart in World War II, can still see a sign on the door of the tournament hotel.

"It said, 'No niggers or dogs allowed.' When I saw that, I knew we were in very big trouble," he said. Luce recalls walking near the hotel and having people come up behind him.

"They were yelling 'You'll get the same thing he's gonna get!' When we were at our workout, they shut the water off on us."

In the 1930s, American Legion baseball was not nearly as widespread as it is now. The 2003 Hampden County season included 18 teams. In 1934, there were just four teams in all of Western Massachusetts. The others were Chicopee Falls, Palmer and Pittsfield.

When first-year coach Babe Steere was putting his Post 21 team together in the late spring, he called for a tryout at Emerson Wight playground.

"There was a real big turnout," said King, a West Springfield native who also served as team captain at Cathedral. "Vic Raschi (later a star pitcher with the Yankees) tried out but he was young then and didn't make it. Joe Zanolli, a heck of a ballplayer, didn't make it, either." Keyes always wondered about that.

"Cutting Joe Zanolli – that had to be a mistake," he said. "He went on to play pro ball, and got as high as Triple A."

Mistakes or not, Steere wound up with quite a ball club, one that could be counted on to continue the post's tradition of baseball excellence. Two years earlier, a Post 21 team sparked by the pitching of Silvio "Moonie" Giovanelli had lost in the national finals in Manchester, New Hampshire.

Coffey, a sneaky-fast right-hander, was King's neighbor and classmate at Cathedral. They lived in the Merrick section of West Springfield.

"In those days, the Depression was on, and we didn't have much," King said. "Every morning, John and I would walk to school – across that bridge, down Main Street and up to Cathedral (then on Elliot Street). And then we'd walk to baseball practice, and walk home."

Coffey, who later in life served several terms as a representative in the state Legislature, pitched for the '32 team at the age of 14. He could have been the team's ace in '34 – but not with Taliaferro around.

"The best athlete I ever saw," said Keyes.

Taliaferro went 19-0 as a Tech pitcher. On the football field, he was a hard-running tailback, rated by longtime coach Chief Walmer as the best player he ever had.

"Bunny not only was the best pitcher around, he was the best hitter," Keyes said. "When we had that infamous workout in Gastonia, Bunny hit six balls over the left field fence in batting practice, but all that did was incite the people in the stands even more."

Post 21 ripped through its Western Massachusetts schedule undefeated in six games. Then it swept past Milford to reach the state finals against Lowell. Post 21 took the title as Taliaferro pitched a 3-1 victory in the deciding game in a best-of-three series.

Then it was on to the New England regional. Taliaferro beat Sanford, Maine, 17–0, as Lombardi belted two home runs. In the championship game, Coffey pitched all 11 innings to beat host St. Albans, Vt., 1–0, on a base hit by Lombardi.

The tenor of the times was such that coverage of Post 21 games often included references to Taliaferro as "the colored pitcher."

His Post 21 teammates remember him as quiet, shy and unimpressed by his talent.

"Bunny grew up on Hickory Street, and I grew up on Hancock Street near Ruth Elizabeth playground," said Lawler, who played with Taliaferro for three years at Tech. "Bunny was such a good kid. He could do anything in sports."

Luce, another longtime admirer of Taliaferro, maintained interest in American Legion baseball years after Gastonia. In the 1950s, he coached some outstanding teams for Brightwood Post 449.

At the age of 85, right fielder Lou Grondalski still wonders what might have been if the team had been able to keep playing.

"It's too bad that we couldn't have shown 'em what we had, but it just got too dangerous. And when somebody said we should send Bunny home, we said 'No way!'"

Like Grondalski, Keyes has that "what if?" feeling about that special team.

"You always think you could have gone all the way (to the national title)," he said. "With Bunny, yes. He was that good, and he just didn't know how to lose. But he was 10, 15 years ahead of the times."

Receiving a national award for coverage of American Legion baseball in 1961

Taliaferro stayed in Springfield after graduating from Tech. He married, worked at a local dairy and for 20 years at Fisk Tire in Chicopee, and raised a family. He played a lot of local baseball in the Triple A Industrial League. In 1967, he died on his 50th birthday.

Post 21 still exists, but its membership has dropped to around 200. After the 1934 ugliness, it never again sponsored a baseball team, not even when the Hampden County American Legion program was directed for many years by a Post 21 member, Jim Denver. His sister, Ruth McBrian, now serves as post commander.

After the decision to leave Gastonia, Post 21 officials and Springfield political leaders made an attempt to force the Legion to give the team a berth in the national finals in Chicago. That effort never got anywhere.

Cumberland, Maryland, won the Gastonia tournament, then lost to New Orleans in the national finals. Cumberland later was challenged by Post 21 to play a game at Pynchon Park with a winner-take-all prize of $10,000. Cumberland declined, and Post 21's season of strife was over.

Edward Hayes, national commander of the American Legion in 1934, promised Post 21 a thorough investigation of the Gastonia incident, but nothing came of it.

"What really hurts is that the Legion never did anything about it," team captain King said. "They never should have scheduled a tournament in a place like that, at a time like that."

Postscript: Dr. Tim Murray and former Springfield mayor William Sullivan, fearful that the Post 21 story might one day be forgotten, led a fund drive to have a monument placed in Forest Park in memory of the 1934 team's stand against racial segregation. The monument, entitled "Brothers All Are We," was dedicated August 22, 2003, on the 69th anniversary of the team's withdrawal from the Gastonia tournament. In June of 2010, Post 21 returned to American Legion baseball after a long absence.

The Old Underwood

It sat on a small, unstable table in the corner of our kitchen. Nowhere else to put it, I guess. Couldn't be in the living room, which featured a bulky Philco radio as its centerpiece. Couldn't be in the bedrooms – too many bureaus and closets.

So there it sat, amid the family's food, sinks and dishes. Out of place, but never out of mind.

It was an Underwood typewriter, a wondrous instrument with an aroma all its own. No, nothing smells quite like used typewriter ribbons, with their heavy dose of black ink.

Anyway, this particular Underwood was already on its way to being an antique – my father told me he thought it was manufactured in 1920. The keys, made of some kind of material that probably doesn't exist today, showed obvious signs of age and wear. They had been pounded so many times, they actually were worn in the middle, giving them a concave shape. The letters on the keys? Some were barely legible.

Still, the old Underwood retained its special place in our house because it was used by my father almost every day in a role dear to his heart – local correspondent for The Springfield Daily News.

Of course, that wasn't his real job. He supported the family by working 40-something years for the U.S. Post Office, serving its Indian Orchard branch as assistant postmaster.

When you meet the public as often as he did in his Post Office job, you get to know your little town and just about everybody in it. Oh, the Orchard technically was part of Springfield, but it really was a village unto itself.

Everything we needed was right there, in our "downtown." We even had The Grand, our own movie theater.

In that environment, my father flourished as a reporter. With all the contacts he had, he managed to collect numerous news items every day. After supper, he would sit at that Underwood and type them, one after the other. Not big news, mind you, but items that people cared about.

Sometimes, the typing would involve weddings. To collect that information, he often would go directly to weddings in the Orchard and pick up all he would need for a full story, including what the bride and her party were wearing.

This was an especially interesting aspect to me, because he often would take me along. As a kid, I attended more wedding receptions than I would ever see as an adult. And, boy, was the food good.

Other times, we would go to club meetings, or stop by Stanley Makuch's bowling alley to pick up the latest league news. I can still hear my dad saying, "Come on, Garry, let's go find out what the Itchybellies up to this week." He had that kind of irreverent sense of humor – the "Itchybellies" was his name for the Daughters of Isabella, an auxiliary of the Knights of Columbus.

After typing up his day's news items, he would take me "downstreet" – that was Orchard talk for going to downtown Springfield. His destination was the Springfield Newspapers building, then on Cypress Street. We would walk up the stairs and into the newspaper office. It was a noisy, fascinating, awesome place, with typewriters clattering and Associated Press and United Press machines tapping out the news of the day. There, he would leave his little pile of stories on the desk of Frank Kelly, managing editor of The Daily News. He could count on Frank to take care of them in the morning.

The next evening, like clockwork, The Daily News would be delivered to our doorstep, and in it would be a page of "news from Indian Orchard" – all of it gathered by my father and typed on that old Underwood.

That typewriter also became a part of my daily life. The first story I ever wrote for print was done in that beloved corner of our kitchen. It was about a woodpecker I had been hearing every morning as I walked to school. My father delivered my little story to the newspaper office, and to my delight, it appeared one night on a weekly page known as "The Junior Daily News."

My introduction to sportswriting – later to be my life's work – came on the old Underwood. It all began when, at the age of 16, I heard a WSPR announcer named Bob Jones doing play-by-play of a Springfield Indians hockey game. His broadcasting captivated me, and I soon rounded up some Orchard friends for Saturday night trips to the

Eastern States Coliseum to watch the games. (My father made it possible by forking over the bus fare and the $1.60 ticket price each week.)

When I would get home, I'd stay up late, sitting in that kitchen corner, writing a story about the game I had just seen. The next day, I would compare my story to those by George B. Kelleher, Howard W. Robbins, Victor N. Wall and Harold W. Heinz in the Sunday Republican sports section. Somehow, theirs were always better than mine, but my father took notice of what I was doing and encouraged me to keep at it. The more I did, the better I would get, he said.

A few years later, I would be going to that familiar newspaper building almost every day – working in The Springfield Union sports department. There, I left the old Underwood far behind.

First came Royal typewriters which were at every desk in the Union office. Later, soon after I attended my own wedding, my bride bought me a wonderful little Olivetti portable typewriter for my road trips to sporting events.

Boy, have times changed. In a career that seemed to travel at warp speed, I went from typing on those office Royals all the way to dashing off stories on a wondrous thing known as...the computer keyboard. And, oh, yes, I've already gone through several generations of those.

Remarkable as they may be, they don't have the special feel, the unique aroma that I remember from that certain corner of our kitchen. The Underwood. I shall never forget it – even though I never did master the fine art of changing a typewriter ribbon.

One For the Railbirds

It happened Nov. 6, 2010. Zenyatta, 19-0 and the darling of the horse racing world, ran against the big boys in the Breeders Cup Classic.

Everything went against her in the early going, but she roared into the stretch, took to a clear path on the outside and came thundering from far behind.

Ah, but an eyelash short. In a photo finish for the ages, Zenyatta lost for the first time, to a horse named Blame.

So, you can blame it on Blame for that disappointing loss for one of the great fillies in the history of horse racing.

Or, you can blame it on Ye Olde Handicapper, the so-called horse racing expert who makes a weekly appearance in Yours Truly's "Hitting to All Fields" column.

Of course, Ye Olde Handicapper picked Zenyatta to win – as did just about every racing writer in America.

Her stunning loss led to a flurry of e-mails, many of them saying that YOH's selection of Zenyatta had doomed her to failure.

One of the mails had a subject line that said "Only you…"

At first glance, I figured the note would be about my favorite Platters song. You know, the one that starts "Only you can make the world seem right…"

Instead, the full e-mail said, "Only you…can take an undefeated horse

and turn her into an also-ran."

Boy, that really hurt. Until I read that, I thought Blame was to blame. Nope. Obviously, the YOH jinx was in full flower. Poor Zenyatta.

Truth to tell, I almost gave up my "Handicapper" disguise after Zenyatta's heartbreaking loss. I was ready to quit picking the horses altogether until I stopped to consider that this particular alter ego of mine has quite a readership. So what if it's mostly negative? At least it provokes readers, which is one of the missions of a columnist.

So, Ye Olde Handicapper rides on, mostly picking losers and drawing horse-laughs from readers.

"You'd better not bet with real money," warned one.

No chance. Not with my wife riding shotgun on the family checkbook.

Actually, we had learned decades ago about the dangers of horse race gambling. Our first such bad experience came at Narrangsett in li'l ol' Rhode Island.

In one of the late-afternoon races, we decided to go across the board on a horse with an intriguing name, Thanatopsis. We liked it, because it also happened to be the title of a William Cullen Bryant poem that we had studied in college.

A check of the Greek roots to Thanatopsis would tell you that it literally means "Meditation upon death." Well, our thoroughbred Thanatopsis didn't die that day, but his jockey just about finished him off by pulling him wide in stretch, thereby dooming him – and our pocketbook – to a last-place finish.

If we needed further reminder that playing the horses can be hazardous, it came a few years later on a 100-degree day at Saratoga. We went 0-for-9 that afternoon – then had to face the long ride home.

Over the years, Ye Olde Handicapper has especially loved trying to pick winners in the sport's signature event – the Kentucky Derby. "Try" is the operative word, because YOH had a decades-long losing streak going in the Derby until Orb finally came through in the 2013 "Run for the Roses."

Of course, he was our choice again in the Preakness, but never made it. A Triple Crown winner for Ye Olde Handicapper? Not likely – ever.

If you want to talk about embarrassing moments in picking the horses, try these: YOH twice has picked a horse to win a race that actually had been run the day before. Lost both times.

Then there are those rare occasions when one of our "best bets" gets scratched. Hey, that's a day without a loser. A good day, indeed.

On a recent trip to the supermarket, an elderly woman stopped me and said, "I have a question for you – is Ye Olde Handicapper about golf?"

Hmm. Maybe it should be.

Tony and the Judge

Tony King played sports at Cathedral High School, then served in the Navy during World War II.

Dan Keyes played baseball as a kid, even after a childhood accident caused him to lose four fingers on his left hand. Later, he went from Classical High School to become a "double Eagle" – graduating from Boston College and Boston College School of Law.

King came back from the Navy, got hired at American Bosch and worked at the Springfield plant for 45 years. Until the age of 35, "when I was getting too heavy to bend over for ground balls," Tony played on Bosch championship teams in the Triple A Industrial League.

At age 28, Keyes became the young-

est judge in Massachusetts, appointed to the Chicopee District Court. As a loyal Democrat from Springfield's Hungry Hill, he also became an active voice in Massachusetts politics.

Yes, Tony King and Dan Keyes took totally different life paths, yet baseball brought them together as teen-agers and reunited them decades later.

In 1934, King played second base and Keyes served as his backup on a Post 21 American Legion team that took a stand against racial segregation on the eve of an Eastern Sectional tournament in Gastonia, N.C.

When the Springfield players, all of them in the 15–16 age bracket, heard that their one African-American teammate, Bunny Taliaferro, would not be allowed to play, they voted unanimously to withdraw, thereby taking a stand against racism while at the same time forfeiting a chance to play for the national championship.

The Post 21 story came back to the public consciousness in 2003, when Dr. Martin Murray and former Springfield mayor William Sullivan led a fund drive to have a stone tablet honoring the team erected down the left field line of Forest Park's main baseball diamond.

The memorial was unveiled on August 22, the very date on which the team's 14 white players had voted to withdraw in support of Taliaferro 69 years before.

Five survivors of that team took part in the dedication of the memorial – Walter "Jimmy" Lawler, Fran Luce, Lou Grondalski, Keyes and King. Names of the team's 15 members are inscribed on the tablet along with those of Post 21 officials at the time.

The memorial's theme – "Brothers All Are We" – was suggested by Keyes. It comes from the song, "Let There Be Peace on Earth."

One of the speakers at the dedication, Congressman Richard E. Neal, wore a Technical High School baseball cap as a tribute to Taliaferro's old school. Neal said the Post 21 team "won a championship without playing, by standing up for brotherhood with great resolve." For Keyes and King, the ceremony served as the start of a beautiful friendship. They became a Springfield version of "The Gold Dust Twins," bonded by their Post 21 background, and often seen together. They especially enjoyed making lunch dates, telling jokes about

each other and recounting their versions of "the good old days" of local sports.

In 2010, when Post 21 made a return to the American Legion baseball scene, Keyes and King were the only survivors from the 1934 team. They were honored at Forest Park in a touching Father's Day ceremony at which Gov. Deval Patrick served as main speaker, with Bunny Taliaferro's family members among the guests.

In 2011, the Post 21 team of '34 was saluted by the Boston Red Sox prior to an August game at Fenway Park – with Keyes and King taking part in an on-field ceremony and drawing an ovation from the crowd.

Now, 78 years after Gastonia, only King, at the age of 94, remains from a team whose actions spoke so eloquently against racism.

Dan Keyes, Tony's pal and traveling companion, died in his sleep October 19, 2012. He was buried October 25, on what would have been his 94th birthday.

"One of the nicest things that has ever happened to me was having Danny as a friend. I thought the world of him," King said. "When we played ball for Post 21, the players weren't really that close because there were guys from all over the city and a couple of us – John Coffey and I – even came from West Springfield. But when they dedicated the memorial and I got to see Danny again, that bonded us, and we had some wonderful years together."

Tony and The Judge – local treasures, teammates, friends – and shining reminders of one of the great chapters in the history of Springfield sports.

Chris Across America

IMAGINE RUNNING A MARATHON – 26 miles, 385 yards.

Now imagine doing four miles more, just for the heck of it.

Now… imagine doing that just about every day for four months.

Imagine all that, and you might get a mind-boggling idea of what Chris Gould, an Amherst Regional High School faculty member, accomplished in 1991, at the age of 25.

His "Chris Across America" run – covering 13 states and 3,000 miles – raised $20,000 for cancer research. The real point of it, though, had to do with Gould's unabashed passion for running, and the need to give himself an adventure he would never forget.

"I had a sentimental love for running, and doing it across America presented a challenge I thought I could handle. It offered an adventure at a time when I felt well suited to try it – not married, with all factors in my life properly aligned," he said.

He could take comfort in the knowledge that cross country runs have been done before.

"I think by now, it's been done by about 400 people," he said. "Those ultra-marathoners can do 70 miles a day," Gould said.

Now 47 years old and a successful coach of cross country and track at the very high school he attended, Gould uses his run across America as a teaching tool, both with his teams and with the students in his history classes.

"I try not to overdo it with the kids, but there are a lot of stories I can tell them about the geography I saw, and the people I met. Also, I want to help my students get off the beaten path, help them appreciate the outdoors, impress upon them to have an idea and go for it," he said.

Gould stands 5-foot-9 and weighs 150 pounds – "same now as I was then," he said.

"I thought I would lose weight on my run across the country, but I didn't because I was constantly eating – including power bars and fig newtons on the road."

Maintaining his weight can be explained, in part, by his compact build as a natural athlete. But a lot of it has to do with the fact that he still runs regularly as a member of the Greater Springfield Harriers, a club which competes all over New England.

"With the Harriers, I'm just one of the runners. Believe me, there are some real studs on that team," he said.

Gould also runs with his high school teams. His present-day athletes will tell you that he's very hard to beat, even though they're some 30 years younger.

He came back to Amherst Regional in 1995, thanks to a "grapevine" that informed him of the impending retirement of Randy Crowley, the man who had coached him as a high school cross country competitor.

"The grapevine actually was my mother," Gould said. "When she told me about Randy's plans, I called him. He went to bat for me, and I got the job."

Amherst has had only two cross country coaches since 1955, thanks to the Crowley-Gould connection.

In his 18 years of cross country coaching, Gould's Amherst boys teams have won the Western Mass. championship 11 times. In 2012, his outdoor track team swept the WMass meet, giving Amherst the 2011–12 triple crown – regional titles in cross country, then indoor and outdoor track.

His daughter Audrey, now a freshman at Tufts, won the Western Mass. indoor mile as a high school senior. His daughter, Lily, now runs the 600 and 1,000 as an Amherst sophomore. His youngest daughter, 8-year-old Bea, attends school in Pelham.

Some of those running genes come from Deborah, whom Gould married soon after his "Across America" adventure.

"Actually, Deb is more suited for that run that I was," he said. "She has done 50-mile runs, and she's a 2:53 marathoner."

When Gould decided to do something about his "infatuation" with the idea of running across America, he wasn't really that well prepared for it.

"At that point, I wasn't exactly an elite runner. I had done two marathons, and I had never run more than 80 miles in a week," he said.

If he needed further inspiration for his run, it came from his older brother, Jeff, who had been diagnosed with stage 3 testicular cancer in 1987.

"Jeff was three years into his recovery, so doing something for cancer research seemed to be an appropriate cause," Gould said, "but even without that, I think I would have done the run."

Twelve years later, Gould also was diagnosed with testicular cancer. Like his brother, he underwent successful treatment. He has been cancer-free for 10 years.

At the time of his decision to do the run, Gould was three years removed from Wesleyan University, where he had run cross country and track, and played varsity baseball.

He left a teaching job at St. Louis Country Day School to join Deborah, who was working in San Francisco, so he could prepare for his cross country trek.

He couldn't have made it without help – good friends who would drive a pickup truck to his next destination. One such, a St. Louis friend named Corbin Hoornbeek, accompanied him part of the way and helped in their quest for lodging and meals.

"That first day – March 1, 1991 – felt eerie, kind of scary, when I got to the Golden Gate Bridge for the start of it," he said.

Then off he went, crossing into Sausalito and eventually into the Sierras. All goes well – until he begins feeling a searing pain in his knee. Friend Corbin had to drive him to a hospital in Reno, where a doctor told him that what he was attempting was "insane." But he did help him with treatments and advice on stretching that enabled him to get back on the road after a week lost to injury.

As it turned out, he somehow managed to stay on the road just about every day after that, although he had to settle for walking at times when the knee – and then painful shins – would demand that he stop running.

"I averaged 4–4 ½ hours a day on the road when I was running, and about 5–8 hours a day when I had to walk," he said.

The only other break in his schedule came when Deborah called to tell him about a teaching job that was open in Oakland.

"I flew back, got the job, and hit the road again two days later," he said.

As injuries and walking impeded his progress, he admits to times when he wondered if he really could do this. All of that changed after he had made it through California, Nevada, Utah, Wyoming and Colorado.

"Then it was into Kansas – and what a relief that was to be running in flat country. All it would be was one town after another with a grain elevator, Grange hall and post office. Along the way, I got a lift from a rock radio station. Once they picked up what I was doing, they stayed with me – had me call in every morning for the last 1,000 miles," he said.

From Kansas, Gould made it into Missouri, where friends from his teaching days picked up his trail and gave him company and encouragement.

"When I reached St. Louis, I knew I could make it. I had 857 miles to go – and I could smell the finish line," he said.

That finish came on the morning of July 8, when he reached the Capitol building. His mother greeted him with a hug and a simple yet touching comment – "You made it!"

Three years later, Gould completed requirements at Wesleyan for a master of arts degree in liberal studies. For his thesis, he submitted a 142-page essay on his cross country run. He concluded it with lines from Walt Whitman's "Song of the Open Road":

"Afoot and light-hearted, I take to the open road,

Healthy, free, the world before me,

The long brown path before me leading wherever I choose…"

Decluttering Days

In one of my recent crossword puzzle ventures, I came across a clue that really hit home.

"Fibber of old-time radio," it said.

That would be Fibber McGee, of course. Heck, anybody who grew up with a huge Philco radio as the living-room centerpiece would know that. After all, the "Fibber McGee and Molly" show ran from 1935 to 1959, making it one of the true treasures of those long-gone radio days.

In his home – at the unforgettable address of 79 Wistful Vista – Fibber had a closet which ranked as one of the great running gags on network radio. Every so often, he would make the mistake of opening his closet door – and chaos would ensue as he would be buried under an avalanche of clutter. It all would be in the listener's mind, courtesy of those geniuses who specialized in sound effects for radio programs.

"I gotta get that closet cleaned out one of these days," Fibber would say when the clutter clatter subsided.

If he were using modern-day lingo, he would have said it was time to "declutter."

Yes, "declutter" has entered our language, maybe not officially, but as one of those buzzwords whose true meaning is crystal clear. It's what you're supposed to do with accumulated junk.

Easy to say, hard to do.

I know, because I've been trying to declutter, after once again coming to the realization that I really don't need all those pants from 20 years ago, when they fit. Why are they still hanging there? Maybe Fibber McGee would know.

Gathering old clothes and bringing them to the nearest collection box is only a small part of the decluttering process.

The hard part comes when you discover relics from your family's past that you forgot you had in the first place. Such a discovery can become difficult to deal with, because nostalgia gets in the way, big-time.

During one of my decluttering forays, I came across a 1986 Baseball Register, published by The Sporting News. A collector's item, you might say? Not really, because I can find everything that the Register contains simply by going to one of the many baseball history sites on the world-wide web.

Still, I cherish that Register, because it's from a time when I was Boston Red Sox beat writer for The Republican. I also cherish it because I'm basically a printed-page guy, as are all newspaper folks of my era (20th century).

OK, but now I also have to wonder what to do about all those Red Sox media guides. They used to be pocket-size, but over the years became bigger and bulkier. I covered the Sox full time for 23 seasons, and that translates into several shelves of old media guides.

After swallowing a large dose of nostalgia, I think I'm now ready to clear them out, tear down the shelves and have that room redecorated.

Ah, yes, redecorating. When that time comes – and it always does – it only increases the need to declutter. Items that have been stuffed indiscriminately in drawers and closets just can't be allowed to stand in the way of ...progress?

Again, easy to say, but how can I throw out that bushel-basketful of kiddie board games – you know, the ones with all kinds of little plastic parts, spinning dials and strange figurines? And how about those jigsaw puzzles, with countless pieces long since lost? Also in that basket, a set of Lincoln logs that were used over and over as we built cabins for our grandkids.

As any grandparent well knows, such artifacts really tug at the heartstrings, until we finally accept reality – our grandkids now range in age from 22 to 17, and we haven't looked at any of those playthings for years.

Decluttering often raises tough questions. Like, how many pictures of our children, grandchildren, Labrador retrievers and other friends and relatives do we really need? Can at least a few of those make it to the Wilbraham Transfer Station?

Maybe, but that's not going to happen. Instead, our 17-year-old granddaughter stands ready to drop by and scan photos into our home computer. She makes it look easy.

Of course, attempts at decluttering sometimes get derailed by a counterproductive process known as "relocating." That is, instead of throwing things out, you simply relocate them. Such relocating – also known as taking the easy way out – has happened all too often in our case. Clean out one closet, overstuff another. Or, shove it under the bed. So it goes over too many years.

Which reminds me again of Fibber – I gotta get that garage cleaned out one of these days.

Sister Joyce Carries On

There I was, standing along the sideline at Emerson Wight playground, watching a Cathedral High School football practice supervised by coach Billy Wise and his faithful aide, Mike Scibelli.

Suddenly, a wide receiver raced past me, heading down the sideline. He looked over his shoulder, reached up and made a nice catch.

"Did you see that?" one of the other Cathedral players shouted. "She must have thrown it 60 yards!"

The "she" happened to be Joyce Wise, teen-age daughter of the Cathedral coach. On game days, I came to know her as the peppiest member of Cathedral's cheerleading squad. On this day, I saw Joyce in an entirely different role – strong-armed passer par excellence. She really could fire that football, which she did quite often during those weekday afternoon drills.

Joyce, you see, was a true athlete. She had the natural physical talent, and the competitor's heart.

Yes, but this was the late 1950s, long before female athletes had the kind of varsity sports opportunities that are now available to them in high school and college. So, Joyce had only one choice: if she wanted to be close to her father's football and basketball teams, she had to be a cheerleader. Naturally, she did that with talent and heart – a true leader of the cheerleaders.

"In our house, you had to know and love sports, or you'd have to move out," she would say.

After graduating from Cathedral in 1959, Joyce chose to devote her life to her church, entering the Sisters of St. Joseph. She recently marked her 56th year in the order. Over that time, she has served many and varying roles – teacher, physical education instructor, probation officer, counselor to jailed females, counselor to at-risk kids, helper to the homeless.

Even as she gave full measure to those roles, she never lost her love for sports. For many a summer, she would step out of her nun's garb to star as a pitcher in local softball leagues.

"I pitched just about my whole life, so much that one arm's longer than the other," she says in the good humor that's typical of her.

Much of her pitching was done for teams that won championships in Springfield and Holyoke leagues. Her teammates included another member of the Sisters of St. Joseph, Sister Frances White of Chicopee. Rumor has it that Sister Franny played a mean third base.

Her years of watching her dad coach three sports at Cathedral also led Sister Joyce into a "second career" as a high school and college basketball referee, which she did for several years.

She retired from softball at the age of 67 because of a nagging foot injury that required surgery.

Her first mission as a young nun came at Holy Rosary in Springfield. "I'd tell my kids to run and cut to the left, then I'd hit 'em with a touchdown pass," she said.

She continued her education at Springfield College, earning a degree in 1975. One of her skills classes included flag football games, in which she excelled, of course.

Her teaching career then took her into physical education assignments at St. Mary's of Longmeadow, Holy Name and Our Lady of the Sacred Heart in Springfield and St. Thomas of West Springfield.

Then it was on to 12 years as a probation officer assigned to Juvenile Court. She also found time to work for a master's degree from Boston College in outreach therapy counseling.

At Forest Park Middle School, she worked for 12 years with at-risk youngsters.

"Then I retired – for a week," she said.

Now, she's still busy at age 74, helping the homeless and counseling jailed females.

Sister Joyce is just one of many Sisters of St. Joseph who remain active well past what would be considered "retirement age."

Ah, but the order also includes aging nuns who no longer can work after years of touching thousands of lives as teachers. Financial constraints have forced the order to give up its quarters at Mont Marie in Holyoke.

Sisters of St. Joseph in the Boston area have reached out, taking in many of the nuns who were forced to relocate.

For decades, the sisters got along without help, all the while remaining true to their vow of poverty. Now, though, volunteers have launched a "Support the Sisters" drive, designed to raise $5 million to cover the gap in the sisters' unfunded retirement needs. Hampden County sheriff Mike Ashe leads the fund drive. He's a graduate of Cathedral High School, and a former football lineman for Sister Joyce's dad.

Meanwhile, the Sisters of St. Joseph and thousands of Cathedral alumni also must face up to drastic changes in the high school they knew and loved.

Cathedral's quarters were rendered useless because of damage done by a tornado which ripped through Springfield on June 1, 2011. Plans finally have been brought forth to rebuild on the Surrey Road site, but the school will be smaller – and will have a different name. No more Cathedral. No more Holyoke Catholic. The two will be merged by the diocese, which has decided on Pope Francis High School as the new name.

As for Sister Joyce Wise, she has come a very long way since those carefree afternoons when she would fire 60-yard passes at her father's football practices.

Her order struggles and her school disappears, but she carries on, with head high.

Beanie Memories

This column ran Aug. 30, 2012 – the 60th wedding anniversary for Garry and Mary Brown,

September, 1951. First day of classes at American International College.

Into Prof. Bill Duffey's 8 a.m. World Literature class walked Joe Cool.

Actually, that was little ol' me, wearing an outfit so bizarre, one of my classmates asked me if I got dressed in the dark.

Hey, what was so wrong with a black-and-yellow plaid beanie? What could be so funny about a lime-green Nehru jacket (without collar, of course)? What could be so hilarious about a clashing shirt of red and brown plaid? Gray-and-black plaid slacks?

Hey, it all made sense to me.

I don't know if it made sense to the beautiful sandy-haired blonde to my right, but at least she didn't giggle when I plunked down into my seat next to her.

Come my next class, there she was again, right next to me. I thought maybe she wanted to sit there because she found me interesting. Nope. I soon came to realize what really brought us together – I was Brown and she was Bukowski, simple as that. Yes, those were the days when college class seating was done by alphabet.

So there we were, also thrown together in Dorothy Spoerl's Psych 101 and Milton Birnbaum's Shakespeare.

It took a while, but one day she asked me why I kept wearing that brown-and-yellow beanie. I mumbled something about it being the only hat I owned, which was true, but didn't explain why I had purchased such a thing in the first place.

Her beanie question raised a red flag, causing me to reassess my clothing style. I was finding her wonderfully attractive, and didn't want to lose her to a wacky wardrobe.

For help, I turned to the man who had steered me back to AIC after a year's absence. That was Joe Napolitan, a sportswriter for The Springfield Union who would go on to international renown as a political consultant.

I had dropped out of AIC after my freshman year, choosing to do so because I was hired – at the ripe age of 18 – to fill a vacancy in The Union's sports department. Joe Nap was only slightly older, but he already had served in the Army and now was established as The Union's high school sports beat writer.

I soon learned that he was going to AIC while working full time. After a few months of serving as my sportswriting mentor, he said, "You're crazy to drop out of school. Go back and get your degree. So you're working six nights a week, so what? It can be done."

I couldn't ignore that advice. After all, he was doing it, so why couldn't I?

Anyway, there I was, in the middle of October, desperately needing more advice – this time on how to dress properly for college. Joe Nap came through again with a simple sentence – "Stop buying plaid."

Into the trash went the "Joe Cool" beanie, along with several shirts and slacks. The Nehru jacket? No, I couldn't let that go.

When I stopped "dressing in the dark," I noticed that the sandy-haired blonde, one Mary Bukowski of Wilbraham, was becoming friendlier by the day. She also got more open with her remarks, which could be pointed at times.

In November, when trying to impress her with my sportswriting job, I proudly announced that I would be covering the big Springfield-AIC football game.

"Oh, what are you covering it with?" she asked, as a couple of her female classmates giggled in the background.

By this time, though, there was no stopping fate. Joe Nap, AIC and the alphabet had brought us together, so falling in love was only a matter of time.

It happened that December, when I finally found the nerve to ask her out – on Christmas Eve, yet.

Yes, that beautiful girl from Wilbraham chose me over "Wigilia" – the Polish celebration of Christmas Eve. Her mother was appalled that her only daughter would pass up an important night for the family, to go on a date... with me?

Actually, it all went wonderfully well, and after a few months, her mother and other family members soon found it in their hearts to forgive me.

By then, we were spending as much time together as school and work would allow. By springtime, we were engaged. By August, we were married.

That was 60 years ago.

Somehow, my beautiful college classmate has stayed the course over good times and bad. She went back to school at age 42, and built a 20-year career as a medical technologist. All the while, she raised a wonderful family with me, despite having to deal with the sometimes-ridiculous demands that daily newspaper work can put on a marriage.

Happy anniversary, darling.

And if you're thinking of buying me something to mark the occasion, this old bald head could use a new beanie.

Plaid, of course.

August 30, 1952

August 30, 2015

He's a Teddy Bear

HAVE YOU EVER...

Won an auto race at Riverside Park Speedway.

Piloted a hot-air balloon.

Visited 80 of the world's 195 countries.

Had a professional hockey tryout on your 50th birthday.

Launched a successful business in the carport of your parents' house.

Acted in *The Graduate* at the Majestic Theater.

Skated with Boston Bruins legend Johnny Bucyk.

Sponsored 250 sports teams, male and female, from ages 6 to 60.

All that, and more, has been part of the life of Ted Hebert, a 60-year-old dynamo who grew up in East Springfield and now is in his 36th year as chief executive of Teddy Bear Pools and Spas, based in Chicopee.

On the local sports scene, you'll find "Teddy Bear" teams playing everything from small fry baseball to senior hockey. He also has become a benefactor of the Chowder Bowl, a high school football fund-raiser for Springfield's Shriners Hospital.

Add to that the 300 or so golf tournaments that have been sponsored by Hebert over the years, and his work with the as a board member of the Make-a-Wish Foundation.

"I love doing it. It's an opportunity to help others. And once I started doing it, it just snowballed. I have a hard time saying no," he said of his constant involvement in local sports.

By the way, the name "Teddy Bear" actually is a play on his own name. (If given its proper French pronunciation, Ted Hebert comes out sounding like "Ted A-bear").

"That goes back to when I was trying to think of a name for my new business. I was talking with my mom (Billie Hebert) about it, and I said, 'How about Pools by Ted?' We didn't like that, so I said, 'Hey, how about Teddy Bear Pools?' My mother said she thought that was a terrible name, but I decided to go with it."

Despite that difference of opinion, Hebert knows how important mom was in his life. She died in 1994.

"I had a great mother. She taught me how to have integrity and work my ass off," he said.

"Mom always gave to charity, even when we didn't have much. I'd ask her why she was doing it and she'd say, 'They need it more than we do.' "

Teddy Bears Pools started in 1975. As the business grew, so did Hebert's interest in sports.

"It goes back to when I was a kid, playing 6–8 baseball for St. Mary's (of East Springfield). I was the guy they kept on the bench until the score was 15–0. At that point, they would let me play right field."

Back then, though, he loved having a uniform.

"I liked them, because they all had the name of some business on the back," he said.

Yes, those were the sponsors, and now Hebert has taken that kind of generosity to a new level.

Don't ask him how much money he pours into sports.

"That doesn't matter. I do it because I can, and I want to," he said.

Hebert became involved in American Legion baseball in the 1990s when Ludlow coach Jeff Garrow asked him if he would pay for one of the team's caps. He did much more than that, and now also acts as the major sponsor of the Chicopee-Aldenville Legion team, and Springfield's Post 21 entry.

Garrow, who now serves as a Post 21 assistant coach, said that Hebert called him last August after reading in The Republican that the team would be looking for sponsors for 2011.

"He told me, 'Anything you need, let me know,'" Garrow said.

Whether it's baseball, basketball, soccer or hockey, you'll find Teddy Bear teams in action – sometimes against each other.

"I like to find the time to go to games. I remember one year I went to see a Small Fry League team play. They didn't win a game, but they were so into it, that it was good to see," he said.

Hebert admits that he wasn't much of an athlete as a kid, or when he went to Classical High School. All the while, though, he had a favorite sport – hockey.

"I remember going to the (Eastern States) Coliseum and having Eddie Shore tell me he'd throw me out if I put my feet on the seat in front of me," he said.

Years later – long after finally learning to skate at the age of 25 – he began playing senior hockey at local arenas. His teammates included Bob Shore and his brother, Eddie, grandsons of the hockey Hall of Famer who operated Springfield's American Hockey League franchise for four decades.

"Sometimes their dad (Ted Shore) would coach our team. That was special. I always thought hockey was a great spectator sport, and I found that it's even greater to play," Hebert said.

He's still at it, three nights a week, mainly because he has an understanding wife. He and the former Barbara Bigos of Chicopee have been married for 24 years.

Of course, the name of his Over 40 League team is Teddy Bear Pools.

"Who else would have me?" he asked.

Hebert long has been a corporate sponsor of the AHL's Springfield Falcons franchise.

"He's a very loyal supporter of our organization," Falcons president/general manager Bruce Landon said.

Their long-time friendship led Landon to pull a surprise on Hebert's 50th birthday.

"He let me have a tryout with the team – I even had to sign a Professional Tryout Agreement for one day. Ralphie Calvanese (Falcons equipment manager) had a game jersey for me with my name on it, and he assigned me a locker in the dressing room. I skated through one of their regular workouts, and I had to do all the calisthenics they do before skating," Hebert said.

Over the years, Hebert has hired Landon's players for part-time jobs during the summers. One of them, Ontario native Rod Willard, settled in the area after his playing career ended. He's now one of Hebert's full-time employees.

Hockey also has given him the opportunity to skate with the stars. In a charity game a few years back, he played with Boston Bruins old-timers, including Johnny Bucyk and Mike Milbury.

Auto racing rates right up there with hockey among Hebert's favorites. His personal highlight came on his 40th birthday, when he won at Riverside in his first race as a pro stock driver.

"That was great, because I had gone four or five years without winning," he said.

He was part of a team that featured Mario Fiore, Reggie Ruggerio and Gentleman Jack Lecuyer – all beloved names in Riverside lore.

In 2000, he had another memorable auto racing experience. His racing team, led by driver Jerry Marquis, won NASCAR's national modified championship, clinching it on the final race of the season at Thompson, Conn., Speedway.

"Jerry nailed it by beating one of my old favorites, Reggie Ruggiero," Hebert said.

On his office wall, he has a photograph of West Springfield's Bob Polverari winning the last feature race before Riverside Speedway closed down in 1999.

"That was a sad night at a great race track," he said.

Hebert bought all the Riverside Speedway seats when the old

facility was demolished, and has them stored in Enfield. He considered using them in the building of a new track in Southwick, but hasn't been able to find a site suitable to him and agreeable to the town.

His willingness to face up to challenges took him down a different path in 2008. At the urging of a friend, he auditioned at the Majestic Theater in West Springfield for the role of Ben's father in "The Graduate" – and got it.

"I had been involved with the Majestic as a sponsor, but now I was in an actual play for the first time in my life. I was so tensed up, I had to have massage therapy. But I wound up doing 36 performances over six weeks, and I've been told that I did okay."

That was a major milestone for a man who had a stuttering problem in his youth. He has gone on to become a motivational speaker.

Yes, that's "Teddy Bear," all right. He always gives it his all, whether he's working, playing, traveling, acting, speaking – or sponsoring teams in sports of all sorts.

My First Day At Fenway

August, 1945. World War II was over, and it was time for me to fall in love – with the Boston Red Sox.

A 23-year-old guy named "Boo" had a lot to do with it. I found him when I stopped reading about war, and turned to a new interest, the sports section.

There he was, getting a lot of attention. Dave "Boo" Ferris, The Morning Union and Daily News told me, was heading for a 20-victory season. As I got more into baseball, I came to understand that winning 20 was quite an achievement.

So began a daily ritual of following what Boo and his Red Sox were doing. Actually, the Sox weren't doing much. They were heading for a seventh-place finish, but Boo kept my interest high.

On Aug. 26 – 11 days after the announcement of Japan's surrender, ending World War II – he went 10 innings to beat the Philadelphia Athletics 4-3 at Fenway Park. It was that 20th victory I had been reading so much about.

He slumped a bit after that, but finished 21-10. My sports section said it was the 28th time that the Sox had a 20-game winner.

The Boo Ferriss season set me up as a Red Sox fan. By spring training of 1946, I eagerly awaited the return of Ted Williams, Johnny Pesky, Bobby Doerr and Dominic DiMaggio from military service.

I kept a scrapbook of every game, leading off with a Morning Union headline that said, "Red Sox Start Right" in winning their opener. If ever a newly-minted baseball fan had a dream season, '46 was it for me. The Sox were so good, they ran away from the rest of the American League.

I followed them daily on the radio, with the voices of Jim Britt and Tom Hussey describing all the action. But that wasn't enough. I wanted to see the Sox play. I wanted a trip to Fenway Park.

My father took careful note of my scrapbook, and realized how much the Red Sox meant to me. He got together with my uncle, my older brother and a co-worker from the Indian Orchard Post Office. I don't know how it all came together, but there we were, on a Wednesday morning in July, piling into the car for a ride to Boston.

My father wanted it to be a special day, so he picked a doubleheader – something you'll only see in baseball today when a rainout forces it. In 1946, though, doubleheaders were part of the regular schedule. On this day, the Sox would be playing two against the Chicago White Sox, and I would be there.

When I first saw Fenway from the street, I was disappointed, because it looked like any old brick building. The magic of the place did not hit me until we walked up a ramp along the third-base line, and I saw a major league baseball field for the first time.

It gleamed, beautiful green, on

a sunny July day. The Red Sox were there, taking infield practice, wearing the most beautiful creamy white uniforms I had ever seen. At that point, I was officially hooked for life. The Red Sox would always be my team, and there would never be a better ballpark than Fenway.

The Wall amazed me. It seemed to be right on top of us as we settled into grandstand seats about two-thirds of the way toward left field. As I would find out later, this was the last season in which advertising would adorn Fenway's left field wall. Calvert Whiskey, Gem Blades to fight that five o'clock shadow (I was 13, and had no idea what that meant) and Vimms, the family vitamins.

Another great day for the Sox. Joe Dobson, who was getting to be my second favorite Red Sox pitcher to Boo, won the first game 3–1 over a lefty named Eddie Lopat. Then came my man Ferriss, winning 6–1.

I recently looked up those two games in The Republican's archives.

The first one took 1:45, the second 1:54. Try that today.

My favorite Red Sox regular, second baseman Bobby Doerr, went 3 for 3 in the second game with a home run.

It was a perfect day, and the Red Sox were a perfect team, as far as I could tell. They did go on to win 104 games, and no Sox team has done that since. Of course, the season came to a bitter end in the World Series, but let's not talk about that.

On the way out of Fenway, my father bought a packet of Red Sox photographs, and handed it to me. At home that night, I thumb-tacked 25 Red Sox players to my bedroom wall, everybody from Ted, Bobby, Dom, Johnny and Boo to guys I hardly knew, like relief pitchers Mike Ryba and Mace Brown.

My mother was not pleased, but she let the photos stay.

I was so grateful that she did so, because they represented a day I shall always cherish. The first trip to Fenway – any Red Sox fan knows the feeling. Unforgettable.

The Boston press corps surprised me with a cake while I was covering the last game of my career as Red Sox beat writer for *The Springfield Republican.* May 10, 2009

The Red Sox said goodbye to me on the Fenway messageboard. May 10, 2009

The Music of Our Lives

Back in the day when the Varsity Spa on State Street in Springfield was just a block away from the American International College campus, it served as the ideal coffee-break spot.

Each booth had its own little juke box, where 25 cents would get you some great music.

Sitting there with my favorite college student – later to be my wife, one particular song seemed to be just right for us. It was done by the man known as "Satchmo," Louis Armstrong.

As he would croon "Dream a Little Dream of Me," complete with one of his awesome trumpet solos, we would be falling in love to the music.

Actually, Armstrong's version (still one of the best in my book) was just one of seven revivals of the song in the early 1950s, including pretty good efforts by Frankie Laine and Vaughn Monroe.

As the music business evolved, there always seemed to be time for "Dream a Little Dream of Me." It was done by a list of big names – Ella Fitzgerald, Nat King Cole, Bing Crosby, Doris Day, Joni James, Dinah Shore and Dean Martin.

Years later, as we listened to the great 1960s era of rock and roll, guess what came floating back to us? None other than "Dream a Little Dream of Me," this time by the Mamas and the Papas, featuring Cass Elliott.

She did such a terrific job on the song that it was re-released as a single and climbed the music charts in the United States and Europe. In Australia, it twice reached No. 1.

Yes, "our song" was so good, so romantic that it somehow managed to become a hit again, even in a time dominated by such rock giants as Bob Dylan, Neil Young, the Beatles, the Beach Boys, the Doors, the Rolling Stones, Creedence Clearwater, the Who, the Band. You go can on and on.

That only affirms a well-known fact in the music business: if a song is good, it doesn't matter how old it is.

Well, this one is REALLY old. Actually, it's my age, which only adds to the song's mystique in our marriage.

Written by Fabian Andre and Wilbur Schwandt, with lyrics by Gus Kahn, it first was performed in 1931 by Ozzie Nelson and his orchestra (an endearing rendition with Ozzie doing the vocal), and quickly covered by the orchestras of Wayne King and the Dorsey brothers. Kate Smith came along to sing it in the late 1930s.

Over the decades, renditions of "Dream a Little Dream of Me" just kept coming. It was performed in 1995 by Chicago, with Paul Shaffer on piano.

In 2002, it was part of "A Wonderful World," an album of duets by Tony Bennett and k.d. Lang that featured several songs which had been made popular by Louis Armstrong.

The song surfaced again in 2004, this time done by Jim James, of My

Morning Jacket, and in 2007, by jazz singer Diana Krall.

Two years ago, Kevin McHale's character in the cast of the TV show "Glee" sang it while confined to a wheelchair. It was a very touching version.

And, just when you might think it finally has run its course, along comes that Canadian crooner, Michael Buble, doing a pretty darn good job on it in 2011. Also that year, Eddie Vedder did a ukulele-backed version of the song.

But wait, there's more.

At our 60th anniversary party, our granddaughter Rayna Brown, of Wilbraham – the girl with the green guitar – brought tears to our eyes when she stepped to center stage at the John Boyle O'Reilly Club and sang, "I Can't Help Falling in Love With You." It was a from-the-heart performance in our honor, and one we shall never forget.

At that point, it seemed that all musical memories and tributes had been exhausted. Not quite.

As we were leaving the hall, our Amherst grandchildren – Sonia, Conlan and Kanya Brown – handed us a CD entitled "Happy Anniversary" that they and their dad had put together for us.

The final track on that disc? Sonia doing "Dream a Little Dream of Me" and artfully accompanied by members of the Brown Family Band. Best version ever of our favorite song? Absolutely.

From Satchmo to Sonia – what a long, wondrous trip for a song that stands alone as the music of our life together:

"Stars shining bright above you;

Night breezes seem to whisper 'I love you.'

Birds singing in the sycamore tree;

Dream a little dream of me…

Carl Beane – An Appreciation

As we tooled along the Masspike, heading for another Red Sox game, the radio blared rock 'n' roll, most of it from the 1960s.

As soon as a song would start, my driver would recognize it.

"Double Shot of My Baby's Love – The Swingin' Medallions, 1966," he would say, in a beautiful booming baritone.

Yes, that was Carl Beane – music aficionado and the best traveling companion a guy could ever hope to have.

The funniest, too.

He couldn't abide Bob Dylan's whining voice, and would gladly do a hilarious impression of "Positively Fourth Street." He idolized The Three Stooges, and could do Curly better than Curly himself.

When we would pull up to a stop light on Storrow Drive, ready to turn for Fenway, we often would see a skinny guy walking between cars, selling artificial flowers. One look at him, and you had to wonder how his pants stayed up.

Carl christened him "Barry No-Ass," and cracked me up beyond belief.

At the time we started covering the Red Sox together, he was doing sports for WARE, a little AM station, and he also covered the Red Sox, Celtics, Bruins and Patriots for various radio outlets around New England. On top of that, he often did play-by-play of Ware High School football and baseball.

In other words, he worked days and far into the night, almost nonstop. That was Carl – a little dynamo with that good old New England work ethic. He could get back from a Red Sox game at 2:30 a.m., and still make his early-morning radio shows, first at WARE and later at WESO-Southbridge.

He had side jobs, too, like turning into "Beanski" as he hosted a WARE hour of polka music on Sundays.

Carl could have had a career in music – he was that good as a drummer.

"I wanted to be Buddy Rich," he would say, speaking of the great drummer of the big-bands era.

Carl once told me why he favored a career behind a microphone.

"I have the perfect face for radio," he said.

Actually, he had the perfect voice for it.

He also happened to be a world-class interviewer. Some of my best stuff came simply from being there with him in the clubhouse and dugouts as he grilled three decades of Red Sox superstars.

After games, when speed was of the essence, Carl could pop into the locker room, get right to the heart of the game story, and come away quickly with quotes from players that gave his listeners real insight into the state of the team.

Our baseball travels often took us to Yankee Stadium, where Carl had the opportunity to meet another idol of his, Yankee public-address announcer Bob Sheppard.

Oh, yes, that was another of his great impressions – sounding exactly like the elegant voice of that Yankee Stadium icon.

When Carl went to Agawam High School, they knew him as "Rocky." I didn't know him then, but I have to believe he was the class clown of 1971.

He knew what he wanted to do, even before he graduated from high school. As a 17-year-old, he had the opportunity to work as an intern at WMAS in Springfield. Soon after he started, he went on his own to the Basketball Hall of Fame to interview Curt Gowdy, who was president of the shrine's Board of Trustees. Gowdy, of course, was better known for his broadcasting work with the Red Sox and later as host of ABC-TV's "The American Sportsman."

Gowdy was so impressed with the way Carl conducted the interview, he praised him and told him to keep at it.

Carl never forgot Gowdy's encouraging words, but then, Carl never forgot anybody. He always kept in touch with his Agawam classmates and often returned to this area to do public appearances and charity work.

"I'll always be a Western Mass. guy," he said, long after he became a major league celebrity as public-address announcer for Red Sox games at Fenway Park, his favorite sports shrine.

In 2010 and 2011, he gladly returned to his roots to help coach Pat Moriarty's fund-raisers on behalf of Cathedral High School baseball. His charismatic presence – complete with his two World Series rings – gave Moriarty's efforts a huge lift.

Carl almost didn't apply for the Fenway Park job when it opened up in 2002, because he wondered if he could do justice to the role that had been filled so well by another idol of his, Sherm Feller.

Everyone who knew Carl knew better, and told him so. Given that kind of encouragement, he tried out for the job – and won it handily.

For nine-plus seasons, his voice served as a comforting background for Fenway's fandom. He did the job so well because he not only knew broadcasting, he knew everything about baseball and the team.

Along the way, he made it into the Baseball Hall of Fame in Cooperstown, N.Y., as lead-off voice in its "The Baseball Experience" exhibit.

In the newspaper business, we often must write a dreaded piece known as an "obit column."

I never thought I would ever be called upon to write this one. Carl was only 59 years old, still a vibrant, funny guy, looking forward to his next Red Sox game when he died Wednesday, felled by a heart attack as he was driving.

Just like other Sox fans across the land, I will miss that voice. Mostly, though, I'll miss the baseball travel buddy who made me laugh every day.

The Kid and the Coach

THEY CAME TOGETHER BY ACCIDENT – a Marine Corps veteran of the Vietnam war, and a college sophomore looking for something to do with his summer.

They met at the Fitness Center of Westover Air Reserve Base in Chicopee, and soon formed a bond based on mutual respect and a passion for a sport known as "the sweet science."

Yes, boxing has changed the lives of Rocky Snow, 61, and Josue Lopez, 21. In July of 1970, Snow came back from Vietnam, angry and depressed. Eventually, he found his way to boxing at the Holyoke Boys Club, and the sport has led him to a new life as dedicated teacher, coach and volunteer for good works.

As for Lopez, boxing has led him to a national championship in the lightweight division, two All-America certificates and the hope of turning pro after he completes his education at the University of Massachusetts. He will go into his senior year carrying a 3.9 grade-point average (4.00 means all A's).

Beyond all that he has accomplished in only two years as a boxer, Lopez has enhanced his already considerable work ethic by training with Rocky, whom he calls "an old-school guy" regarding conditioning.

"I'm never going to lose because I didn't run that extra mile or do that extra sparring," he said. "As Rocky says, you win the fight before you go into the ring."

Both men are from South Hadley, but never knew each other until one morning in the summer of 2010, when a friend who had access to the Westover Fitness Center invited Lopez to work out with him.

"That's when I met Rocky, and after talking to him, I got interested in boxing. I liked basketball as a kid, but I was really more interested in a one-on-one kind of sport. In the ring, there's no one to blame but yourself if you lose, and no one to thank but yourself if you win."

Sensing Lopez's interest in the sport, Snow asked him if he wanted to start a boxing team at UMass.

"I loved the idea. I never even knew intercollegiate boxing existed until Rocky told me about it. He knew, because he had experience coaching college teams at Western New England and Central Connecticut," Lopez said.

In the first season with the UMass boxing club, Lopez convinced Snow that he was ready for national competition.

"I won't put a kid into a tournament until he's ready, and Josh was. Now he has teammates who could be ready by next season. I think we're going to have a smokin' UMass team in 2013," Snow said.

Lopez was so ready, he made it all the way to the 2011 national intercollegiate tournament, conducted at the U.S. Military Academy in West Point, N.Y. "Josh came in third and made All-America," Snow said. "Not too bad for a first-year guy."

From there, Lopez continued to improve, concentrating on the techniques and training provided by his mentor.

That training sometimes includes sparring with him.

"Can I beat coach? Nobody beats coach," Lopez said. "He's 61 and he can take anybody on our team."

In advance of the 2012 intercollegiate tournament, Snow knew what he had in Lopez, so he arranged bouts with top competition.

"Rocky set up a fight on November 21 with the defending NCAA champion, and I beat him," Lopez said. "Then on January 28, I fought the national runnerup, and beat him, too."

His buildup for the nationals continued in March, when he went against the fourth-place finisher from 2011. Another victory for Lopez.

All of that gave him a No. 1 ranking going into the eastern regionals. He drew a bye, won the championship and in April headed for the NCAA tournament at the Air Force Academy in Colorado Springs, Colo.

"I won three fights at the nationals, and brought home the championship belt. I can't wear it, though. Too big for me," he said.

UMass does not recognize boxing as a varsity sport, but that didn't stop Snow from doing what was necessary for his club team.

"If there's a fight, we'll go, and don't worry about the money," he said.

"Josh's championship belt and All-America certificates aren't on display at UMass – they're here, at Westover. That's because my team does all its work here, and considers this home."

All the training done by Lopez – as much as three to four hours a day – serves him well in the ring.

"In college, the fights are three two-minute rounds. That means each round is a sprint – you have to go all out every second. A lot of guys are good fighters for one round – we call them one-round wonders – but it's the third round that usually makes the difference. I explode in the third round, and I win a lot of fights decisively."

The training that Lopez gets at Westover is merely a part of what Snow does – often putting in eight hours a day, providing help in the gym for military personnel, both male and female, along with the time he gives to the UMass team.

Snow, who is retired from the Marine Corps and the Post Office, does all of that as a volunteer.

"A while back, we got some boxing apparatus," said Westover's Fitness Center director, Janice Wheeler. "I said, why not use it?"

Then Rocky came along, and started working with Army Staff Sgt. Luis Delgado, a fighter he had known years before at Holyoke Boys Club. Soon, other base personnel began joining in, and boxing at Westover just took off.

"Rocky has such a humble attitude about what he's doing, people love him for it," Wheeler said. "And he sure knows how to work them. People don't realize how out of shape they are until he puts them on our rock-climbing wall,"

Snow specializes in giving back. In 2006, he donated a kidney to JoAnn Dion, a 50-year-old nurse from West Springfield whom he did not even know.

Over the years, he has done 17,000 hours of volunteer work for the Veterans Administration, helping his brothers in arms. He also serves as president of the Pioneer Valley Chapter of the Leathernecks Motorcycle Club. His bike's custom paint job includes a replica of the unforgettable World War II scene at the peak of Iwo Jima's Mt. Suribachi, when four Marines planted the American flag.

"My bike also carries the name of my unit – First Battalion, Third Marines," he said.

When he came home from the war as a 20-year-old corporal who had seen combat, there was no heartfelt greeting, no warm welcome, no parade.

Coach Rocky Snow works with his two-time national collegiate champion, Josh Lopez. (Photo by Don Treeger, *Springfield Republican*)

It was a time of social upheaval, including public demonstrations against U.S. involvement in Vietnam. Such strong anti-war feelings often were misdirected, with homecoming veterans as the target.

"People looked down at us. They spit at us. Go for a job interview, and they asked you to roll up your sleeve. They expected to see heroin tracks.

"We served as honorably as our troops did in any war. But people didn't like this war, so we were the enemy."

He spent time in a U.S. Naval hospital – "Nothing physical, but I was messed up from things that happened over there," he said.

Now, 42 years after his service in Vietnam, Snow has evolved dramatically from the seething, bitter young man he once was.

How did he deal with the anger issues that nearly consumed him?

"When I first got back, I used to get into fights – I had so much hostility. Then one day I decided to check out what was happening at the Holyoke Boys Club. I thought it might help if I could swim or play some basketball," he said.

That was in 1975, the year he ran across Pat Bartlett, a boxing man who trained many a Golden Gloves fighter when the HBC hosted the New England Tournament each February.

"Pat saw me one day and said, 'Hey, you want to box? I got a guy here who needs a sparring partner.' I did it, and I liked it so much, I came back the next day, and it just went on from there. I can truthfully say that getting into boxing at the Holyoke Boys Club saved me."

He proved to be perfectly suited for the sport, from the nickname "Rocky" to the talent and fortitude he brought to the ring. Soon, he was fighting Golden Gloves matches as a 126-pound featherweight. He turned pro at age 24, fighting for 10 years in the 135- and 147-pound weight classes.

"Was I a champion? No, but that wasn't the point. For me, boxing was therapeutic, a way to keep my life balanced," he said.

While he was pursuing his pro career, HBC director Bruce Thompson — a former Marine Corps captain — asked him about working with youngsters at the club.

"It was a rule that you couldn't start in Golden Gloves until you were 16. Bruce wanted something for the younger kids. So I got involved in a Junior Olympic program, training kids from the ages of 8 to 15. We wound up having the No. 1 team in New England five years in a row."

He went on to become a college coach, and now looks forward to seeing his UMass team members when they get back from their summer away from school. He expects them to train, hard.

"They can tell me they ran, but I'll take them in the ring and I'll know if they ran," he said.

He doesn't have to wonder about Lopez. They will be together over the summer, aiming toward another national championship.

"Josh is a natural, and he's left-handed. I don't know what it is, but there's something special about left-handed fighters," Snow said.

For both Snow and Lopez, boxing is much more than it might seem to be to the general public.

"People think of boxing as two guys in a barroom. It's nothing like that. It's like chess, and the idea is to score points without being scored upon," Snow said.

Lopez, who hopes for a career in law enforcement after his boxing days are over, firmly believes in the value of his chosen sport as an art in itself.

"People think boxing is a brutal and masochistic sport," he said, "but to me, there's nothing more honorable than stepping into the ring, going one-on-one, and seeing who is the better man."

Sonia and Pedro

Late winter, 2004. Our grand-daughter, Sonia Marie Brown, signs up for her second season in the Amherst Little League. Yes, girls are welcome, thanks to the Amherst league's open-minded director, Stan Ziomek.

Sonia makes a team called the Mets. She plays right field most of the time. At the plate, her speed helps her get on base. When she comes around to score, her male teammates are right there, giving her the high-five.

On an evening in late May, we take a ride to Amherst to watch Sonia play. Before the game, her dad takes a photograph of her. She poses on one knee, with bat in hand, looking like a hitter on deck. It's a beautiful picture, a family keepsake.

Sonia's interest in baseball also includes the Red Sox. Her favorite player is Pedro Martinez, the team's Cy Young Award-winning pitcher.

At the time, I was covering the Red Sox for The Springfield Republican. I worked almost every home game at Fenway Park.

One day, Sonia hit me with a tough question: "Grandpa, can you get Pedro's autograph for me?"

First let it be said that it's a major no-no for baseball beat writers to ask players for autographs. I tried to explain that to Sonia, but she wasn't buying it.

"What if I give Pedro an autographed picture of me in my baseball uniform? Would he do one for me?" she said.

Well, that put grandpa directly on the spot – but it also sounded like a really good idea.

"OK, let's try it," I said.

Sonia went directly to her room, and came back with her baseball picture, neatly autographed, as follows:

"Best wishes to Pedro Martinez, my favorite baseball player. Sonia Brown, Amherst Little League."

On my next trip to Fenway, I sidled up to Pedro's locker. He had his back to me, buttoning his uniform shirt. Then he turned, gave me that million-dollar smile and said, "So how's my old man doing?"

Okay, so I was 73 years old and still working full time, but when Pedro called me his "old man," he meant that in a good way. He often called me that when I would approach him for an interview.

This time, I didn't want an interview. This time, I handed him Sonia's picture, and told him what a great fan she was. And, yes, I also mentioned that she would love to have his autograph.

Pedro smiled as he studied the photo. Then he turned and put it in an upper compartment of his locker. By then, it was time for him to get onto the field to do his running (pitchers do a lot of that between starts).

Over his shoulder he said, "We will talk later."

Two days later, I walked into the clubhouse for the daily interview time. Pedro saw me and called me to his locker. Without a word, he handed me a brown envelope.

As soon as I could, I hurried up to my seat in the pressbox. To go to work? No, to see what was in the envelope.

Eureka – there it was. An 8 by 10 color photograph of Pedro, with this autograph: "To Sonia...Pedro Martinez CY 97-98-00." (a reference to the years he won his three Cy Young Awards). What a treasure.

When I delivered Pedro's picture to Sonia, she gave it suitable star treatment on her bedroom door.

All of that happened in June of '04. As the pennant race and playoffs unfolded, Pedro's autographed photo became a symbol in our family of a world championship that will live forever in Red Sox lore.

Meanwhile, Sonia finished her Little League season, then took part in a local tournament. In what would be the final game of her baseball career, she made a nice running catch of a foul fly down the right field line for the game's last out.

After baseball, she went on to compete in volleyball and track at Amherst Regional and Smith College.

Now, her favorite baseball player is heading to Cooperstown, N.Y., where he belongs. In July, he will be enshrined in the Baseball Hall of Fame.

Throughout his illustrious career, Pedro was known for having two personalities – warrior on the field, gentleman away from it.

In my years on the Red Sox beat, I came to know Pedro as a friendly sort in the clubhouse, and a consummate artist on the mound. Without question, he's the greatest pitcher I ever saw in person. I also saw him as a man who cared about the feelings of a Little Leaguer from a small town.

A Hall of Famer? Yes, in every way.

Sonia hitting away for Smith College   Pedro at his Hall of Fame induction

Lunch with Mr. Hockey

I had lunch the other day with Eddie Shore…staring at me.

Yes, there he was, "Mr. Hockey" himself, in a super-large photograph. It shows him in full regalia as a player for the Springfield Indians of the American Hockey League. A notation in the lower right corner explains that the picture was taken in 1942.

It hangs on a wall at the Friendly's restaurant on Boston Road, near the Wilbraham town line. Being a curious sort, I had to know why the photo was there. The Friendly's manager explained that it was part of several photographs from an Eastern States Exposition collection that were used as wall decorations when the restaurant interior underwent an extreme makeover.

Yes, but that's only part of the story – and I know the rest of it after spending years as a sportswriter covering various hockey doings at the Eastern States Coliseum. That great old building was ruled by Shore for 40-something years in his tenure as owner of Springfield's AHL franchise. Before all that, of course, he had a Hall of Fame career as a defenseman for the Boston Bruins. He was a key member of Stanley Cup championship teams in 1929 and '39, won the National Hockey League's most valuable player award four times, and made the All-Star team eight times in a 13-year career.

Yes, but why would an NHL super-star of Shore's magnitude be wearing a Springfield Indians uniform? Well, what hockey fans of younger generations may not know is that he made hockey history on Jan. 20, 1940, when he became the first franchise owner to play for his team. He did that for parts of three seasons before retiring as a player – at the age of 39 – after the 1941–42 season.

Some of this happened amid controversy. It began when, at the age of 37, he struck a deal to purchase the financially-troubled Springfield franchise on July 11, 1939. That decision infuriated Art Ross, general manager of the Bruins, who still had Shore under contract as a player.

Then, it only got worse when Shore told Ross that he planned to play for both the Bruins AND the Indians during the 1939–40 season. Of course, Eddie got his way because there was nothing in his Bruins contract to prevent him from playing for his own minor league team.

Basically, Shore's new arrangement called for him to play home games in both the NHL and AHL. That, in turn, caused protests among other AHL owners, who wanted Shore to make at least one playing appearance in each city. After all, they reasoned, he would be a huge drawing card as a reigning NHL star.

With so much haggling delaying Shore's plans to play, he got into only four games with the Bruins before Ross could stand no more. With Eddie in full agreement, Ross traded him to the New York Americans, an NHL franchise of the '40s. In return, the Bruins received $5,000 and journeyman forward Eddie Wiseman.

In New York, Shore got to play for one of his long-time friends, Red Dutton. However, the season had grown late by then, and he wound up playing only 10 games for Amerks, plus three as they were knocked out in the first round of the playoffs.

Meanwhile, back in Springfield, Shore made his Indians debut five days before the Bruins traded him. The news that Shore would be in the lineup brought a crowd of 5,200 to the Coliseum, where they saw the Indians play a 1–1 tie with the Philadelphia Ramblers.

Shore played 14 more games for the Indians that season, including road appearances at Cleveland. Indianapolis and Providence. He also played three playoff games for the Indians.

"As I remember it, the six playoff games he played between Springfield and New York were on successive nights," said Shore's son, Ted.

"I was only nine years old when my father started playing for the Indians, but I can remember him being at the rink all day, coming home for a nap at 3:30, then having a steak at 4:30 before going back to play a game," Ted said.

Shore retired as an NHL player after the 1939–40 season, but still had a lot of hockey left in him. With his Indians of 1940–41, he played all 56 of their games, plus three in the playoffs. Shore's partner on defense, Frank Beisler, was the only Shore teammate to play 56.

His playing career wound down in 1941–42, when he played 35 games for the Indians as they won the AHL's Eastern Division title before losing in the playoffs.

Now, you'll find a photo of Mr. Hockey looming large on a restaurant wall. He makes quite a companion for lunch.

Rocking Along

As I scanned my wife's recent copy of Rolling Stone magazine (yes, she's been a subscriber for years), I happened to see a page devoted to Leonard Cohen's latest studio album, which came out in September.

"Leonard Cohen's still going? How old is he, anyway?" I asked across the breakfast table.

For that, I received a proper rejoinder from my soulmate of 62 years: "You've got a nerve to ask that. How old are you?"

Ouch. Point well taken. Who was I to talk, when I'm still writing for publication at the age of 83?

My wife then reminded me of Duke Ellington's pithy response to an interviewer who asked him when he was planning to retire.

"Retire to what?" The Duke said.

Again, point well taken. Why should that master of the jazz world have to retire from what he loved to do – writing and playing music? Instead, he continued to lead his orchestra until he passed away at the age of 75.

By the way, to answer my own question – Leonard Cohen celebrated his 80th birthday on Sept. 21. He was still touring as recently as 2013.

Recently, as I had morning coffee with my Springfield Republican, a Page 2 headline grabbed me. It said, "Fleetwood Mac's 'dream girl' is back"

Wow. Seventeen years after Christine McVie "retired" from the band,

there she was on stage at Madison Square Garden, back at her keyboard. With her return, a band that had formed 40-something years ago had its five key members together again as she teamed with Mick Fleetwood on drums, Lindsey Buckingham on guitar, John McVie on bass and Stevie Nicks, doing her dreamy vocals. They rocked the house for two and a half hours.

You want to talk about old age? Well, Christine McVie at 71 qualifies as Fleetwood Mac's "senior citizen." The other four band members are well into their 60s but they still can deliver such great hits as "Don't Stop."

Neil Diamond certainly doesn't stop. At the age of 73, he has a new album that will serve as prelude to a 2015 tour that includes band members and backup singers who have been with him for more than 30 years. In 2008, my wife and I attended a Neil Diamond concert at Fenway Park – and, yes, he did "Sweet Caroline" three times for a very appreciative full house.

The beat goes on for aging rockers who don't want to consider that "R" word (retirement). How about Sir Paul McCartney? 'tis said that he was 16 years old when he wrote a terrific song entitled "When I'm 64." Now, he's eight years beyond that age and still sounding like Paul of the '60s.

Then we have Sir Mick Jagger, a mere 71 years old. He once was quoted as saying, "If I'm still singing 'Satisfaction' when I'm 45 – shoot me." Well, he and the Rolling Stones have gone about a quarter-century beyond that deadline.

How about one of my all-time favorites in popular music, Tony Bennett? He's so old – 88 on Oct. 3 – that he fought in the Battle of the Bulge in World War II. Now, with no plan for retirement, he's singing duets with some slightly-younger female stars. If you haven't heard Tony and Lady Gaga do "The Lady Is a Tramp," you're really missing something.

Over the hill? Never say that about Frankie Valli, that 80-year-old Jersey Boy. He's still out there, telling the world that "Big Girls Don't Cry." And don't forget Mike Love. He's 73, but in his heart he's still a "Beach Boy."

As for the always-busy Neil Young, a line he sang in 1972 rings somewhat truer today than it did then: "Keeps me searching for a heart of gold, and I'm getting old" (69 on Nov. 12, to be exact).

One of my favorite golden oldies is Springfield's own Phil Woods, renowned in the world of jazz. He's 82, with no plan to hang up that alto sax. Graduates of dear old Technical High School can be very proud of this member of the class of 1950.

If I had to pick an all-time favorite, it would be Bob Dylan. However, knowing that he's now 73 years old, it can be teary-eyes time when you listen to him sing " ...May your heart always be joyful, and may your song always be sung. May you stay forever young."

Yes, tears at times, I will keep listening because Bobby D, Tony Bennett, Sir Paul and all the rest remind me that some labors of love have no official stopping point.

Oh, I am officially retired after 59 years of full-time newspaper work. But when editors of The Republican invited me to keep writing as a free-lancer, I thought about Duke Ellington's answer. I was retiring...to what?

I soon decided that it's better to keep busy at something I love. After all, I haven't run out of words yet, so it's much better for me to keep on keepin' on.

Hey, it works for Leonard Cohen.

Jim Thorpe's Springfield Game

IT WAS 1912, THE YEAR JIM THORPE ASTOUNDED the sports world by winning gold medals in both the pentathlon and decathlon at the Summer Olympics in Stockholm.

It was four months after King Gustav of Sweden had said to him, 'You, sir, are the greatest athlete in the world" to which he responded with a classic: "Thanks, King."

Yes, it was 100 years ago this week – Nov. 23, 1912 – that Jim Thorpe came to Springfield with the football team representing the Carlisle Indian Industrial School of Pennsylvania. At that point of Thorpe's sensational athletic career, Coach Glenn "Pop" Warner's Carlisle Indians could play with anybody in the country.

On that particular day in 1912, the schedule called for them to play in Springfield against the School for Christian Workers, also known in the press of the day as "YMCA College" and later to be known world-wide as Springfield College.

This unusual matchup came about because of a close friendship between Warner and Springfield coach James McCurdy. Warner accepted the challenge of playing in Springfield because it fit well into his itinerary, which called for a season-ending game at Brown University in Providence on Thanksgiving Day.

Springfield College football archives show that Warner planned to play Thorpe only in the first quarter, in order to keep him fresh for the game at Brown.

Instead, the home team battled so hard that Carlisle needed Thorpe to play the full game – and be at his best. He delivered, scoring four touchdowns, and kicking three extra points and a field goal. It took all of that for Carlisle to prevail, 30–24.

"No Springfield team ever fought harder from whistle to whistle than coach McCurdy's moleskin-wearers did this day. Capt.

Dan Kelly and his teammates gave a sterling performance," *The Springfield Republican* reported.

In the weeks prior to their Springfield trip, Thorpe and his teammates had rolled up a 10-1-1 record. Carlisle did have two bad weeks – a scoreless tie with Washington & Jefferson and a 36–24 loss to Penn – but when they stormed onto Pratt Field to face McCurdy's team, a serious mismatch seemed in store.

The Carlisle Indians had outscored their opponents 443–96. That included a 65–0 pounding of Villanova, then one of intercollegiate football's elite teams, and a huge 27–6 victory over a proud Army team that featured one Dwight D. Eisenhower as its star running back/linebacker.

As for YMCA College, it came into the game with a 5-3 record that included losses to Williams and Amherst, and a victory over the Mass. Agricultural College (the forerunner of UMass).

Thorpe's visit to Springfield so captivated the local sporting populace that a crowd of 7,000 packed Pratt Field (where Amos Alonzo Stagg Field now stands on the SC campus).

That throng of football fans cheered for an innovative Springfield offense directed by quarterback Les Mann, one of the college's all-time great athletes. He completed 10 of 12 passes, setting up his team's three touchdowns. He also kicked three extra points and a field goal.

Coach McCurdy's attack featured line shifts, speed and the aerial game – the very attributes that made Carlisle teams so successful.

"It would be no exaggeration to say that no team this season has given a finer exhibition of working the forward pass than the local eleven, keeping Springfield right in the running," *The Republican* reported. "The game produced thrill following thrill, with the rapidity of a motion picture film."

Thorpe scored early, but Mann passed Springfield into a 14–7 lead. Thorpe kept coming, though, and ran for the tieing touch-down just before halftime.

In the second half, as hard as Springfield fought, it could not contain Thorpe.

"The athletic marvel of the age certainly was the chief stum-bling block in Springfield's path to winning the laurels," *The Republican* said. "The Olympic champion was a Hercules on offense, and more than once he was the one defender to stand between a Springfield runner and a touchdown. As a ball carrier, he gave a wonderful exhibition of straight-arm work."

After getting out of Springfield with that hard-earned victory, coach Warner's team went on to trounce Brown 32–0.

In what was his last season of intercollegiate football, Thor-pe scored 29 touchdowns, kicked 38 extra points and added four field goals (all done with the old "dropkick" style) for a total of 224 points. As a running back, he averaged 9.8 yards per carry.

For the 1911 and '12 seasons, Carlisle had a combined record of 23-2-1.

The 1912 season marked the first for college football under a series of rules changes which made the game what it basically still is – four downs to make 10 yards; touchdowns worth six points instead of the previous five; and the field changed from 110 yards to 100.

Under that format, Harvard was declared the first national champion in 1912, finishing with a 9-0-0 record. Penn State ranked second at 8-0-0, followed by Carlisle.

Thorpe went on to play professional football and baseball at the major league level, and basketball as leader of a barnstorming team. He retired from athletic competition at the age of 41.

Because it was found that Thorpe had played two summers of minor league baseball while in school, he was stripped of his medals as the International Olympic Committee enforced its then-strict rules regarding amateurism. Thorpe died, poverty-stricken, in 1953 at the age of 64. Through the laborious efforts of friends and family members, Thorpe's Olympic medals eventually were restored in 1982. A town in Pennsylvania now bears his name.

Pop Warner had a coaching career which started at the University of Georgia, then took him to Cornell, Carlisle, Pitt, Stanford and Temple. His lifetime record of 319-106-32, led to his election to the College Football Hall of Fame in 1951. He's also remembered for starting the Pop Warner League, a national program for kids' football teams.

Les Mann, the Springfield star against Carlisle, went right from college to the Boston Braves in 1913 for the start of what would be a 16-year career as a major league baseball outfielder. He became part of the "Miracle Braves" as they went from last place on July 4 to a sweep of the Philadelphia A's in the World Series. Mann also played in the 1918 World Series for the Chicago Cubs against the Boston Red Sox.

McCurdy, the friend who gave Pop Warner all he could handle on the football field, coached at the School for Christian Workers from 1896 through 1916.

Jim Thorpe, Les Mann, Pop Warner, James McCurdy...they all came together 100 years ago, giving Springfield the greatest football show this city has ever seen.

Revisiting the Mother of Women's Basketball

"I went down to the demonstration,
To get my fair share of abuse…"
From "You Can't Always Get What
You Want," by Mick Jagger and Keith
Richards

On an October night in 1984, some 25 members of the National Organization for Women (NOW) took more than their fair share of abuse from male basketball fans as they demonstrated on behalf of equal rights regarding the Basketball Hall of Fame, a Springfield institution since 1968. They wanted the world to know that basketball's Valhalla really was nothing more than a male-only club which completely ignored the women's game.

At the time, the Springfield Civic Center was hosting the Boston Celtics and Utah Jazz in an NBA exhibition played for the benefit of the Hall of Fame. Two hours before the doors opened, NOW members and sympathizers gathered outside the arena's main entrance.

One of them carried a sign which read, "Biggest shutout in basketball history, 143–0." That said it all – 143 men elected to the Hall of Fame, and no women.

Abuse? One of the protesters was told, "Wear your bra tighter." That remark was made by a male basketball fan to Dr. Mimi Murray of Springfield College, a nationally-respected coach and educator. Another heckler said, "Women can't dribble." Still an-

other shouted, "Build your own Hall of Fame."

Well, never underestimate the power of protest. Only five months after NOW's demonstration, the Basketball Hall of Fame's Honors Committee announced that Senda Berenson Abbott, Margaret Wade and Bertha Teague would be part of its Class of 1985.

Berenson Abbott of Smith College would go in as the duly recognized "mother of women's basketball." Wade was elected as a highly-successful coach at Delta State in Mississippi. Teague was recognized for her long and illustrious career as a high school coach in Byng, Okla.

There they were – the Basketball Hall of Fame's first women. The election of Berenson Abbott was especially significant, because she had taught basketball to her phys-ed classes in January of 1892, less than a month after she visited James Naismith at the Springfield YMCA Training School (now Springfield College) to talk about the game he had just invented. In March of 1893, she organized and refereed the first public women's basketball game. Then, for 20 years, she served as national editor of the women's basketball rulebook.

The Hall of Fame began its elections in 1959. While other pioneers were recognized in the first and second elections, Berenson's pioneering work went unnoticed for 26 years.

In late June of 1985, the Hall of Fame finally became what it had always claimed to be – a shrine for all of basketball – with the induction of its Class of 1985 at Chez Josef in Agawam. At last, the Hall of Fame had shed its "unisex" label.

Now, as women's basketball celebrates the 30th anniversary of that breakthrough, it's a proper time to remember the people who made it happen.

Foremost among them would be Agnes Stillman, a 1971 Smith College graduate. For her master's thesis in physical education, she chose to tell the life story of Senda Berenson, and all that she had accomplished in her 20 years at Smith. When Stillman finished the thesis, she wondered . . . why isn't Senda in the Basketball Hall of Fame?

So, Stillman began nominating her, but after four such attempts, she never did get a reply. Finally, in frustration, she wrote to The Sunday Republican, letting it be known that the Hall of Fame was ignoring her.

Meanwhile, a basketball dad named Ed Pomeroy was bombarding the Hall of Fame with letters demanding that the women's game be recognized. He was inspired by his daughter, who had played at Chicopee High.

The Stillman and Pomeroy protests brought action from The Sunday Republican. Columnist Gerry Finn interviewed director Lee Williams about the Hall of Fame's male-only aspect. In his response, Williams said, "If James Naismith is the father of basketball, then Senda Berenson is the mother of women's basketball," but he pointed out that he had no say with the Honors Committee.

After the Williams interview, this newspaper continued to press the issue, and caught the attention of NOW. Meanette Vermes, the local chapter president, pointed out that public funds were being used to build a new Hall of Fame on Columbus Avenue (the predecessor to the current facility), and that meant women had to be part of it. She and Maxine Garber organized the Civic Center protest.

On enshrinement night, the crowd applauding the election of women included Agnes Stillman and her family. As she told Yours Truly, "I am so glad. I thought it would never happen. Senda was such a great lady, my fear was that the memory of her eventually would fade, that the world would lose sight of what she had done."

Well, thanks to her and advocates like her, Senda is well remembered now, and the Hall of Fame continues to honor women among its electees.

Since 1985, a total of 29 women and two women's teams have been elected. Not a great number considering the scope of women's basketball, but certainly better than that 143-0 "shutout" of 1984.

Postscript: Two years after her induction into the Springfield shrine, Senda Berenson Abbott was elected to the International Jewish Sports Hall of Fame. In 1999, she was elected to the Women's Basketball Hall of Fame in Knoxville, Tenn. In 2012, when the Smith College Athletic Hall of Fame was formed, she was part of the first class to be enshrined. In addition, the edge of Smith's basketball floor bears an italic inscription in large letters, "Senda Berenson Court."

Changing Times for a Cellar Dweller

One day, I suddenly realized that three once-thriving sports leagues had folded when I wasn't looking. No notice. No fanfare. No farewells. Year by year, they just quietly slipped away, finding their places in the dustbin of our family's history.

Yes, gone are the WCBA (Wilbraham Cellar Basketball Association), the WCHL (Wilbraham Cellar Hockey League) and my all-time favorite, the WFYWL (Wilbraham Front-Yard Wiffleball League).

Gone, simply because they have run out of players.

Those Wilbraham "leagues" began some years ago, when our three kids – Melissa, Peter and Paul – would take to the front yard (too many trees to play out back) for games of pepper and catch. In those days, when Dad was younger and more mobile, we used real baseballs. And we had the perfect ballchaser – a black Labrador retriever.

League play subsided for a few years, but came roaring back when our four grand-children – Sonia, Conlan, Kanya and Rayna – moved into the starting lineups.

Well, those lineups play no more. Two of the starters have gone on to college. The other two are high school juniors, far too busy (and too tall) for cellar and/or front-yard sports.

While they lasted, the Brown family cellar leagues played busy schedules. At holiday time, they were booked solid. Many a typical Christmas Day would include hockey and basketball before dinner, then more of both after dinner, intermingled with cheesecake breaks.

All of the sports action pitted grandkids against grandpa – and you know the outcome. It can be said without question that I never won a game, but loved every minute of the losing.

Hockey was a favorite, because it usually came down to a one-on-one challenge between me and our grandson, Conlan. The fact that he was born in Sherbrooke, Quebec (while his dad served as a postdoctoral fellow in the Department of Mathematics at Universite de Sherbrooke) might have something to do with his love for the slapshot. He drilled many of those at me (and past me) in our hours of cellar hockey. Luckily for me, we used a tennis ball instead of a puck.

We also used a family heirloom – a genuine NHL stick that had been signed by most of the "Big Bad Bruins" of 1970. A beloved friend of ours, Edwin "Soupy" Tulik of Ludlow, knew many of the Bruins players, and got them to sign the stick as a gift to our 10-year-old son when he was a patient at Children's Hospital in Boston.

Now there was his son, a generation later, playing cellar hockey with a stick bearing the autographs of Bobby Orr, Phil Esposito, Kenny Hodge, Wayne Cashman, Johnny Bucyk and all the rest. Many a sports collector would have paid handsomely for that stick. In our family, though, it wasn't meant for memorabilia. It was meant for slap shots.

Hey, the use of autographed equipment runs in the family. Back in those pepper-game days, I often brought out a baseball autographed by Jim Lonborg, Cy Young Award winner for the "Impossible Dream" Boston Red Sox of 1967. So the autographed ball became grass-stained and slippery with dog saliva – so what?

If cellar hockey generally was a "guy thing," cellar basketball was for everyone. It all began when Grandpa decorated one wall with a miniature hoop-and-backboard. For some years, I would lift each grandkid, in turn, so he/ she could dunk the ball. Later, as they grew, games of "horse" became the rule, and you know who lost most of those.

One day, I handed the little basketball to our youngest grand-daughter and told her to pass it back to me, then head for the hoop. I fed her a nice bounce-pass, and she slam-dunked it. I told her that she had just completed the oldest play in basketball – give-and-go, New York style. She loved it. Many more give-and-go moments fol-

lowed, all of them now stored in my memory bank.

We even played some baseball in the cellar – dart baseball, that is. In that game, you could do outlandish things, like hitting into a double play as the leadoff man. It all depended on dart accuracy. Or inaccuracy.

The grandkids also reveled in wiffleball. They especially loved hitting line drives back at the pitcher (me). Of course, the taller they grew, the harder the hits. Many of them landed on our neighbor's roof, but it was all in the game.

Oh, yes, there also were occasional attempts at outdoor bowling (a real challenge in our slanted driveway) and many an after-dinner game at croquet.

This all came to mind the other day, when I tried, yet again, to get rid of some of our garage junk. The first thing I dug out from beneath a one-time picnic table? A bucketful of sports equipment, including a beautiful bat obtained on a long-ago visit to the Cooperstown, N.Y., Bat Company.

Sorry, but I can't bring myself to throw that bat away. It will stay with me, along with all those memories of little games, and the players who made them precious.

Downtown Theater Days

Across the aisle sat Maxwell Anderson. Next to him, Robert Sherwood. Two celebrated playwrights, settling in to watch a performance at the Court Square Theater in the heart of downtown Springfield.

No, we're not talking about downtown as we know it today. That particular celebrity sighting took place Nov. 12, 1954, in a wonderful theater that had opened on Elm St. in September of 1892. Less than two years after Anderson and Sherwood came to town, the Court Square Theater would be closed, then demolished.

For my wife Mary and I, being in the presence of those playwrighting giants carried special significance, because we both had studied their work with Prof. Jack Gaffney at American International College. Memories of his drama classes in the garret of Lee Hall remain dear to our hearts.

For two nights in that long-ago November, the Court Square Theater offered Anderson's new play, "The Bad Seed" before it opened on Broadway.

In the vernacular of show business, that was known as "an out-of-town tryout," a chance to test the play before New York audiences got to see it. Anderson came to Springfield mainly to determine what rewriting, if any, his play might need. Sherwood, an imposing figure at 6-feet-8 inches tall, came along as his confidant and well-meaning critic.

Also in the audience that night sat Louise Mace, who had a long and illustrious career as a theater and movie critic for The Springfield Union. In her review of "The Bad Seed," which ran in the next morning's paper, she gave the play a four-star rating, with a gentle suggestion that the beginning scenes could use some editing. She had high praise for Nancy Kelly, who played a mother faced with the chilling realization that her 6-year-old daughter is a demonic, cold-hearted killer. Patty Mc-Cormack so impressed Mace that she predicted "a long career of success in the theater" for her.

How do I remember all this? Well, seeing a Broadway play in little ol' Springfield, Mass., certainly is memorable enough, but I did need help with the details. The internet told me that the play opened on Broadway Dec. 8, 1954, running for a year (334 performances) before it was made into a movie.

Then, turning to newspaper archives, I was able to find the dates it played on stage at the Court Square.

The archives also stirred memories of a time when a Springfield movie-goer had so many choices. At the time when "The Bad Seed" was live and on-stage at the Court Square, only two blocks away the Capitol Theater was showing "A Star Is Born," starring Judy Garland. "White Christmas," starring Bing Crosby, was playing at the Paramount.

Right next door at the Art Theater, Alec Guiness was on-screen in "The Lavender Hill Mob."

Worthington Street had two theaters – the Bijou and Loew's Poli. Bridge Street had the Broadway Theater. On Main Street, in Springfield's South End, stood the Garden Theater. State Street had the Arcade, just around the corner and up the hill from main street. By the way, the Arcade's headliner in that November of 1954, was Jack Webb, starring in his old radio vehicle, "Dragnet."

With "The Bad Seed" due to leave town after two performances, the Court Square Theater already was trumpeting coming events. One newspaper ad told theater-goers not to miss Jose Greco, the premier Flamenco dancer of his era, who would be at the Court Square later in November. And the theater's next stage play? "The Caine Mutiny Court Martial," starring Paul Douglas and Springfield's own Wendell Corey, directed by the esteemed Charles Laughton.

So much has changed in downtown Springfield since then. The only theater still in place is the Paramount – now known as the Hippodrome. Ah, but its once-wondrous marquee which beckoned movie-goers stands in a state of disrepair.

Springfield's "theater district" began disappearing in the '50s. By 1968, when the Capitol fell victim to the city's "urban renewal" project, only the Arcade and Paramount remained. In 1971, the Arcade closed. A year later, it was demolished.

As the old theaters – with their dazzling lobbies, high ceilings and beautiful balconies – faded from the local scene, they were replaced by something known as the "cineplex," which offers a lot of movies rolled into one building. Very nice, very glitzy and very 21st century.

Yes, but you'll pardon movie-goers with long memories if they yearn for the good old days of downtown theaters with their continuous showings, and little neighborhood theaters with movie schedules that changed every three days.

Meanwhile, the Browns cherish their memories of that wondrous night at the Court Square, when Nancy Kelly and Patty McCormack showed us drama at its best.

And remember, Maxwell Anderson and Robert Sherwood sat right across the aisle, taking notes.

A Guy Named Breezer

SOON AFTER PAUL BRISSETTE ENTERED FIRST GRADE at Springfield Street School in Agawam, one of his classmates gave him a nickname: "Breezer."

The name seemed just right. It was a play on his last name, but it also fit his personality – a free-and-easy kid who seemed to enjoy every day.

He was one of five children in the family of Paul Brissette Sr. and the former Mary Vivenzio of Springfield. In 1943, when he was 12 years old, the family moved to Springfield's Forest Park section. He began to play baseball on the sandlots with the Forest Park Aces and basketball at the old Springfield Boys Club on Chestnut Street.

As he dominated all the games he would play, the Breezer nickname fit evenbetter.

Yes, athletic competition seemed to be a breeze for him. Nobody around him could play shortstop better. Nobody around him could handle the basketball better.

After years of high school and college stardom, and a brief time in professional baseball, he came home and settled into what would prove to be a remarkable life as a television executive.

That, too, seemed to be a breeze for him. He started as an ad salesman at Springfield's WWLP-Channel 22, gradually moving into management and ownership. Years later, when he sold the last of his holdings which at various times included 32 television stations, he retired as a millionaire.

"I was fortunate to be able to make a better life for myself and my family. I hit a home run in television, especially in the Raleigh (North Carolina) market," he said.

Brissette met his future wife, Estelle Cook, while he was playing summer ball in Nova Scotia. They married in 1953, were divorced in 1980. After 30 years apart, they remarried last January.

In his current hometown of Wilmington, N.C., Brissette has been a positive force in the community. He has won Wilmington's "Citizen of the Year" award, and last May he and his family were honored with the "Living and Giving" Award for their work in the fight against juvenile diabetes.

However, life is no longer a breeze for him.

As he arrived at a gym for a workout one morning in December 2009, a friend said, "Paul, you look yellow."

That revelation of a jaundiced condition led him to Duke University Medical Center, where he was diagnosed with pancreatic cancer, which has been characterized as inoperable.

Despite living with a condition which doctors consider to be terminal, he faces life with a clear mind and strong will.

"I decided to go public about my cancer because I have nothing to hide and nothing to be embarrassed about," he said.

"Maybe something good will come from this, maybe more progress with pancreatic cancer research. It's called the silent killer, because for a long time you don't know you have it," he said,

"I had 78 years of good health. I am at peace with myself and I have made all my funeral arrangements. The cancer is dormant right now, and I have some good days. I go to the gym and work out. I stay positive, and I get support from so many people."

Brissette has made countless friends over the years. He credits that to what he calls "the brotherhood of athletes."

As a glittering star in that brotherhood, he became a unique high school player, then went on to become part of what is now a legendary 1952 Holy Cross baseball team – the only one from New England to win the College World Series.

Brissette's status in Western Mass. high school basketball is special, indeed. He's the only player to be part of back-to-back

Western Massachusetts championship teams at different schools.

His desperation shot in the closing seconds of the 1948 final was rebounded into the basket by one of his all-time favorite teammates, Carl Binsky, as Classical became the first city school to win the WM Tournament.

Those Bulldogs of 62 years ago also featured Buzz Wagner, Bob Spears and Doug Jenkins in a starting five coached by Sid Burr.

"We surprised everybody, including ourselves, I think, because at that time Cathedral had a great team with Frank Korbut and Tech had a great team with Lefty Ferrero and Elvin Eady," Brissette recalled.

Carmen DeCosmo, a long-time coach of youth sports in Springfield – best known for his West Street Atomics football teams – prevailed upon Brissette to transfer to Cathedral after the '48 basketball season.

That put him in the hands of Billy Wise, Cathedral's one-of-a-kind coach.

The Breezer joined a Cathedral basketball team that had Korbut, Jerry Cavanaugh, Pete Pashko, Fred Karam and Abe Moses. Together, they won the WMass championship in 1949, and Korbut won the Lahovich Award for the second time. "Billy Wise was terrific, a man who coached three sports for so many years. I owe a lot to him. He helped me get into Holy Cross," Brissette said.

Now, he gets "a letter and a prayer" each week from Coach Wise's daughter, Joyce, who is in her 51st year as a member of the Sisters of St. Joseph.

"The outpouring from Sister Joyce and so many others is very uplifting," he said. "So many people from the Springfield area have contacted me and come to see me. It's nice to know that they never forget."

Brissette also has heard from Willie Manzi, who played with and against him as they were growing up. Manzi is retired after an exemplary career as coach and administrator at Springfield Technical Community College.

"Willie sent me one of the most beautiful letters I have ever read," Brissette said.

He recently received two visits from Eddie and Carol Hurley of Wilbraham. They go back to 1950, when Brissette was a senior at Cathedral and Hurley a star second baseman at Holyoke High. After helping HHS win the state championship, Hurley went to Deerfield Academy for a year.

When he graduated from Deerfield in 1951, he had college offers to consider. It came down to Holy Cross and Notre Dame.

"By then, Paul was at Holy Cross. I thought about him playing second base, and I knew I'd better go to Notre Dame," Hurley said.

They never forget Brissette at Holy Cross, either. He gets telephone calls every week from Ronnie Perry, Togo Palazzi and Don Prohovich of Ware – all stars on HC's National Invitation Tournament basketball champs of 1954. Perry also played a lot of baseball, excelling as one of the pitchers on that College World Series team.

"The Omaha paper did a story about us on our 50th anniversary. They pointed out that we hold records that will never be broken," Brisssette said.

Yes, Holy Cross is the only team in College World Series history to go through an entire tournament with its eight starters playing every inning, and its pitchers working complete games in every start.

The '52 Crusaders were coached by Jack Barry, who had a 40-year career at Mt. St. James after playing shortstop for the Philadelphia Athletics as part of Connie Mack's "$100,000 infield."

"When we went to Omaha, our school had, shall we say, an austere budget for athletics," Brissette recalled. "So we stayed at a little hotel that had no air conditioning. It was so hot, we wound up spending most of the nights sleeping outside, on the lawn at Creighton University. It was great for camaraderie."

That HC team went 6-1 to win the championship in the dou-ble-elimination tournament. Its lone loss, in the third game, came 1–0 to Missouri, which was held to one hit by Barry's No. 3 starter Jackie Lonergan.

Barry's national champions had another Springfield player – third baseman Frank Matrango.

He went to Holy Cross after serving in the Navy in World War II, then went on to become an outstanding basketball coach at little St. Joseph's of North Adams. Later, he served as a state represen-tative.

"A few years after we got out of school, I had my College World Series ring stolen while I was on a business trip," Brissette recalled.

"Frank was so upset about that, he made a crusade of trying to find it, or replace it. When he died (in 1996), his wife, Theresa, called me and said, 'Paul, Frank left something for you in his will.' I knew right away what it was – Frank's College World Series ring. I wear it every day in honor of him, and when I go, it will be returned to the Matrango family."

Brissette told that beautiful story of friendship on the night of the '52 team's 50th reunion banquet.

"There wasn't a dry eye in the house," he said.

He and Matrango played in an HC infield with Jack Concan-non at shortstop and Fran Dyson at first. The outfield had Johnny Turco in left, Artie Moosman in center, Dick Hogan in right. Catch-er Pete Naton worked with a staff of three – Lonergan, Perry and the College World Series MVP Jim O'Neill.

Brissette had come out of high school as a shortstop, a position he played since 10–12 sandlot ball. After his freshman year at HC, he had the opportunity to spend the summer in the Blackstone Val-ley League, a circuit much like the Cape Cod League.

He wound up on a roster that also had Joe Morgan, a Walpole kid who would go on to manage the Boston Red Sox (1988–92).

Morgan was Boston College's starting shortstop at the time, and didn't want to move.

So Brissette became his Blackstone Valley League second baseman. He excelled at that position, and stayed with it for the rest of his career in college, pro ball and finally in the Tri-County League.

Brissette signed with the White Sox after his graduation, but Army duty came first. He served for two years, then played the 1956 and '57 seasons with Chicago's Triple A club in Colorado Springs.

"I hit .310 my second year, but I lost time when I tore up my ankle. I was 26 years old, I had the injury and I had Nellie Fox (a future Hall of Famer) in front of me, so I took a voluntary retirement in 1958 and came back to Springfield," he said.

"The funny thing was, when I was 43 years old, out of the blue I got a letter from the White Sox telling me, 'You are now released from our roster.'"

He worked for a time as an underwriter at MassMutual, then moved into the world of television, starting at Springfield's WWLP-Channel 22. That was the start of what would be a brilliant career in the broadcasting industry.

"They wanted me to do sports at Channel 22, but I said I'd rather have a change of image, so I took a sales job, and eventually became sales manager," he said.

While working locally, he played basketball and baseball. As usual, his teams were winners.

He joined a friend, Milton Bradley executive Jake O'Donnell, on a team sponsored by Jinxey's Café of Springfield. That team won the Holyoke Allies Tournament against a strong field. O'Donnell had been a standout at Cathedral and AIC.

In the business world, he rose to become president of Milton Bradley's East Longmeadow division.

"When Paul came back to this area after retiring from pro ball, he hadn't played basketball for about nine years. You'd never know it," O'Donnell said.

Brissette also played for Royal Typewriter in the Holyoke City League.

"We would win it every year," he said.

His teammates included Dan Della Giustina and Bob Tourtelotte of AIC, former pro player Bob Hubbard of West Springfield, and former city stars Jack Dineen and Bobby Blinn. They were coached by Ed Kosior, a former AIC star.

Brissette also played for the Springfield Acorns with a couple of Holy Cross greats – Palazzi and Jack "The Shot" Foley.

In baseball, he played for a star-studded Buick Aces entry in the Tri-County League. His teammates there included Bobby Findlater, Bill Quinn, Eddie Hurley, Ace Bailey, Bill Quigley, Lou Giammarino, Bill Lynch and Bill Mullins – later to become a state rep. The Mullins Center at UMass bears his name.

Brissette also played locally for Bay Diner and its impresario, Socrates Babacas.

"We had Wayne Upson, my brother Larry and Nick Buoniconti (yes, the NFL Hall of Famer). And I brought in some Holy Cross talent – pitcher Hal Dietz, shortstop Ron Liptak and catcher Larry Rancourt."

When his basketball/baseball days were over, Brissette turned to golf and handball, and excelled at both.

In later life, he never forgot his years as an athlete, or the places that helped him succeed.

At Cathedral, he has donated to the Billy Wise Hall of Fame. At Holy Cross, he has established an endowment that takes care of the baseball coach's salary.

In September, he plans to come back to Springfield for the Joe Salvon Memorial Golf Tournament, a fund-raiser which honors a Cathedral athlete and brother of another lifelong friend, the late Ralph Salvon, who had a long career with the Baltimore Orioles as their head trainer.

Now, as Brissette faces a serious physical condition, he does so with the fighting heart of a true competitor.

"I'm hanging in there, and I'm optimistic. I'm not looking at how long, I'm looking at quality of life. I'm still going to the gym. You gotta keep on truckin'," he said.

Note: This story appeared in The Springfield Republican *June 10, 2010. Paul Brissette passed away three months later.*

Facing Life Without Yaz

Note: This column, written on the last weekend of Carl Yastrzemski's baseball career, was selected by The Sporting News *for publication in "Best Sports Stories of 1983."*

BOSTON – To understand the impact of Carl Yastrzemski's baseball career, one simply has to consider the thousands of people who have never known the Boston Red Sox without him.

Let us assume, for instance, that the earliest a person can get hooked on baseball is at age 6 or 7. That means this country is populated by thousands of baseball fans age 28 or under who cannot envision a Red Sox team without Yaz.

If you want to carry it further and assume that most baseball fans get hooked on the game around the age of 10 or 12, you can add thousands of folks up to 34 who have never known baseball without No. 8 playing for the Red Sox.

Therefore, the trauma will be deep and lasting when Yaz plays Game No. 3,308 today – the final one in a 23-season career which began on April 11, 1961.

That last at-bat will be an emotional experience for him, and it will be something of a culture shock to those thousands who have come to think that Yastrzemski has always played for the Red Sox and always will.

These children of the Yaz era knew him before they knew the Beatles and he outlasted them by 13 years. They knew Yastrzemski before Bob Dylan told them that the times they were

a-changin.' The times did change, but Yastrzemski didn't. He was always there, the bat dangling loosely as he awaited the pitch. The hard eyes staring out at that adversary on the mound. The vicious, all-out swing so often producing drama and excitement.

These children of the '50s and '60s knew Yaz before they knew the Rolling Stones. Long before Woodstock, there was Yaz, playing left field and swinging his heart out for the Red Sox.

As the 34-and-unders grew up through the tumultuous '60s and war-torn '70s, they always knew they could rely on him. They lost John F. Kennedy and they couldn't count on Richard Nixon, but they knew that Yaz would not let them down. And if they had the slightest doubt about that, he reassured them in 1967 and 1975. No. 8 was there, doing the job and doing it right. If the game-winning hit or rally-killing throw were needed, they looked to No. 8 and he delivered.

There have, of course, been greater ballplayers than Yastrzemski. Egad, Ty Cobb hit .367 for 22 years. Hank Aaron and Babe Ruth hit a lot more homers than Yastrzemski, and No. 9 looked a lot better at the plate than No. 8 ever could. Joe DiMaggio played the outfield better. Willie Mays ran the bases better and Al Kaline looked better throwing the ball.

None of this matters to the people who grew up with Yaz as their left fielder. Sure, they know Williams must have been great. They know about Aaron's and Ruth's home run records and DiMaggio's hitting streak. They respect the careers of Willie Mays and Al Kaline. But, in their eyes, Yaz is above and beyond them all, because he has been theirs for a lifetime. They love him, because when it became fashionable to jump from club to club, he did not leave them. He was no baseball vagabond. He stayed with them, in one place and in one uniform. They could always count on No. 8.

They love him, too, because they know it was not all that easy for him. They know about the all-winter workouts. They know that he had to sweat and strain to remain in the game. They know he had to tinker constantly with his swing to offset the advancing years.

Mostly, though, they love him because they knew he always gave them an honest effort. He brought to baseball what the Polish immigrants brought to this country – a deep-seated work ethic, a willingness to sacrifice, a desire to excel. A day's work for a day's pay.

They love him, too, because they know how much he loved what he was doing. How could they want him to leave? They know he wanted one more pennant, one World Series ring.

So now, they know he has to go. They are here this weekend to cheer, and maybe shed a tear. That is the case with Michael Toscano, an 18-year-old UMass student from Revere. He was at the gate early Saturday, waiting for a look at his hero.

"I've loved the guy since I was 10 years old," he said. "He's the greatest player in the history of the American League."

Don't argue. Don't try to talk to them about other eras and other heroes. The children of the '60s and '70s are losing theirs. The times they are a-changin.'

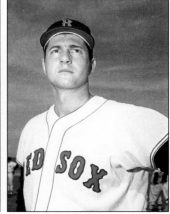

In 1967, Yastrzemski led the Red Sox to the American League pennant for the first time in over two decades. Voted the American League MVP, he was the last winner of the Triple Crown for batters in the Major Leagues until 2012.

Learning From a Rink Rat

There I sat, in the press box of the old Boston Arena, a jittery 20-year-old cub sportswriter for The Springfield Union, facing deadline pressure for the first time.

West Springfield was playing Walpole in the semifinal round of the 1952 state high school hockey tournament. It was the second semi, meaning a late finish and not much time to get the story done.

Lucky for me, I had an old pro at my side. He not only knew the newspaper business, he knew hockey, and he knew every kid on that West Side team. With him as friend and adviser, I really couldn't go wrong.

I got the story done and he quickly checked it for me. He made several suggestions that improved it, and I finished well before my morning paper's first-edition deadline.

He had his own story to write that night. He was covering for The Springfield Daily News, an evening paper, but before he settled in to doing his own work, he made sure mine was done, and done right.

He did the same in the championship game as we shared the joy of writing about the first WMass team to win a state hockey title.

So it was with Sam Pompei and me. He was my idol, my friend and my mentor then, and he remained so for the rest of his life.

Sam was only 34 years old when we covered that '52 state tournament, but to me even then he was like an ageless sage, a consummate newspaperman always willing to help the young kid.

Oh, he helped another kid at that tournament too. Junie Fontana, a former West Side hockey-football star who had moved to Agawam, came to Boston to watch his buddies play.

The trouble was, he didn't have a place to stay. Sam and I had a room at a little hotel on Huntington Avenue, a block away from the Boston Arena. He solved Junie's problem by inviting him to sleep on the floor in our room during the tournament. And he even got him a seat in the press box.

Junie came from Sam's Memorial Avenue neighborhood in West Springfield, across the street from the Eastern States Coliseum. The "old barn" was a second home to all the kids who grew up there, from Sam's generation down through the "rink rats" who brought home the state crown.

Sam loved his little neighborhood, and never left it. He stayed for a lifetime right there on Heywood Avenue, a short walk from the hockey world he so loved.

Failing eyesight forced him into retirement when he was only 56, but he never lost his passion for sports and the newspaper game.

Sam always stayed in touch. He often would call me with story ideas — and they were good ones. Sometimes, he'd call to point out something in one of my stories that I could have done better. Always the beloved mentor.

He also would call to chat about his favorite teams, the Red Sox and Patriots, usually with complaints about what they were doing wrong.

When Sam was active, you couldn't beat him. Case in point: His "The Man and the Myth" series on Springfield Indians owner Eddie Shore ranks as a classic in hockey writing.

I loved working with – and sometimes against – this man because he had such a passion for what he was doing, and a sense of humor to go with it.

One of Sam's favorite anecdotes came from his years of covering Shore's junior hockey league on Saturday mornings at the Coliseum. In those days, The Sunday Republican would run full box scores on each junior game, complete with penalties.

Sam got a chuckle one Saturday morning when a 10-year-old junior player walked up to him and said, "Hey, mister, you made a mistake in the paper last week. You gypped me out of a penalty."

Through all his years on the sports beat, Sam always had time to be a great family man. He adored his wife, Marge, and their children, Pat and Sandy.

Sam's kids have their own precious memories. As Pat tells one, his dad had his own secret way of getting into the Coliseum after hours.

"Sometimes, on Sunday nights, he would bring us over there and we'd have the ice to ourselves. We'd skate and skate, with only one light on in the whole place – somewhere high above us in the rafters."

That was Sam Pompei, king of the Coliseum in his own right.

We lost him February 20, 2011, just short of his 93rd birthday. A "rink rat" for the ages.

The Haydenville Kid

There she poses in a semi-crouch, hands on knees, cap tipped jauntily to one side. She looks ready to play... hardball?

Hey, she has the uniform for it. Pants rolled tightly at the knees, black socks high. As for that auburn hair, it protrudes beautifully from beneath her cap, catching the afternoon sun.

That uniform? It's a perfect fit, with short sleeves and high-buttoned collar. To the left, the shirt bears a "Cubs" logo – obviously a copy of the well-known insignia of the National League's Chicago Cubs.

The cap completes her sartorial elegance. Just above its short bill, the cap is emblazoned with "H."

What an outfit. Put her in, coach, she's ready to play today.

Actually, she never played an inning. She probably could have, but young ladies of her day just didn't engage in such a sweaty and dusty activity as baseball.

No, she never played baseball or softball, because she was a child of the late 19th century, born in 1892.

OK, but that didn't stop her from having a bit of fun on a Sunday afternoon at Walpole's Field in dear old Haydenville. She was there to cheer for her boyfriend, a resolute right-hander who was pitching for her favorite team, the Haydenville Cubs.

As usual, he pitched the whole game. Hey, he didn't have much choice, considering that the Haydenville roster consisted of 10 boyhood pals, and no bullpen. After it was over, she began kidding him. I want to wear your uniform, she said. I want to feel like a ballplayer.

Oh, she could be persuasive, all right. With those Irish eyes smiling at him, and that auburn hair glistening in the sunlight, he didn't have a chance. He finally agreed – but she would have to wait until the next weekend. He wanted to take his woolly uniform home, and let it air out on the clothesline before he would hand it over to the girl of his dreams.

So it was, on the following Saturday, that he produced his precious Cubbies outfit, somewhat fresh and ready to wear. She took it home, put it on, and came back to Walpole's Field. To play ball? No – to pose for a picture. She wanted the camera to record this magic moment in the colorful history of Haydenville baseball.

As she posed, the pitcher studied her and could truthfully say that the uniform looked far better on her than it did on him.

It is hard to know exactly when that photograph was taken. An educated guess would be that she probably was 16 years old when she struck her baseball pose. If that's correct, in seven more years, she would be married to that ace of the Haydenville Cubs pitching staff.

Today, one of those baseball photographs has a place on the desk where I do a lot of writing at home on my trusty laptop. As I tap away, the sight of her in a baseball uniform makes me smile and at the same time makes me wonder what the grand olde game must have been like in the small towns of America in that simpler time.

The Haydenville Cubs played every weekend, sometimes at Walpole's Field, sometimes elsewhere in Hampshire County. Their No. 1 pitcher often told me about his team's arch-rivalry games with kids from Skinnerville. If Haydenville won on Skinnerville's home field, those Cubbies would be stoned out of town. At least that was the pitcher's colorful version of what happened.

Haydenville's rubber-armed right-hander later moved up from the Cubs – a junior team – to the New Haydenville Nine. He played a couple of seasons, but his baseball days ended all too soon. At a time of life when he might have been at the peak of his pitching prowess, he took a job at the United States Post Office in Indian Orchard, got married and soon was moving a long way from Walpole's Field, so he could walk to work in the morning. Family life and a steady job became more important than the Haydenville-Skinnerville baseball rivalry.

My mother, Marguerite Mary Connell, as a 16-year-old, modeling the Haydenville Cubs baseball uniform of her boyfriend, Jeremiah James Brown (my dad).

Over the years, the photograph of his sweetheart in his baseball uniform has been copied and recopied many times so various members of our family can share it. The photo becomes especially precious in May, when we say "Happy Mother's Day" to the loving memory of Marguerite Mary Connell Brown.

I'll bet she would have made a terrific second baseman.

Danny D On the Court

IN DECEMBER OF 1962, the first Chicopee Comprehensive High School basketball team opened its schedule at Springfield Trade.

Halftime score: Trade 38, Comp 1.

"The final score was something like 71–15, and that was with their coach, Ed Kosior, taking it easy on us," said Dan Dulchinos, the living legend of Comp coaching who will retire at the end of this season.

Dan D is best known as a baseball man, the winner of 600-plus games and the Western Mass. record-holder for coaching longevity – 50 years. But for the first seven years of Comp's varsity existence, he also coached the basketball team, and while he was at it, produced one of the great stories in Western Mass. high school sports.

That story unfolded in March of 1965, when those Comp Colts stunned Springfield Tech 53–49 at the Springfield College Field House to win the Western Mass. championship.

It was the year of the first state tournament, which replaced the old New Englands at Boston Garden. Comp went on to beat Oliver Ames of North Easton in the state quarterfinals, then lost to Eastern Mass. power Durfee of Fall River in the semifinal round.

With that, Comp closed with a 20-5 record, including a 14–2 to win the Valley League in its first season of membership. Only two seasons earlier, the team had gone 3-16 and lost by such outlandish scores as 65–25 (Cathedral) and 90–30 (Commerce).

"It was a special team that learned to play together from the ground up," Dulchinos said. "When we started, all the junior and senior athletes were allowed to stay at Chicopee High to finish out their school careers. So we had freshmen and sophomores, and they stayed together for three years to become a team I'll never forget."

Johnny Graham, Comp's first star athlete, served as the cornerstone of Dulchinos' building job. He teamed with Alex Popp, Bill LaPointe, John Kitchen, Ed Matulewicz and Vic Anop to form the core of a team that would first learn how to play the game, then how to win it.

The Colts learned the hard way, playing an independent schedule over their first two seasons that included all the Springfield schools, plus smaller powers like Longmeadow, Smith Academy, Arms Academy and Holyoke Catholic.

"I think the turning point came six games into the 1964 season, when we played in the Commerce gym," Dulchinos said. "Going in, I was figuring that if we could lose by less than 30 it would be a big improvement and a moral victory."

With six minutes to play, Comp was doing all right – trailing by 17 points. Then Commerce started to miss, Comp started to score and suddenly the home team was in trouble. Comp won a stunner, 75–72.

"That was the game when things started to fall into place for us," said Popp, a big forward who went on to become a star at Westfield State.

The Colts finished that season at a respectable 12-8, and were on their way to the heights.

"Coach Dan never gave up on us, even when we were so bad and facing utter adversity at the beginning," Popp said.

"When we were seniors, we went into the tournament knowing that Cathedral was the team to beat, but they lost to Drury (of North Adams) and that opened the door for us. I still reflect on it, a magical time playing in a great setting like the Field House."

Popp said that Dulchinos always stressed the fundamentals, and made his players work on improving their individual skills.

"He could torture us bigger guys with rebounding drills, but after we learned how to do it, we had no fear," Popp said.

In their championship season, Dulchinos' preaching about teamwork showed in the final scoring stats – Popp 14.3 points per game, LaPointe 11.5, Graham 11.4, Kitchen 11.3 and Matulewicz 7.9.

"After all these years, I still have to call him Mr. D, because I have so much respect for him," Matulewicz said. "He was a great coach because he cared about you as a person and a player. He was a great motivator, too. Let's face it, he's an icon in Chicopee."

In winning Western Mass., Comp had to beat a Tech team led by Lahovich Award winner Dwight Durante.

"I think Dwight was the best I ever played against, even flashier than Henry Payne and Gene Ryzewicz," Matulewicz said, referencing the Commerce and Cathedral stars who shared the Lahovich Award in 1964.

"Dwight was hampered a bit against us by a foot infection, but he was so quick we still couldn't hope to guard him man to man. So the coach gave us a 1-2-2 zone, and it worked."

It worked so well, Comp became the first Chicopee team to win a Western Mass. basketball title.

Now, you'll find Graham, Popp, Kitchen and Matulewicz in the Chicopee Athletic Hall of Fame. There, you'll also find Dan Dulchinos – a baseball coach who did all right on the basketball court, too.

Bobby Doerr, No. 1

News item: With the death of Lou Lucier on Oct. 18, 2014, Hall of Famer Bobby Doerr becomes the oldest living Red Sox player. He is 96 and six months old; Lucier died at 96 and seven months.

Summer, 1941. Time for another day of baseball in Cottage Hill Park, just across from our house on Myrtle Street, Indian Orchard.

Cottage Hill wasn't really meant for baseball, but our neighborhood crew found a way. A park bench served as first base, two scrub pines as second and third. Home? I took care of that simply by drawing an outline in the dirt with a stick.

We didn't dare "swing away" with houses so nearby. Matter of fact, we even devised a rule that said, "into the street is out." That posed a problem to Marty Rickson, our only left-handed hitter, because Myrtle Street was right there, along the first-base line (imaginary, of course). Marty would whine a bit, then concentrate on trying to hit the ball back through the middle.

We didn't have a full nine, but we did have enough for a pitcher, catcher, two infielders and a lonely outfielder who had to play his way around various trees and shrubs.

I opted for second base, simply because that's where Bobby Doerr played for the Boston Red Sox. Although I was only nine-plus years old, I already had decided that Bobby was my favorite ballplayer. I listened to Sox games on the radio, and he always seemed to be hitting the ball off the left field wall. Besides, I liked the way the announcers talked about him, sometimes referring to him by his full name – Robert Pershing Doerr. I loved that. And I loved the fact that he wore No. 1, which seemed just right for him.

So it was that second base became the place for me. I played it next to the scrub pine, and I played it in pickup games at Goodwin Park. As my baseball career began to unfold, I could see the future. Bobby Doerr would play second base for the Red Sox until he got old, then I would replace him.

Not quite. I peaked as a second baseman at the age of 12, and never got any better. By the time I went to high school at Springfield Tech, I had no chance of even going out for a spot on the bench.

Never mind. I still followed the Red Sox – and especially my man Bobby – even to the point of keeping a scrapbook of the entire 1946 season. The Sox won 104 games that year, then lost a heartbreaking World Series to the St. Louis Cardinals. My man Bobby did his part by hitting .409.

Heartbreak? I really felt it on the last day of the 1948 season (playoff loss to the Cleveland Indians) and the last day of the '49 season (loss to the Yankees with the pennant on the line). Springfield's own Vic Raschi won that showdown, but Bobby socked a two-run triple as the Sox tried to rally in the ninth.

A year later, I was an 18-year-old rookie in The Springfield Union's sports department. The Sox were still dear to me, but they failed in '50 and '51 because they just didn't have the pitching to back powerhouse lineups.

More heartbreak came in September of '51, when my man Bobby incurred a back injury which put him out for the rest of the season. Fearful of causing further damage, he chose to retire at the age of 33.

Fast forward to 1967. Dick Williams gets hired to manage the Red Sox, and asks Bobby Doerr to be his first base coach. A nice job for him, and the break of a lifetime for me. When The Union started covering those "Impossible Dream" Red Sox in their pennant drive, I met Bobby Doerr in person. After I got up the nerve to approach him, he gave me a nice interview, all the while reaffirming what I had always thought about him. The man was a class act.

I had another memorable interview with him in 1981, when he came back to Fenway Park for Old-Timers Day.

Colleague Fran Sypek snapped a picture of me interviewing my idol. It still hangs on a wall at home.

In July of 1986, still another interview with Bobby on the day of his induction into the Baseball Hall of Fame in Cooperstown, N.Y. Then, in 1988 came another special moment – the retiring of Bobby's No. 1 by the Red Sox at Fenway Park. After that ceremony, I broke a personal rule against asking for autographs. I asked Bobby, and he signed a poster for me. Of course, that's on the wall at home, too.

Career stats? He did all right there – 14 seasons, 1,865 games, .288 average, 223 homers, 1,247 RBI. And try this one: He struck out an average of 43 times per season.

Just think. He was 18 years old when he went to his first spring training in 1937 – and he made the opening day lineup as leadoff man (he had turned 19 by then). Now, in his new status as the oldest living Sox player, he's a perfect fit for the role. And he still has that great head of silvery hair.

To this aging fan, Bobby Doerr will always be what baseball is all about. He was "Mr. Team" for the Red Sox of my baseball dreams.

Interviewing my all-time favorite ballplayer, Bobby Doerr of the Boston Red Sox. Old-Timers Day, Fenway Park, June 1981. Photo taken by my old friend and colleague, Fran Sypek.

Keepers of the Game

Baseball endures because of certain heroes.

We might think of them as larger-than-life types with unforgettable names. The Sultan of Swat, the Iron Horse, the Georgia Peach. Matty. Three-Finger. Ol' Pete. The Big Train. The Splendid Splinter. The Yankee Clipper. Yaz. Reggie. Willie. The Mick. The Duke.

Larger than life and colorfully named, for sure, but even they are not the heroes that enable baseball to endure. Even they could not carry The Grande Olde Game this far.

Baseball endures, not because of Hall of Famers, but because of the heroes we honor on Father's Day. In every ballpark of every professional league, attention should be paid to this special occasion, because fathers are keepers of baseball's flame.

Look back across the generations of baseball, and you see fathers in the backyards and vacant lots of America, playing with their sons – and daughters, too.

Look back, and you see them teaching their kids how to play the game, respect the game, love the game. You see them bringing baseball home.

Baseball does not always mean a domed stadium filled with 50,000 roaring fans. It does not always mean professional teams manned by multi-million dollar superstars.

Baseball also means a father play-ing catch with his kids. It means a game of pepper in a nearby park. It means pickup, with three or four on a side and beautiful rules like "into the street is out."

Yes, baseball also means junior programs of all kinds, but here again, those depend on the local heroes who work to keep things going. We can only hope that they make the game fun for the youngsters – uniforms, umpires and tournaments notwithstanding.

The most fun I ever had playing baseball happened on a shimmering beach in Wells, Maine. We stayed next to a cottage owned by Leo Cloutier, a retired sports editor of the Manchester, N.H., Union Leader.

At low tide, he would show up on the beach, carrying a bat and a ball tightly wrapped in adhesive tape. He would stand there, hitting grounders, line drives – and best of all – towering high flies – to anybody who wanted to join in, glove or not.

He would be there for a couple of hours, constantly hitting the ball out of his hand, taking aim at each "player" in turn, and thoroughly enjoying the spectacle of it all.

The daily crowd that would gather for Leo's version of "beachball" includ-ed three of his grandchildren. The five-year-old got to be pretty good at han-dling one-hoppers.

Yours Truly did all right, too. My best play came on a liner to my right.

I speared it backhand, my momentum taking me for an unexpected dip in the surf. Leo loved it.

In the second decade of the 20th century, my father was a kid pitching for the Haydenville Cubs, a junior team of some repute in the Connecticut Valley. Later, Dad moved into the "bigtime," pitching for the Haydenville Nine in an old-time version of the Tri-County League. (He used to talk about his team getting stoned out of town any time they beat Skinnerville).

This man taught me to love baseball, calling it "the greatest game ever invented." Furthermore, he taught me all the intricacies of keeping a scorebook. His games of catch never led me to the big leagues as a player, but his lessons in scorekeeping served me well over a long career of covering games for The Springfield Republican

My dad took me to my first Boston Red Sox game in 1946. Some 20 years later, we took our family for their first look at that green jewel, Fenway Park. They got to see Catfish Hunter, a brash rookie right-hander, get knocked out of the box by the Red Sox in the third inning. That was a few years before he became a blue-chip starter for the Oakland A's and New York Yankees.

Fenway memories of childhood and fatherhood remain special, of course, but the most precious for me came right in our own front yard. We couldn't play out back – too many trees in the way – but the front lawn offered a perfect setting for pepper games. Everybody played, regardless of age, gender or condition of glove. Even our black Labrador retriever took part. She chased down everything that our "fielders" missed. Ah, there's nothing quite like grabbing a grimy baseball slathered in dog saliva.

Our games weren't always at home. Sometimes, we would march up the hill and around the corner to a neighborhood park. As we went, we tended to draw a crowd. By the time we reached the park, we'd have nearly a "full squad" of players.

Years later, our front-lawn pepper game scene was replayed, over and over, with our grandchildren moving into the starting lineup. At that stage, we switched to wiffleball, giving them the chance to swing away without fear of window breakage. Also, they had the great fun of striking out grandpa.

All of the above reminds me of 1972, when our eight-year-old son gave me a Father's Day present – a little book entitled "What Is a Father?" It contained a series of drawings and statements by kids, relating to the trials and joys of fatherhood, like "A father is the man you go to when you're in a tough spot."

On the back inside cover, our son used a black magic marker to add his own statement, one that I treasure to this day: "A father is a man who takes you out to play baseball."

Happy Father's Day, gents. Let's go outside and have a catch.

Remotely Challenged

Back in the '80s, we purchased our first color television set. It really was more like a piece of furniture, with a large wooden cabinet encasing the screen.

Those were the days when TV sets still had knobs, needed for the necessities: switching channels, controlling volume, adjusting the color, brightening the picture.

In the early '90s, when our first grand-child was crawling and curious, she became enamored of that TV set. For the cartoons on the screen? No – for the knobs.

Place her on our living room carpet, and she'd immediately head for the TV set. She kneeled in front of it, turning all the knobs back and forth, over and over. Sometimes, she'd spin the knobs until they became loose. Eventually, she not only removed all the knobs, she managed to make them disappear.

What to do? Well, her grandmother solved the problem by placing a pair of pliers atop the TV set. We used them to turn all the "knobs," which now had only metal protrusions where the actual knobs used to be.

Years later, the old color TV finally gave way to a spiffy new one. Along with it came a remarkable device known as "the remote." Operating it took some practice for the technically challenged (me), but I finally mastered it, only once needing a visit from "the cable guy" to tell me why I was getting a screen full of snow instead of the local news.

We since have disposed of that second TV and acquired a new one. All went well, remote-wise, until last November, when our cable company delivered an upgrade. With it came a whole new set of channels, so many that I have no chance of seeing them all.

The upgrade meant another new remote, which I found to be workable only in certain situations, like watching regular programming. Now, if I want to do anything more than that, well, would you believe that I actually have four remotes lined up on our living-room coffee table – and they're all needed at one time or other.

The complications grew when our son gave us a "sound bar" for Christmas. It's a wondrous thing, enhancing the sound on our TV set. Ah, but you guessed it – the sound bar gets activated only by its very own remote.

Our DVD player adds to the remote difficulties. To activate it, I need a different remote that has an "input" button. Press that, and you get a 10-item menu which can baffle people who happen to have technical difficulties (me). My first encounter with the menu was so confusing, it was time for another visit from the cable guy.

"Looks like somebody at our end messed up the program here," he said, after viewing the input menu. Well, that made me feel a little better. At least it wasn't ALL my fault.

As he pointed out, the listings didn't match the functions.

"If you want the DVD, don't press DVD. Press cable box. If you want the cable box, press HDM1," he said.

Clear? To him, maybe.

At least his visit explained why I would get a black screen when I'd press DVD. Worse yet, the black screen came with a ominous message down in the right corner – "no signal."

All of that was enough to make me ignore the DVD player for several months. Heck, that was easier than trying to make it work.

Finally, though, I had to face up to it. Our daughter visited, and brought along a DVD of a movie she wanted us to see. Luckily, I somehow remembered what the cable guy taught me. I actually got the DVD player going, but when I hit "play," nothing happened.

"Maybe you need another remote," our daughter said. She wasn't trying to be funny. She actually was right. Rummaging through our pile of remotes (we have seven altogether), she came up with one labeled "Samsung," which was the brand of the DVD player.

She found a "play" button on that one, and pressed it. Voila – the movie started. Trouble was, no sound.

I grabbed the sound-bar remote, thinking that was the problem. But it was already on. Help!

At this point, my wife picked up the regular TV remote, and out of desperation, hit the volume button, Wow – the sound came through, loud and clear.

So, after wrestling with four remotes – each of which performed a needed function – we sat back and enjoyed a movie that was made in 1970.

By the time we want to watch another movie on DVD, I'll probably need a refresher course in how to use the four remotes in proper sequence – one to turn on the TV, one to activate the DVD, one to get it to play, and two to take care of the volume.

Somewhere, there must be a better way, an easier way. How about one remote that takes care of everything?

Or, how about a TV set with those good old dependable knobs? Our granddaughter is 22 now, so we can assume that she wouldn't lose them again.

The Writing Wrestler

Rodney Smith's road to an Olympic Games bronze medal in Greco-Roman wrestling began in a corridor of Springfield's Putnam Vocational High School.

As he walked along with classmates, he talked way too loudly about his accomplishments as a running back on the football team. As fate would have it, he also walked into Bill Borecki, coach of the school's wrestling team.

"Why don't you take that mouth down to the wrestling room, and we'll get a good look at you," Borecki said.

Smith bristled at the challenge.

"Sure, I'll go down there. And I'll whip everybody," he said.

Not quite.

"Coach put me up against a kid who weighed about 120 pounds. I kind of laughed, and figured it would be easy. No way. It took that kid about 30 seconds to turn me into a pretzel," Smith said.

"That kid" was Wayne Stevens, one of the 31 Western Mass. champions that Borecki produced in his 16 years as Putnam's wrestling coach (1973–88). "Little did I know," Smith said with a wry smile.

Actually, Smith had done some wrestling at Kennedy Junior High, but the Putnam program was a big step up – and he decided to stick with it.

"Rodney was a solid block of muscle when he came to us, but he needed to learn technique and endurance. He needed to learn that wrestling often comes down to the final minute, and you have to be ready to handle it," Borecki said.

"The upside for him was that he had undeveloped potential that just blossomed."

It took a while.

"Rodney wrestled with us for two years. When he was a junior, he got beat up pretty good, but he won Western Mass. (140-pound class) as a senior in 1984 and finished second in the state."

Putnam's culture of success in wrestling had long-lasting positive effects on Smith.

"My grades were up, my outlook changed. I started thinking about college, the Olympics, and being a writer," he said.

So it was that Smith went to Western New England College (now University), where he became a two-time All-America under the guidance of Bob Skelton, respected hereabouts as "the father of WNE wrestling."

Smith made it into Skelton's program with a big assist from the United States Marine Corps.

"At Putnam, I applied to Springfield College and Western New England. One day I got a letter saying that Springfield had turned me down. I got upset, and decided to forget college, so I went down and joined the Marines."

Two days before his reporting date, he received a letter saying that he had been accepted at WNEC.

"It took a lot of doing, but when I told the Marines that I got accepted at college, they gave me a deferment on the condition that I would go into the military – not necessarily the Marine Corps – after I graduated."

Smith fulfilled his commitment, joining the Army soon after his commencement day in 1988.

By 1989, he was stationed in Atlanta, a place which served him well as a wrestler, and as a student of writing.

"While I was there, the Army developed a training program aimed at producing world-class wrestlers that could be candidates for the Olympic team," he said. "I got the chance to be part of that. At the same time, I was able to attend Georgia State University part-time in a journalism master's program."

In the wrestling department, Smith soon showed the Army that it had a winner. "I was dedicated, and I won some Army tournaments, then a silver medal in an all-Armed Forces tournament, and then a military world championship in 1991," he said.

From there, he was on a fast track for the Olympics.

"The training I had as a soldier made me a very fit, and it helped me with my mindset and endurance. I could focus on the match, no matter what the competition was," he said.

When Smith was training for the Olympics, he had a face-to-face meeting with Gen. Norman Schwartzkopf, commander of coalition forces in the Gulf War of 1991.

"He told me that my mission was to go to the Olympics and win a medal," Smith said. "He saw it as a chance to give a big morale boost to troops serving in combat."

At the Summer Olympics in Barcelona, Smith wrestled in the 149.5-pound class and lost only one match – to Attila Repko of Hungary, who wound up winning the Greco-Roman gold.

Smith's quest for a medal came down to a match with Cecilio Rodriguez of Cuba. Smith trailed 3-0 with only 90 seconds left, but made a miracle comeback to win the match 6-3.

It was a performance mindful of coach Borecki's words about "being ready for the last minute."

In retrospect, Smith says the medal ceremony was "bittersweet" as he was awarded the bronze.

"That's because in my mind, my only mission was to win the gold. I love my country, and my mom is very patriotic, so it was kind of hard to stand there and listen to the Hungarian national anthem being played."

Smith also made the Olympic team in 1996, but did not medal.

He spent 10 years in the Army, and still works closely with its wrestling program, which now is based in Colorado Springs, Colo.

"I've been coaching some of the wrestlers, and three of my guys are going to London. I'll be there with them," he said.

Smith's soldiers on the Olympic roster are Spenser Mango, in the 121-pound class; Justin Lester, 145.5; and Dremiel Byers, in the super heavyweight.

Along with his Army wrestling commitments, Smith teaches at the Hampden Charter School of Science in Chicopee. Among his duties – coach of the wrestling team.

He also works with junior wrestlers at the Martin Luther King Family Center in Springfield.

As he goes about his coaching duties, he never forgets what Putnam's Borecki told him back in the late 1980s.

"Coach always said we should let our efforts on the mat speak for us. Don't talk like a champ until you prove you are one – and never underestimate an opponent," Smith said.

As for his master's degree in writing, he puts it to good use. He keeps a daily journal that he calls "the road map of my life," and writes poetry and short stories.

Wrestling, coaching and writing – Springfield's own Rodney Smith has all of his talents well in hand.

Going To Baseball School

No doubt about it, the gentleman who ran Indian Orchard's Goodwin Park had a commanding presence.

His booming voice carried all the way across Sullivan's Pond and into our backyard. When Tom McCarthy barked orders or worked a Goodwin Park ballgame as plate umpire, everybody in the neighborhood knew it.

With his shock of white hair, ruddy face and strong build, "Mac" was an unforgettable character.

He didn't own Goodwin Park, it just seemed that way. He was always there, caring for the infield with its unusual skin diamond; making sure the park's old grandstand was always clear of trash; and keeping an eye on the tennis courts, as well.

In summers of the long ago, I would ride my bike down Myrtle Street, on to Berkshire Avenue, then into Goodwin Park. One day, "Mac" cornered me. He had seen me playing catch with a couple of friends, and knew I needed help.

"You're in my baseball school," he said. "Be here Monday morning at 9 – and I mean 9 sharp."

Mac knew who he was collaring, all right. He knew my dad, who worked at the Post Office; and he knew that one of my older brothers was a best pal of his twin sons – Tom Jr. and Gene.

The fact that he wanted me in his baseball school was both intimidating and exciting. For instance, it was very scary to realize that Mac had his eye on me. On the other hand, it was quite an honor to be "enrolled" in his baseball school, even though, at the age of 10, I had no say in the matter.

Actually, Tom McCarthy's baseball school ranked as an Orchard tradition, a summer staple for 25 years. As time went on, kids who took part in his school would come back and help him, serving as assistant instructors. There was no doubt, though, about who was in charge.

Many neighborhood kids who learned the basics in that baseball school went on to become varsity players on Springfield high school teams. No, that did not include me, even though in my boyhood daydreams, I would see myself wearing a Tech Tigers uniform.

On my first morning in baseball school, the professor told me to get in a line of kids that stretched from third base to first around Goodwin Park's infield. I'm not sure if it was by chance, or by design, but my place in the line turned out to be the normal spot for a shortstop.

Then it began. With machine-like accuracy, he began hitting ground balls. One by one, we would be tested. Out there, on that skin infield, with no place to hide, we took turns trying to field hot grounders off the crack of his bat.

The first ball hit to me went right through the wickets, as Mac growled something about getting that glove down. Second time around, same thing. Third time? Yes, the same thing again. Baseball school had barely started, and I already had three errors marked against my name.

Mac had a gruffness about him, but as I came to learn, he also had patience. The fourth time around, I did get the glove down, and the ball hopped right into it as he yelled, "That's the way!"

By the end of that first session of Ground Balls 101, I had fielded six out of 10. In my mind, I began comparing myself to Dave Garrow, the slick shortstop for my favorite local team, Chapman Valve. Heck, a few more sessions with Mac, and I'd be on my way.

Well, not quite. I did learn a lot about baseball fundamentals from him in my summer of '41, but an instructor can do only so much if the raw talent just isn't there.

Tom McCarthy knew that, but he also knew I came to play every day, and tried my best to do what he demanded of the kids in his care.

Because of all that, I stepped front and center on the final day of baseball school to accept an award.

Handing me a brand-new bat (wooden, of course), Mac intoned, "This goes to you as my baseball school's most-improved player."

What a thrill, but alas, it didn't last. As I rode my bike home, Marty Rickson rode along with me. For a time, I reveled in my award as we pedaled along in silence. Marty finally had something to say:

"You know why you won that? Because you were so lousy when you started."

Ouch. You can always count on your best friend to tell you the truth, even when it hurts. Marty was right, of course, and deep in my heart, I knew it. Still, I cherished that bat, and kept it for years.

Tom McCarthy's MIP – me, in a shimmering summer of baseball at my all-time favorite park.

Postscript: At the height of Goodwin Park's popularity, it would host 100 games a year, everything from 10–12 sandlots to the Triple A Industrial League. Tom McCarthy Sr. served the city as director of Goodwin Park and Myrtle Street playground until he retired at the age of 70. Tom Jr. succeeded him for a time, then left the Orchard to become director of parks and recreation in West Springfield. Goodwin Park, with its quaint grandstand and beautiful skin infield, no longer exists. John F. Kennedy Middle School stands in its place.

Hitting Away for 40 Years

What? Come on now, that can't be true.

November 19, 1973?

Wait a darn minute. If that date is correct, it would mean that I have been writing "Hitting to All Fields" for...40 years?

Egad!

Yes, after due research by our son Peter, Ye Olde Sports Columnist has found that his first "Hitting to All Fields" column ran 40 years ago on November 19 in a Monday edition of this newspaper (then called The Springfield Union).

So, happy anniversary to...Favorite sports names:

Honking
Getting old if
You take-I'll take
The hard life of Ye Olde Handicapper
Numbers of the week
Trying to get a field named for Billy
 Wise
  Saluting local teams and athletes
  Tracking Labrador retrievers
  And tons more – most of it fun

Forty years? No wonder well-meaning little old ladies stop me in the supermarket to say, "I've been reading your column since I was a little girl."

Of course, not all of the feedback offers praise or encouragement. For instance, after years of writing about Labrador retrievers, I ran across this e-mail: "It's just a dog – get over it."

Ooh, that hurt, but it didn't stop me. Now, I chronicle the foibles of our son's family dog, Venus the Labrador retriever. Heck, she's so popular, she even has her own Facebook page, with 1,181 friends.

By the way, the first Labrador retriever reference in "Hitting" appeared Feb. 18, 1975, as follows:

"Mets pitcher Tom Seaver and I have something in common. He is rich, famous and owns a Labrador retriever. I, too, own a Labrador retriever."

That brought enough mail to make me realize that Labs (and their antics) deserved to be mentioned more often.

Then there was the day I wrote something positive about Tampa Bay third baseman Evan Longoria. A reader offered this response: "You take Evan Longoria, I'll take Eva Longoria."

Dang – wish I had written that.

Forty years. Talk about being in a rut. In this business, though, it happens. One of my favorites, The Washington Post's Shirley Povich, wrote a sports column entitled "This Morning" until he passed away in 1997 at the age of 92.

For the record, the first "Hitting" item said: "Just sitting and wondering if Fran Tarkenton will march through Georgia tonight."

At the time, Tarkenton quarterbacked the undefeated Minnesota Vikings. Of course, they lost that Monday night game to the Atlanta Falcons, thereby setting the tone for decades of faulty predictions by Yours Truly.

"Hitting" hit the big-time in 1990,

when somebody at the Comedy Central network in New York picked up on this line: "Paul Provenza might be the funniest person on TV." It referred to the comedian who hosted an ingenious talk show called "Comics Only."

In response, Provenza devoted a large segment of his next show to a tongue-in-cheek bit dedicated to me and my little ol' column. I still have the tape.

Another time, after praising the stand-up work of comic Richard Belzer, I received a note of thanks from a Longmeadow reader who informed me that "The Belz" was her nephew.

The column's "you're getting old if..." items often refer to athletes I covered during my years on the high school beat. One of them mentioned Marty Wilkes of Smith Academy 1961 basketball, and brought this response from him: "Here I am living in Australia, and I can't believe my name is in the Springfield paper."

Yes, "Hitting" gets around.

On many occasions, I have sat and wondered why the column draws so much interest. Of course, my wife has the ready answer.

"It's the only column you can read from the bottom up." Hmm. She's probably right. Always is.

By the way, let it be said that while my version of "Hitting to All Fields" has become a staple in the sports section, it did have predecessors. My old boss, Dutch Robbins, wrote a local notes column entitled "Hitting to All Fields" in 1948-50. And my long-time colleague, Gerry Finn, did a notes column for a time in the 1960s that carried the same title.

As for the idea of a column consisting of short one-liners on a variety of subjects, we must give a tip of the hat to Jimmy Cannon. His "Nobody asked me, but..." columns in the old New York Journal American established that as a workable format.

Hey, all of this reminds me – another "Hitting" deadline looms, as of Tuesday evening. Time to start collecting more one-liners.

Can anybody spare a favorite sports name? After 40 years, Ye Olde Columnist needs all the help he can get.

Grand-daughter Rayna helps me write "Hitting." January, 1998.

My First 'Hitting to All Fields'

Note: This first edition of "Hitting to All Fields" ran in The Springfield Union of Nov. 19, 1973. It has been running ever since as a staple of the sports section.

Just sitting and wondering if Fran Tarkenton will march through Georgia tonight.

Why didn't someone think to include a "sudden death" proviso in that East Longmeadow-Fitchburg football matchup.

Now we're back to those dastardly ratings.

"You wonder why we can't do this every week," said Jim Plunkett after passing Patriots past Packers.

Yes, Jim, we wonder.

A guy called for Ted Williams' age. The record book says 55, but that must be a misprint.

Are the Western Mass. Pioneers moving from Holyoke to Waterbury?

Does anybody care?

What the American Hockey League needs is more players like Derek Sanderson.

Can't help loving "Angie" by the Rolling Stones.

Confidential to Jeff White: you can play again next week.

Will those auto racers keep it at 50?

Just when Yale's Dick Jauron wondered if he could cut it in the NFL, he zipped 95 yards for a TD on an interception for the Detroit Lions.

Philosophy from UCLA's Pepper Rodgers: "Every coach needs a dog, because a dog doesn't care whether you win or lose."

Just when the Giants win a game, their fans get blacked out.

Don't be surprised if Tommy Harper winds up as the Red Sox' designated hitter.

If Kareem Abdul-Jabbar would hustle half as much as Dave Cowens does, he'd be the best basketball player ever.

Joe Namath's back, passing 'em dizzy and ripping the officials. He hasn't changed.

Williams College always seems to save its best football for last – when it plays Amherst.

If Phil Esposito keeps it up, he'll have to go to a higher league.

Ohio State and Michigan will draw 104,000 for their Big Ten showdown. And who said the NFL is big time?

Hats off to the Chicopee High's soccer boys, best in the state again. Probably best in New England, too, but nobody invited them.

If you can get up early on the next three Sundays, there's some excellent touch football playoff action available. Those guys play for real.

I wonder what would happen if a boy demanded to play in that new Springfield girls hockey league?

Poor Ben Crenshaw. All he got for second place in the World Open was $44,000. Maybe someday he'll hit the big time.

Pats play Houston next. A two-game win streak in the making?

Cheer up, baseball fans, only 13 weeks to go to spring training.

'Hitting To All Fields' — 42 Years Later

Note: This edition of "Hitting" ran Oct. 14, 2015. And the column is still going.

Just sitting and wondering if Dave Dombrowski can lift the Red Sox out of last place.

Bring on the Hershey Bears, and that Falcons home opener.

Pats over Cowboys? No doubt about it.

UMass scouting report: Bowling Green (3-2) has scored 182 points, allowed 180.

News item: Pair of Bruces, Landon and Cline, elected to American Hockey League Hall of Fame. Yes, Springfield scores again.

We'll miss you, Don Orsillo.

Where's Frank Vatrano? With the Providence Bruins.

Say hello to the WNEU Golden Bears, 5-0 in football.

Speediest high school QB in Western Mass. Try Minnechaug's Kyle Trombley.

Farewell, Phil Woods. Your music lives on.

Toronto's Kevin Pillar belongs on the list of baseball's elite center fielders.

Still waiting for the kickoffs at Ted Plumb and Billy Wise fields.

New junior welterweight champ? Viktor "The Iceman" Postol.

What? Ye Olde Handicapper's horse finished last?

The Houston Astros: No. 2 in AL West, No. 29 on the salary list.

You're getting old if you saw Jim and Tim Rooney in a Ludlow High backfield.

Indiana Fever's favorite movie: "Hoosiers."

Number of the week: 2,146 (Career points for NFL place-kicker Adam Vinatieri).

Crimson-tide Dept.: Harvard (3-0) has outscored its foes 139-37.

Who's No. 1? Ohio State, for the 101st time in AP poll history.

That's more like it, Big Blue.

Oct. 9, 1916: Babe Ruth pitches 14 innings as Red Sox beat Brooklyn 2–1 in Game 2 of World Series.

Luckily, the Revs have two weeks to shake off that 3–1 loss at Chicago.

Venus the Labrador retriever's latest sidewalk find: Two full slices of pizza.

News item: Washington Nationals fire manager Matt Williams and his coaching staff. Great expectations, no results.

Grandpa tips his cap to the Western Mass. Golf Hall of Fame.

Paris Hilton as Big E deejay? Yes, indeed.

Chasen A Mason 5K, anyone? (Saturday, 9:30, Turners Falls Masonic Lodge.)

Happy 23d birthday, Mookie Betts.

You take "Madam Secretary." I'll take "Veep."

The other Williams – Venus – is still a winner.

Add Lucas Lessio (Falcons forward) to my list of favorite sports names.

Where have you gone, Sam Cunningham?

Hi At 100

How old is Hy Neigher?

So old, that...

He played basketball in the days of the center jump.

He played against Honey Lahovich, for whom a Western Mass. basketball award is named.

He played baseball in an exhibition game against Rabbit Maranville, Springfield's only electee to the Hall of Fame in Cooperstown, N.Y.

He saw Babe Ruth and Lou Gehrig slug for barnstorming teams at Pynchon Park.

He was a neighborhood marbles star at a time when Springfield would send shooters to the national tournament.

He excelled for the Fro-Joys, a basketball power in the days when local teams flourished.

He saw the Harlem Globetrotters play basketball outdoors at Pynchon Park, and the All-American Redheads play basketball indoors at the Springfield Boys Club. Both teams are enshrined in the Basketball Hall of Fame.

How old must a guy be to have done and seen all that? Well, try 100 – a milestone that Hy Neigher will reach on Sunday, Sept. 14.

Yes, Hy has been around, all right. He has been to Hollywood and back as an illustrator. He has been a newspaperman and an advertising man, bringing boundless energy and good humor to whatever was the task at hand.

Hy could have been a standup comic, but he didn't have time.

Example: "I played golf today at Twin Hills. A good round – found three balls."

Yes, Hy always loved to laugh at the world, and at himself.

And he loved to tell stories. Like the one about meeting Ethel, the love of his life, when he fell into her lap in the old gym at the High School of Commerce. She was in the stands. He was on the court. Someone pushed him out of bounds, and there was Ethel, making a catch that would lead to 70-plus years of marriage.

Then there was the Young Men's Hebrew Association national tournament in New York City. Hy played on a Springfield team that made the finals, only to be disqualified when one of its players blessed himself before taking a free throw. The kid was a ringer – and a Catholic one, at that. The YMHA simply could not allow such duplicity.

That's Hy's story, and he stuck to it for years. Hey, why not? Every time he would tell it – and that was often - he would draw guffaws. He once told it at a reunion of Lahovich Award winners. Jesse Spinks laughed so hard he had to find a bathroom in a hurry.

The truth about Hy Neigher is this – he is an absolute treasure among us, one who can take us back to the '20s when he was a kid, and to the '30s when he was the best left-handed athlete Commerce had ever seen.

Back to the '20s? Yes, Hy could tell you how he won that neighborhood marbles title at the age of 13, and thus earned an opportunity to play for the city championship against a little kid named Howard "Dutch" Robbins. The winner would go to Wildwood, N.J., for the nationals.

"We played on a Sunday afternoon in Forest Park," Hy would say. "Dutchie won the lag, and cleaned the ring every time. I'm playing in the city finals, and I never got a shot."

Hy felt a little better about it when Robbins went on to become the city's first national marbles champion. Later, he became sports editor of The Springfield Union.

Back to the '30s? Yes, Hy can tell you all about those Commerce basketball and baseball days with his teammate and boyhood friend, Izzy Cohen, Class of 1933. Red Raider basketball has been very good over the years – and it started with those teams of 80 years ago.

Then there was Hy's "Betty Boop era," when his talents as an illustrator led him to a job in Hollywood. He drew Betty. He drew Popeye. He also drew for Walt Disney's remarkable "Fantasia" film, then he came back east, lured by love for his hometown. He and Ethel raised a family of bright and successful kids.

Even after he left Hollywood, Hy continued to draw every day – and he was full of surprises, too. My wife and I know that well, because she received a "Betty Boop" drawing from Hy, and I received a "Popeye" – both masterworks, and both autographed by our favorite artist.

In 2007, when the Springfield Public Schools Sports Hall of Fame conducted its first enshrinement, Commerce had worthy representation, led by Hy and Izzy. When Hy received his plaque, he was introduced as the Hall of Fame's "oldest living electee." He was a mere 93 at the time.

Happy 100th, Hi. You are, indeed, a Hall of Famer – a Red Raider for the ages.

Note: Hi Neigher passed away in 2015, surrounded by his loving family.

The Eye and I

As I browsed the world-wide web one morning, I happened upon a full-screen photograph of the vice-president of talent management at Time Inc.

Big job, big smile, big picture – and it left me absolutely stunned.

Is that Bucky Keady? Of the Longmeadow Keadys?

Is that the person who, as a bright-eyed high school senior, asked me to start a student newspaper at Springfield's Ursuline Academy of fortysomething years ago?

Indeed it is.

She's now in her 14th year at Time Inc. after working for 15 years at Conde Nast. While her main concern is in Human Resources, she also writes a career advice column in Real Simple magazine.

I first met her in September of 1970. There she was, sitting in the front row and smiling widely as I walked into a scary new venture – trying to teach journalism to a class of teen-age girls.

Thanks to such superstar kids as Bucky Keady, Maryann "Koko" Kokoszyna, Katie Curran, Valerie Dixon, Judy Rapisarda, Meg Gorman and our daughter Melissa, my first venture into teaching went well.

It was supposed to be a writing class, with special emphasis on the basics of journalism, but one day in late September, the class took on an added purpose. It happened when Ms. Keady raised her hand and asked, "Mr.

Brown, can we have a school newspaper?"

What a great idea. Actually, she had hit upon what the class really should be about. Instead of merely learning the basics of newspaper work, why not use them to produce an actual newspaper?

Maryann Kokoszyna took it from there. As we bandied about ideas for our newspaper's name, she hit it.

"Let's call it The Eye, because our paper will see all that's happening in our school," she said.

Maybe a little over-reaching there, but she certainly had the right idea.

When she came to the next class, Koko showed us a drawing she had done of a beautiful big eye. It became part of our "flag" – the nameplate that would appear on Page One of our paper.

Of course, our plans needed to get clearance from headquarters. That happened quickly. Sister Brenda, Ursuline's principal, loved the idea and encouraged us to proceed.

So it began. Classes included the extra work of talking about story ideas, selecting some for print, then going out and getting them done. I wanted our paper to have at least four pages in a four-column format – and filling that amount of space would be a major challenge.

At that time, my real job was sports editor of The Springfield Union. As such, I was able to convince the paper's chief photographer, Steve Van Meter, to come to one of my classes for a talk about photo-journalism. Once we had him in our clutches, we had no trouble convincing him to donate his services to The Eye. He made several trips to the school, each time taking photographs to go with stories we were doing.

With Bucky and Koko as co-editors, the first issue of The Ursuline Eye reached print in mid-November of 1970 — just in time for us to give advance coverage to the school's annual Christmas Bazaar, a major fund-raising project. A photo of Sister Claveria Laflamme, standing beside a large Christmas Bazaar poster, anchored our first front page.

Bucky became our chief editorial writer, and she would crack me up each time she signed her work, "By Margaret Drake Keady III." You need to think about that for a minute to realize how funny it is.

Luckily, that talented class also included a graphic artist. Judy Rapisarda's pen-and-ink drawings dressed up our editorial page, and other stories, as well.

In The Ursuline Eye's first academic year, the class produced four issues. The paper looked so good and read so well, I suggested to Sister Brenda that we enter it in the Columbia Scholastic Press Association's annual contest. The Eye scored well, leading to a second-place rating. Not bad for our first effort.

Sad to say, the dedicated Ursuline nuns who ran the Springfield high school were forced to close it in June of 1973. Their building at 965 Plumtree Road was converted into a school for grades 1 through 8.

That meant a new challenge for Ye Olde journalism teacher. The school's new principal, Sister Anne Maynard, decided that The Eye could continue, but with the journalism class restricted to eighth-graders. They would prove themselves to be well suited to carry forth what the high school students had started.

The eighth-graders who produced the paper over the next several years did so well, in fact, that Ursuline Eye entries won medalist honors (first place) six times in the Columbia Scholastic Press Association contest.

Hampered by a dwindling membership in their religious order, the Ursuline nuns of Springfield eventually had to close their Plumtree Road school. With that heart-wrenching decision, The Eye faded away.

Memories of all that came flooding back when I saw the stylish photograph of Bucky Keady, shot against a backdrop of Time Inc. publication covers.

A quick exchange of e-mails made it clear that she well remembers journalism class on Plumtree Road, and her considerable contributions to it.

Yes, that's Margaret Drake Keady III of Time Inc. — coming a very long way from her editorial-writing days with the dear old Ursuline Eye.

Nuns Day at Fenway

They were talking baseball. They knew the game, loved the game, and thoroughly enjoyed the second-guessing that goes with it.

"What did that pitcher think? You can't keep throwing fastballs to hitters like Ortiz and Napoli," said one.

"Do that, and they're going to time it, and hit it a long way," said another.

These smart second-guessers were seated on a bus bound for Holyoke. One of them, Sister Irene Fontaine of Chicopee, belongs to the Sisters of St. Joseph, a religious community now facing hard times.

The other second-guesser? Sister Irene's sister, Christine Woz, who accompanied her as they enjoyed a Boston Red Sox offering known as "Nuns Day at Fenway."

After it was over, they sat back on the bus, relaxed and savored the game they had just witnessed – a 2–1, 10-inning victory for the Red Sox over the Minnesota Twins.

"You couldn't make up a better story than that," Sister Irene said.

Yes, baseball had given them something they had never seen, and may never see again – back-to-back home runs to produce a walkoff victory. Those homers came off the bats of their favorite fastball hitters, David Ortiz and Dan Napoli. Until then, the Red Sox had one hit for their afternoon's work. Unbelievable.

Altogether, some 300 nuns – including 43 from the Springfield area – took part in the trip as guests of the Red Sox, who provided free tickets and lunch. Sister Janet Eisner – the longtime president of Emmanuel College - threw a strike on the ceremonial first pitch.

"Nuns Day," a Fenway tradition which had been dropped in the 1970s, was reinstituted in 2013 by Red Sox president Larry Lucchino. His top assistant, Sarah Keaney McKenna, grew up in West Springfield. She arranged for the Western Mass. nuns to attend, under the leadership of Chris Keaney – Sarah's mom – and Mary Jo Salvon of Springfield.

The baseball trip had its edge of sadness, because 14 aging nuns now living at the St. Joseph order's Mont Marie Mother House in Holyoke will be leaving to take up residences in the Boston area as a cost-saving move.

"I look upon it as a new adventure," said Sister Mary Lyons, a Holyoke native now in her 66th year as a religious.

With an attitude like hers generally in place, the nuns were able to enjoy their baseball day.

"I don't get to see many games in person, but I'm a diehard fan. I follow the Red Sox closely on TV," Sister Mary said.

For the record, the nuns stand 2-0 at Fenway. On their trip last June, they saw the Red Sox top the Colorado Rockies 5–3.

"Isn't that something? We saw John Lackey beat the Rockies last year, and today we saw him pitch again, and he had a great game. He didn't get the win, but he was terrific for nine innings."

That bit of baseball wisdom came from Sister Ginny ("Don't call me Virginia") Maitland, a Pawtucket, R. I. native who serves on the St. Joseph order's leadership council.

"I grew up near McCoy Stadium (in Pawtucket), so naturally I came to love baseball. That's such a great minor league park. I can remember how the park's lights would brighten up our neighborhood," she said.

By the way, Sister Ginny wants the world to know that natives pronounce it "Puh-tucket," not "Paw-tucket."

She spoke lovingly of the sisters who soon will be moving, leaving behind surroundings they have known since entering the order.

"They are remarkable, and we are all in awe at the faith and sprit of these women," she said. "Some of them have never lived anywhere outside of the Springfield area, but they know what must be done, and they're meeting the challenge."

Sister Frances White, another Red Sox diehard, has been in the St. Joseph order for 52 years. She's not moving, but admires those who are.

"They offer an example to all of us, the gracious way they are handling this. They see it as a way of opening new doors," Sister Frances said.

On the way to Fenway, the nuns' Peter Pan bus made a stop a State Police barracks in Framingham. There, two troopers insisted on giving the bus a police escort to the ballpark.

"They must have gone to Catholic school," Chris Keaney said.

That quip hit squarely at what these nuns are all about. Sisters of St. Joseph have educated (and disciplined) generations of students – from elementary grades to high school – all across Western Mass. Their impact on the region cannot be measured.

Sister Maxyne Schneider, president of the Sisters of St. Joseph of Springfield, grew up in North Adams, where she attended the now-defunct St. Joseph's High School.

"It was a small school, with 83 in our class, and everybody knew everybody. Later on, in the 1960s, I taught at Cathedral in Springfield, which had something like 2,800 students."

Now, Cathedral's enrollment is less than 300 – and it faces a rebuilding job following the damage done to its Surrey Road quarters by the June 1 tornado of 2011.

Sister Maxyne, a 54-year member of the order, sees the changing landscape of Catholic education and the changing lives of her elderly colleagues as an example of what is happening all across the country.

"We're dealing with difficulty, and a community decision that we do not take lightly. Our sisters are ready to move on, though with some sadness. Those who are able, continue our ministry. Our order is still alive and caring."

Sister Maxyne admits that she's not baseball-savvy like many of the other nuns on the Fenway trip, but she certainly understands the value of this day in the Back Bay sun.

"It's a baseball diversion, very welcome at this time," she said.

The Old Neighborhood

Directly across Memorial Avenue from the Eastern States Exposition Coliseum, a little neighborhood made a huge mark on the American sports scene.

From that neighborhood came...

– Angelo Bertelli, the only Western Massachusetts football player to win the Heisman Trophy. He did that as Notre Dame's quarterback in 1943.

– Pete "The Hermit" Bessone, a defenseman who starred in European hockey of the early '30s, then returned home to play for 10 years in the American Hockey League.

– Amo "Betts" Bessone, Pete's younger brother, who at Michigan State became the first coach from Western Mass. to win an NCAA championship (1966). He was the only one until Springfield's Rick Bennett won at Union College last spring. High school hockey's Bessone Award is named for Amo.

– Gene Grazia, the only WMass native to win an Olympic gold medal in hockey. He did it as a member of the 1960 team which shocked the Soviet Union in the finals at Squaw Valley, Calif.

The Bessones and Grazia all have places in the U.S. Hockey Hall of Fame at Eveleth, Minn. Pete Bessone was enshrined in 1978, Amo in 1992 and Grazia in 2000 along with all of his 1960 teammates.

"The Bessones and Eugene lived on the same block, and Angelo grew up around the corner. It's unbelievable, when you think about it," said Harold Passerini, another Memorial Avenue old-time "hockey guy."

That remarkable neighborhood was brought to mind with the sad news that Gene Grazia had passed away at his Florida residence. When I first saw Gene, he was a young teen, pulling a huge tank of hot water across the Coliseum's ice surface between periods of a Springfield Indians game.

In those days before the Zamboni, Gene and his neighborhood buddies scraped the ice with snow shovels, then put down a fresh sheet for the next period. They were "rink rats," doing every kind of odd job in return for the opportunity to skate on that Coliseum ice.

As a bonus, they often would get one-on-one instructions from their boss, Indians franchise owner Eddie Shore. Lessons from a Hall of Famer helped the West Side kids become the first Western Mass. team to win a state championship.

They did it in 1952, at the old Boston Arena. In their march to glory, they beat Lexington 5–1, Newton 4–0, Walpole 5–3 and Stoneham 4–3 in a tense title game.

That team had a nucleus of six accomplished players known as "The Iron Dukes" – Grazia, Ebby Donaldson, Richie Frasco, Rudy Basilone, Fred Orlosk and Leo Fiorini. Sam Pompei, who also lived across from the Coliseum, gave them their nickname as a hockey writer for The Springfield Daily News.

They were iron, all right, rarely coming off the ice.

"We would just rotate with little rest, and we'd all take turns playing defense," Fiorini recalled. "Graz was on D in the third period when he took a shot from the point. The rebound landed right on my stick, and I put it in for the winning goal."

Fiorini also recalls the important role that backup goaltender Al Klein and sophomore forward Al Collins played in that finale. Although West Side rarely substituted, Collins did get a few shifts – and he scored twice.

"To me, that was amazing. I didn't think Al was on the ice that much, but he gave us those two big ones," Fiorini said.

After that unforgettable senior year, Grazia went on to play for Amo Bessone at Michigan State. In 1960, he made the Olympic team coached by West Point's Jack Riley. The last player cut? Herb Brooks, who 20 years later would coach Uncle Sam's "Miracle on Ice" team in the Lake Placid Olympics.

Now, the old West Side neighborhood has undergone many a change over time. So has the Coliseum, which stopped functioning as a hockey arena when its ice-making system was shut down in 1991. Still, fond memories remain from the those "good old days," when the likes of Bertelli, Bessone and Grazia brought fame to the old neighborhood.

Note: Gene Grazia passed away November 9, 2014. He was 80 years old.

When the Red Sox Played at Pynchon

IMAGINE BEING 14 YEARS OLD AND SITTING STARRY-EYED in the clubhouse among Boston Red Sox players. Ted Williams to your left, Bobby Doerr to your right, Vern Stephens and Johnny Pesky across the room, pitchers Mel Parnell and Ellis Kinder a few lockers down the line.

That's how it was for Paul Whitlock, a retired Cathedral High School cross country and track coach who lived his own "impossible dream" as a teenager in the springs of 1951 and '52.

Whitlock, now 75 years old and living in Florida, had the unique honor of serving for three seasons as visiting batboy at Pynchon Park when the Springfield Cubs played in the Triple A International League.

In 1951 and '52, the Red Sox came to town to play the Cubs in exhibition games prior to the opening of their American League season.

The Red Sox visit to Pynchon Park on April 12, 1951, drew a paid attendance of 10,736 – to this day the largest crowd ever to see a baseball game in Springfield.

The second Red Sox visit on April 9, 1952, also was a very big deal and drew 9,160.

Now, in this 60th anniversary month of the last Red Sox visit to Springfield, Whitlock looks back on a time he will never forget.

"It was so long ago, yet I can remember so many details. That was one of the most wonderful times of my life," he said.

How did he wind up serving as batboy for the Red Sox on those two wondrous April days?

"It all goes back to a contest run by the *Springfield Daily News*," he said. "You filled out an entry blank, and if your name was picked, you could be batboy during a homestand for the Springfield Cubs."

Whitlock won one of the contests in the summer of 1950.

"I got there early for the first game, and I was sitting in the Springfield dugout alone when one of the Cubs players came out. He walked over to me, shook my hand and said, 'Hi, I'm Smokey Burgess.' I thought that was great," he said.

Burgess hit .327 as Springfield's catcher that season, and went on to an 18-year big league career.

Stan Hack Jr. – son of the Springfield Cubs manager – served as home batboy for most of the '50 season, but had to leave near the end to get back to school.

"I got a call from somebody at Pynchon Park asking if I wanted a batboy job for the rest of the season. I jumped at it, and stayed with it for two more years," Whitlock said.

When Hack's son left, the regular visiting batboy took over his role as home batboy. That left the visiting team job to Whitlock.

"Little did I know then that the first game I would work in 1951 would be with the Red Sox," he said.

"I remember being in the clubhouse before the game, listening to Red Sox players talk back and forth. And they talked to me, too."

Whitlock has a dear memory of kneeling near the on-deck circle as Williams awaited his first turn at bat.

"He was swinging to warm up, and he told me I'd better back up so I wouldn't get hit. Then, when he was at the plate, he fouled several pitches back to the screen. I had to chase them down, and I remember thinking, 'I'm picking up baseballs that Ted Williams hit.' It was quite a feeling."

After the 1951 game, Whitlock remembers being in the Sox clubhouse, watching the team prepare for its trip to Boston.

"Vern Stephens (then the starting shortstop), handed me a bat. 'This bat is cracked, and I can't use it any more. It's yours if you want it,' he said. I was really thrilled that he would take the time to do that for me," Whitlock recalled.

During both Red Sox visits, Whitlock had the opportunity to shag balls in the outfield during batting practice.

"Imagine me out there with Dominic DiMaggio and Jimmy Piersall? What an experience," he said.

The 1951 game drew such a crowd that an area in left field had to be roped off to accommodate standees.

"I went to a 50th reunion of my Tech High class, and one of my classmates reminded me that he was in that crowd. He thanked me for getting him some Red Sox autographs," Whitlock said.

For the record, the Red Sox beat the Cubs 5–2 in 1951, and 6–1 in 1952.

Williams and Walt Dropo had two hits each in the '51 game. In the '52 game, Doerr and Dropo hit home runs and Williams went 3 for 4. A month later, he would be back in the Marine Corps, recalled for service in the Korean War.

Holyoke's Ed Hurley, an American League umpire for 19 years, worked first base in the '51 game.

In 1953, after Whitlock gave up his batboy job, he went to a Cubs game and sat in the left field stands.

"Jack Wallasea, one of my favorite Cubs, was playing left field. He saw me and gave me a wave. I loved it," Whitlock recalled.

The Chicago Cubs had placed their top farm club here in 1950, and stayed through the 1953 season, when their Springfield club lost 102 games, finished last and drew an average of 1,107 fans per home game. All of that led to the city losing Triple A ball.

The Springfield Giants came along to operate in the Eastern League from 1957 through '65 before dwindling attendance ended their time here. In August of 1966, Pynchon Park burned to the ground.

Pro ball has been gone from Springfield for 47 years, but for Paul Whitlock, his Pynchon Park days remain precious – especially those two afternoons in April, when the Boston Red Sox came to town.

Freddy and His Kids

There I was, a wide-eyed 18-year-old freshman surrouned by veterans of World War II. Yes, every class I attended at American International College in the fall of 1949 had its share of older students, taking full advantage of the GI Bill.

In a U.S. history class taught by professor John Mitchell, I met Joe Buchholz, a freshman who had served as a navigator on bombers in the Pacific Theater. In a psychology class taught by professor Dorothy Spoerl, I met Freddy Zanetti, a 28-year-old senior who had toured the South Pacific as a pharmacist's mate in Uncle Sam's Navy.

Joe B and Freddy Z shared another bond – hockey. Yes, they were part of American International's first varsity hockey program, started by coach Bill Turner. Buchholz became one of the leading scorers in the nation, while Zanetti was a rock on defense and served as team captain.

Lucky for me, I got to write about those two for the Yellow Jacket, the school's weekly newspaper. Watching them give their all for dear old AIC was inspiring, indeed.

Give their all? In many a game, Buchholz and Zanetti rarely came off the ice. Iron men playing their hearts out for a team short on manpower.

In those days, AIC played a major schedule – Boston College, Boston University, Yale, Princeton, Brown, Rensselaer Polytechnic Institute. Athletic director Hank Butova saw to that, giving Turner a chance to put his teams on the national hockey map.

Zanetti often talked about a game at the old Eastern States Coliseum when AIC came within a goal of upsetting BC, which was as a national power then, just as it is now. "I heard their coach say, 'You going to let this bunch of rink rats beat you?' And we almost did," Freddy would say with a hearty laugh.

When he stopped skating as an active player, Zanetti stayed on the ice as a referee, working high-school and college games. His officiating partner? None other than Joe B. Zanetti graduated from AIC in 1950. Four years later, he became an elementary-school principal, marking the start of an illustrious 44-year career as an educator.

He spent 40 of those years as principal of Howard Street School. The school later was named in his honor, and the name was transferred when the school relocated into the former Our Lady of Hope School building on Armory Street after the 2011 tornado devastated Springfield's South End neighborhood.

Over the years, I would run into Fred on many a special occasion. I was there the night the Springfield Falcons honored him with their first "Golden Stripes" award, which is presented to officials who have made significant contributions to local hockey. I was there, too, the night he and Joe B were inducted into the AIC Athletic Hall of Fame.

I last saw Fred in February, when he was guest of honor in a kindergarten event at Alfred G. Zanetti Montessori Magnet School. The pupils were duly impressed when they were informed that their school is named for the white-haired gentleman who was sitting in front of them. At that point, he drew an ovation.

In response, he said, "My career in education was never about me – it was about the kids. It was the kind of job where I never woke up grumbling about having to go to work. I looked forward to spending each day with the kids."

Fred Zanetti passed away May 25, 2014, at the age of 92.

A legion of "his kids" will never forget him. Nor will his AIC classmates, war vets and 18-year-olds alike.

Where Are They Now –
The Brothers Bedard

FROM 1966 TO 1977, IT SEEMED THAT TECHNICAL HIGH School and East Springfield Post 420 American Legion baseball teams always had a Bedard in the lineup.

Sometimes, more than one.

They were brothers – five of them – and they grew up playing sandlot baseball for the Our Lady of Sacred Heart Orioles, then high school and Legion ball for coach Howie Burns.

The Bedard boys – Rich, Billy, Johnny, Jimmy and Tommy – all loved the game and played it well. Their passion for baseball carried into college, then into the Tri-County League.

Case in point would be Billy Bedard, who played on a state championship team at Tech, served as baseball captain at Boston College – and then played and managed Tri-County ball for 22 years.

Billy, 62, recently retired after serving 31 years as an assistant to American International College's Hall of Fame softball coach, Judy Groff.

Brother Jim pitched for Tech, Post 420 and the University of Massachusetts, then played Tri-County ball until the age of 40. He's now 58, working as a mail carrier for the U.S. Post Office.

He has always stayed close to the game, doing coaching stints at UMass and AIC, and helping Burns with his Legion teams. He was his top assistant when his '74 team won a state title. There were seasons, too, when Jimmy would throw batting practice at UMass just to help out an old friend, the late Elaine Sortino, the Hall of Fame coach who passed away August 18.

Tommy, the youngest, pitched for Tech, Post 420 and Siena College, where he still holds the record for victories by a lefty. He's now 54 years old, working as a manager in retail sales.

As the Brothers Bedard look back to their days playing together on the Glickman Elementary School playground, they share a lifetime bond.

"We had caring parents, and grandparents. They supported us when we played, and they did so without hovering. Our mom and dad were always there for us," said Johnny, now 61 years old. He lives in Watertown, New York, where he runs his own fuel treatment business.

Al and Mary Bedard, both in their 80s and still living in their old homestead in Sixteen Acres, believed in letting their kids play. Mary and her one daughter, Tina, ranked as the Bedard boys' most faithful fans. 'Tis said that in one particular summer, they saw 70 ballgames. Al was always there, too, whenever he could get away from his work as a carpenter.

Al and Mary started going to ballgames in 1957, when Rich began playing, and kept it up until 1995, when Tommy closed out his Tri-County League career.

"That's 38 years, and then they did 15 more watching the grandchildren play. Baseball is in our blood, no question about it," Jimmy said.

Mary's brothers, Mel and Johnny Pasteris, were outstanding players. Mel played for a time in the New York Yankees system. Johnny starred as a first baseman at Tech, then played on a UMass team that reached the College World Series in 1954.

"Our dad was a good ballplayer, too. He played for Tech in 1944, before going into the service in World War II," Jimmy said.

Johnny would rank as the most high-profile of the Bedard boys, reaching celebrity status in 1970 when the Pittsburgh Pirates made him their first-round pick in the June draft – the 13th player chosen in the nation.

Shortly after that draft, Johnny helped Tech win its third

straight state title. He pitched six innings, then caught the last three as the Tigers nipped New Bedford 3–2. With that, coach Burns completed a three-year baseball binge in which his teams went 55-5 with 41-game winning streak.

Johnny Bedard's ability to excel both as pitcher and catcher worked against him in pro ball. He loved catching, but the Pirates already had Manny Sanguillen and Milt May coming up, so they decided that Bedard should pitch.

"I just wanted to play, so I did what I was told, even though most people – including me – thought I should be a catcher," Johnny said.

The first week after he signed, he hurt his shoulder. He still tried to pitch, but as he compensated for the injury, his pitching mechanics got out of whack.

"I felt the pressure of being a No. 1 draft pick, so I kept on pitching. I could still throw hard, but not the way I wanted to. And in those days, sports medicine wasn't what it is today," he said.

So it was that his career lasted only five seasons. He went 15-28, never getting above Class A, before the Pirates released him. He hooked on with the Houston Astros, but soon was released by them, too.

For one season, at least, he had the fun of playing pro ball with his brother Rich, who signed with the Pirates after his graduation from Amherst College. They spent the summer of 1971 together, with Niagara Falls of the short-season New York-Penn League.

Johnny went to UMass after his stint in the minors and earned his degree in 1977.

Rich left pro ball after that Niagara Falls season, intent on pursuing a career in coaching. After serving as an apprentice at Amherst, he did a 10-year stint as baseball coach at American International College before moving into the administrative side of the athletic department. In June of 2006, he succeeded the retiring

Bob Burke as athletic director, a position he holds today.

"I had bad timing at Tech – I missed those championship teams. We lost in 1966 to Pittsfield and Tommy Grieve, and in 1967, my senior year, to Westfield and Jimmy Jachym," he said.

Rich still was eligible for Legion ball after his freshman year at Amherst – and that meant four Bedards would be together on one team for the first and only time.

"Rich, Billy and Johnny played, and I was the batboy," Jimmy said.

That '68 Post 420 team won state and northeast championships before losing in the Legion World Series at Manchester, New Hampshire.

The Brothers Bedard had the good fortune to play for coaching legends...Burns at Tech and in Legion ball, Bill Thurston at Amherst, Eddie Pellagrini at BC, Dick Bergquist at UMass, Tony Rossi at Siena College.

"There were some great baseball guys we played for in Tri-County, too," Billy Bedard said. "...Eddie Pooler, Bobby Findlater Sr., Randy Smith, Floyd Narcisse, Chris Corkum..."

Now, as the Brothers Bedard head toward senior citizenry, they can count their blessings – 16 grandchildren and one great-grandchild.

"Growing up, we played a lot of different sports. In the end, though, baseball was the game," Johnny said.

In their blood. No doubt about it.

A Sergeant's Story

For three-plus decades, Springfield native Paul Letourneau never talked about his service with the U.S. Army in Vietnam. Never talked about leading men into battle as a sergeant, just barely 20 years old.

Nor did he ever talk about the demoralizing feelings he had when he returned in 1969 to find much of the American public despising Vietnam vets, rather than welcoming them home.

In 2001, after the 9/11 attacks and the first Gulf War, he felt it was time to tell his story. His wife, Kathleen, urged him to write it down so their children and grand-children would know about that defining time of his life.

Once he decided to write about his service in Vietnam, it took him all of 13 days.

"My wife and I were on a cruise when I wrote the outline of what I wanted to say. When I got back, I used more vacation time from my job to write it all down – and I did it in long-hand," he said.

Some time later, he had his original manuscript edited by a professional writer. "She wore out three No. 2 pencils making the necessary changes," he said.

Finally, his story of service under fire became a book, "My Vietnam Conflicts." It was first published in 2002, then reissued in 2005. His "grunt's-eye view" of that controversial war won the Barclay Arts Council's Bryan Bur-

rough Award for nonfiction.

Letourneau and his book resurfaced locally in November, when he returned to his hometown to be enshrined in the Springfield Public Schools Sports Hall of Fame.

He gladly made the trip from his 40-year residence in Sun City, Texas, because he never lost affection for his hometown and his old high school – Springfield Tech. His wife also grew up in this city, graduating from Commerce in 1967.

Hall of Fame night was a reunion for members of Tech's 1965 hockey team – the school's first to win a Western Mass. championship. It was one of 12 inducted under the Hall of Fame's new policy of enshrining teams along with individuals. Letourneau and teammate Chris Robbins also were inducted as players who twice made The Sunday Republican's all-Western Mass. hockey team.

Letourneau excelled as rangy center, Robbins as a goaltender.

At the conclusion of his Hall of Fame night, Letourneau signed and gave out several copies of his book.

"Springfield was such a great place to grow up when we were kids, and the Coliseum was a great place to play hockey. I remember playing for the 10–12 Forest Park Panthers at 8 o'clock on Saturday morning. It was so early, the lights weren't even on yet," he said.

Letourneau's memories of Springfield also include an unforgettable set of coaches, led by his high school hockey mentor, Ed Mason, whom he remembers as "a great motivator."

His other coaching favorites? Ray Tuller in hockey, Mush Lawler and Pete Siciliano in baseball, Norm Superneau and Charlie Stagnaro in soccer.

At Tech, Letourneau centered a "French Connection" line with his brother John at left wing and John Abair at right wing.

Paul's hockey talent led him to a scholarship at American International College.

"The trouble was, I had to keep up the academics, and I didn't do that. So I drew academic probation, and they asked me to step out for a semester," he said.

That was in the spring of 1967 – and young men who didn't have college deferments were eligible for the military draft and two years of service.

Nobody would hire him because of the draft, so he decided to enlist for a three-year hitch. He entered the Army in March of 1967. After service in Germany – during which time he married Kathleen and earned promotion to sergeant – he got the news that he would be going to Vietnam. He arrived in Saigon on Jan. 1, 1968, and soon was facing firefights with the Viet Cong as a sergeant in the 11th Armored Cavalry.

As he noted in his book, when he was assigned to Bravo Troop, a master sergeant said to him, "War is hell, and welcome to hell. This sure ain't heaven."

Letourneau's writings do not touch on the politics or the policies of the

U.S. government during that tumultuous time. But he does reveal that, to this day, his wife questions why he went to Vietnam. When he returned, she burned his uniforms, medals and even the letters he wrote to her.

"She did it because she loved me, and she despised the time we lost together because of Vietnam," he wrote in his book.

After service, Letourneau began what would be a 34-year career with RJ Reynolds. When he retired, he had risen to become the company's national director of accounts. He said that after what he went through in wartime, he had no trouble meeting the challenges of the business world.

Now, he lives a peaceful life with his loving family. Sometimes, he plays softball on a senior citizens team. Their annual games with the University of Texas women's varsity have been known to get coverage on ESPN.

As he reflects on the approach he took to his Vietnam book, he says he wanted "to tell the story of young men who were real people, and were soldiers not because they wanted to be, but because they were called."

Paul Letourneau was called only 21 months after his graduation from Tech. As a schoolboy, he knew the special brotherhood that develops on a hockey team. All too soon, he came to know the special brotherhood that develops among soldiers in combat.

To one reviewer, his book is "a valuable contribution to military history." To the Letourneau family, it's a story they needed to know – about a time that should not be forgotten.

Our Crossword Friends

Melvin Thomas Ott of Gretna, La., signed with the New York Giants out of high school. He played his first major league baseball game at the age of 17 and went on to hit 511 home runs. After 22 seasons, he retired as an active player at the age of 38, and was on his way to the Hall of Fame.

So what, you ask?

Good question, because Mel Ott has been out of the public consciousness for nearly 70 years.

Yet, whenever my wife and I tackle a crossword puzzle (we have learned that working together produces better results), good old Mel Ott shows up more often than not.

You really need to be an old-time baseball fan or a crossword nut – I qualify on both counts – to know Mel Ott. Yet, there he is, on the puzzle pages day after day. The clues may vary, but the answer remains the same.

He sometimes appears as "Master Melvin of the Giants." Or, simply as "Slugging Giant." Or, if the crossword constructor feels devilish, he might clue him as "Leo Durocher's target." Yes, Leo the Lip, then managing the Brooklyn Dodgers of 1941, was talking about good ol' Mel when he famously said, "Nice guys finish last."

Mel Ott is just one example of names from the long, long ago that show up daily in crossword puzzles. They make it simply because they're handy three- or four-letter answers

that no crossword puzzle constructor can do without.

Sometimes, the puzzlers give Mel a rest and use his substitute. That would be Ed Ott, a journeyman catcher whose one big year happened with the world champion Pittsburgh Pirates of 1979.

Of course, the No. 1 three-letter man in crossword land is Bobby Orr, the all-time great defenseman of the Boston Bruins.

Our most recent confrontation with him came in a clue which was ridiculously easy: "Bobby on ice." By this time, even crossword solvers who never heard of hockey have come to know what to answer when they see clues like "Boston's No. 4."

Music and the movies also give crossword constructors plenty of help. You have to wonder where they'd be without celebrities like Uma (Thurman), Yma (Sumac), Eno (Brian), Niro (Laura) and Fey (Tina). Furthermore, no puzzle-maker can resist answers like "DRNO" (007 adversary) or "MRT" (A-Team grouch).

Sometimes, though, they go so far back, even senior citizens can be baffled. For instance, try this clue: "Silent vamp." Consider yourself a student of film history if you know the answer is "Bara" – as in Theda Bara, an early sex symbol who made her last movie in 1926.

Oh, yes, there's more. How many movie-goers of today ever heard of "The

Thin Man" series? They were detective stories from the '30s and early '40s, yet they are constantly referenced in 21st century crossword puzzles. Why? Two reasons: One of the stars was Myrna Loy (nice three-letter word) and her resident pet was a pooch named Asta (a four-letter gem in the world of crossword design).

When it comes to rock 'n' roll, we often face a dilemma caused by obscure clues with three-letter answers. Hmm. Is the correct response "ELO," "REM" or maybe even "REO" (as in REO Speedwagon?) As for clues related to rappers, we're pretty much lost if "DRDRE" or "ICET" doesn't fit.

The world of academia also helps the crossword constructors. They get a lot of mileage from clues like "high school hurdle" (SAT) and "law school hurdle" (LSAT). They also have a favorite institution of higher learning. That would be Elon (four-letter beauty), a small college little known outside of North Carolina until it hit the crossword grids.

Certain answers fit more than one kind of crossword clue. Case in point: Eli, which can be Peyton's brother or New Haven Ivy. Be on the lookout.

Food? Try "crunchy sandwich" – a BLT. Geography? Puzzlers can't resist the battle-scarred French city of St. Lo, which appears over and over. They also love Tokyo's previous name, a nice little fit – Edo.

Where did this all begin? Well, several sources on the internet tell me that the first published crossword puzzle was created by a journalist named Arthur Wynne from Liverpool, England. His first puzzle appeared Dec. 21, 1913, in The New York World. By the 1920s, crossword puzzles were featured in most American newspapers.

Puzzling has come a long way since the fairly-easy offerings of Arthur Wynne. Now we have to deal with experts who seem to take fiendish delight in designing clues guaranteed to lead solvers down the wrong path.

Example: A recent clue – "Plain variety" – had us baffled. Did that refer to something to drink? Or vanilla ice cream, maybe? Only after staring at the puzzle squares for far too long did the answer dawn on us – "prairie."

Ooh, that hurt. But not enough to make us stop. Rather, we're ready to tackle the next puzzle, no matter how misleading and difficult it may be.

We're ready, too, for our old friends, Mel Ott and Bobby Orr. We know we can count on them.

The Fabulous Falcons of Smith Academy

FIFTY YEARS AGO, WESTERN MASSACHUSETTS had its own version of "Hoosiers."

Just like Gene Hackman's team from that memorable 1986 movie, the players came out of a small town to win a big-time championship.

They were the "Fabulous Falcons" of Smith Academy, a Hatfield school with only 57 boys in grades seven through 12.

This is golden anniversary time for those Smithies, who twice stormed the old field house at Springfield College to win the Western Massachusetts Tournament.

Until Smith's remarkable run, no small school had ever won this region's biggest basketball tourney – and no school had ever won it twice in a row.

Smith took care of all that with teams built around a powerhouse scorer and rebounder – 6-8 center Bob Kovalski. They called him "Jingles," and his name remains familiar to basketball fans who remember the teams he led to glory in 1960 and 1961.

Kovalski got his nickname from John Skarzynski, a triple-threat administrator who served as Hatfield's superintendent of schools, principal of Smith Academy and, oh yes, head basketball coach.

"I used to like to walk around with a lot of change in my pocket," Kovalski recalled. "One day, I was coming down the school steps and I dropped some quarters. Coach Skar saw that and said, 'Hey, Jingles, pick up your change' and the name stuck from there."

Today, at the age of 68, Kovalski lives in an apartment directly across the street from the site of the original Smith Academy, a school founded in 1870 by Hatfield resident Sophia Smith. She also served as the benefactor and founder of Smith College in

Northampton. The old school in Hatfield was torn down soon after the present building was dedicated in the fall of 1980.

"We had a nice school (with 25 students in his senior class). Nobody ever got in trouble. We loved each other," Kovalski said.

The Smith Academy of today has better quarters. But it isn't really much different from what it was in Kovalski's time. With 202 students in grades seven through 12, it's the second-smallest public school in the state.

"Provincetown is smaller, but they're going regional. When that happens, we'll be the smallest again," said Scott Goldman, Smith's principal.

It's fair to say that Smith of the '60s wouldn't have had its "Hoosiers" moments without Kovalski, but it's also fair to say that it wouldn't have had them without gritty supporting players around him and dedicated coaches who made them realize they really could win Western Mass.

To appreciate fully Smith Academy's accomplishments, consider what the Western Mass. Interscholastic Basketball Tournament was in those days:

– An open championship, at a time before Divisions I-II-III were established.

– Open, but limited to only eight teams.

– Open, but also including schools from Worcester County under the "Western Mass" umbrella.

– Open, but limited, in that the Connecticut Valley and Worcester County each got three berths, Berkshire County two.

Under that strict format, it was almost impossible for small schools in the Connecticut Valley to be selected.

In 1956, Hopkins Academy of Hadley put together a Western Massachusetts record 42-game winning streak and had the regional scoring leader in John Pipczynski. That did catch the attention of the WMass selection committee, which gave Hopkins one of the Connecticut Valley's three spots.

The Hadley kids played their hearts out before a sellout crowd at Springfield College, but lost a one-point overtime quarterfinal to the eventual champion, Worcester Commerce.

Four seasons later, along came Smith.

"We began to realize what we had when we played St. Mary's (of Westfield) early in the season. They had a good 6-7 kid named (Tom) Baker, but we beat them," Kovalski said.

With Kovalski averaging 29 points per game and once hitting 50, the Falcons rolled to a 19-1 record. They twice tallied 101 points and surpassed 90 in four other games. They went before the selection committee as Hampshire League champions, and could not be overlooked.

"Skar did a great job of preparing us. He took us away from our little place (the Hatfield Town Hall, where Smith played all of its home games) and had us scrimmage teams like Longmeadow and Deerfield Academy on bigger courts," Kovalski said.

"We were much better on a big floor, and when we got to the field house, we were ready. I loved playing there. Something about it, the netting at each end of the court, the crowds."

Once on that big stage, that 1960 Smith team showed true grit to go with its talent. Matched against an Adams team that came into the tournament with 20 victories and the Berkshire County title, Smith prevailed 44–43 in its first tournament test.

"We fell behind 10–0 and Skar called time. We went out and got the next four points, and we were all right after that," Kovalski recalled.

In the semifinals, the Falcons outlasted a perennial powerhouse, St. John's of Shrewsbury, in a 59–58 cliffhanger that left the field house crowd emotionally drained.

After those thrillers, Smith had a slightly easier time in the final, holding off Pittsfield 65–57 as Kovalski hit 29 points – right on his season average.

On nights when Smith played at the field house, Hatfield closed down and everybody went to the games.

"The crowds were behind us all the way. You couldn't get a ticket. I remember people from Hatfield driving to Pittsfield to buy tickets when we were going to play them in the finals," Kovalski said.

In their 1960 victory, he had plenty of help from a solid group of seniors. Team captain Ken Kulesza was a cool and efficient force in the backcourt, along with Tony Symanski. Up front, Jim Southard, Jim Majeskey and Ed Malinowski gave Kovalski strong support.

In those days, a state tournament had not yet been established (it started in 1965). Instead, the WMass champion went to the New England Tournament at Boston Garden. There, Smith's season ended in a 61–59 loss to Westerly, Rhode Island.

Still, the Falcons had a 22-2 record – and they had Kovalski coming back for his senior year.

Dick Harubin, still a Hatfield resident, was an underclassman and bench player on both of Smith's championship teams. He remembers going to a basketball camp at Worcester Academy during the summer of 1960, along with Kovalski and several other Smith players.

"A big star from Worcester Commerce (Pete Ranucci) was at the camp, but Jingles was the best player there," Harubin said. "At the end, the Worcester kid said, 'We'll see you guys in the Western Mass'."

How right he was. Smith won its 1961 title at the expense of Ranucci and W-Commerce in a 50–48 thriller settled by Kovalski's rebound basket.

In Smith's return to the tournament, Big K was its only constant.

With Skarzynski stepping aside to concentrate on his administrative duties, the Falcons had a new coach, Skarzynski's former assistant, Max Moczulewski.

"With Skar, you couldn't get away with anything. If he thought we weren't playing well enough, he'd have us run, run, run in practice. Maxie was a different personality, but they were both great coaches and they knew their hoop," Kovalski said.

Around him, Moczulewski assembled a new cast – Marty Wilkes and Charlie Symanski (younger brother of Tony) in the backcourt, and Bill Celatka, Bernie Pelis and Terry Michaloski up front.

"Jingles – he was the best around," said Pelis, now a retired construction worker, then Smith's sixth man. "He could shoot from anywhere. He was a three-point shooter before the three-point shot."

Kovalski was so dominating as a senior, and the Smith team so efficient, he never played a full game until tournament time.

"He'd play three quarters and get his 40," Pelis said.

This second edition of the Fabulous Falcons set a Smith record with 108 points against St. Michael's of Northampton on its way to a 19-0 season, making it an easy choice for a tournament berth.

Smith cruised past Southern Berkshire champion Lee 78–37 in the first round as Kovalski hit 42 points, then the tourney record. In the semifinals, Smith defeated Worcester South 49–43.

In the championship game, Kovalski dominated with 18 points and 29 rebounds, but the Falcons also owed their title to Celatka, a tenacious forward whose in-your-face defense held the dangerous Ranucci to 13 points.

So there it was, another championship for a team representing the then-smallest public school in the state.

Smith took a 22-0 record into the New Englands, but was overmatched against Hartford Public and lost 63–43 in the first round.

Kovalski? He had a spectacular senior season – 865 points, a 37.6 average and a Western Mass. single-game record of 63 points in a Hampshire League victory over Hopkins.

He went on to Providence College, and was on the Joe Mullaney squad that won the National Invitation Tournament in 1963.

Today, as a retiree, he still loves basketball, especially on ESPN.

"I watch three-four games a day," he said.

And he remembers everything – scores, people he played against, wondrous nights at the old Town Hall, when people would start lining up at 4:30 for seats in its little gym.

They came to cheer Smith Academy's basketball boys, and they followed them on their two magical rides to Springfield.

Yes, it all happened fifty years ago – when Falcons became Hoosiers to earn a special place in the history of Western Massachusetts sports.

When Old Foes Meet To Eat

There they sat, side by side, in a booth at The Fort in downtown Springfield.

A couple of phone calls had brought them together Tuesday, October 13, 2013, for the first time since 1979 – and 49 years after they captivated Western Massachusetts in a magical high school basketball season.

The year was 1964, in which Henry Payne of Commerce and Gene Ryzewicz of Cathedral were so outstanding, so evenly matched that they became the first co-winners of the John "Honey" Lahovich Award, which goes to the top high school player in the Connecticut Valley.

A lot of schoolboy stars have come along since their day, but the early '60s have to rank as one of the golden eras for basketball in Western Mass. A cluster of strong teams – Cathedral, Commerce, Chicopee, Holyoke, Pittsfield, West Springfield – were matched during the Payne-Ryzewicz years.

"I don't know about high school basketball here now, but I can't imagine anything more exciting than those Friday night doubleheaders at the (Springfield College) Field House," Ryzewicz said.

"That's all I would hear about – Commerce going against Cathedral, me going against Gene," Payne said.

As they chatted, they came to the conclusion that this was the first time they had been together since a 1979 retirement party for Hawk Connery, a beloved coach who shaped both their lives.

Both players put together stellar high school careers. Payne's was shorter, because Springfield public high schools had only three grades. Thus, Payne did not get to play a ninth-grade varsity season, as Ryzewicz did at Cathedral.

In Payne's three seasons, Commerce teams went 49-12. In Ryzewicz's four years at Cathedral, the record was 54-27.

As the basketball fates would have it, neither played on a Western Mass. championship team. However, in that senior season of '64, both players lit up the Field House in remarkable performances at tournament time.

Ryzewicz set a tourney and Field House record when he swished 51 points in a semifinal victory over David Prouty of Spencer. In the first round, Payne had scorched Prouty with 41 points in a heartbreaking 93-92 loss.

Cathedral had defeated Commerce 65–63 in their first meeting of '64. The second time around, the Purple Panthers got caught in a Payne blitz, suffering a 97–65 loss before a packed Field House crowd.

"I remember a lot about playing against Henry, but the one play that really stands out came in that 97-point game," Ryzewicz said. "Commerce broke up a fast break, and somebody whipped the ball to Henry. He took one step, right at the foul line, then with his back to the basket, tossed the ball up – and swished it. He never looked. I would have felt a little better about it if he at least had peeked over his shoulder, but no, he just swished it while looking down at the floor."

As seniors, both players outdid anything they had done as underclassmen. Payne scored 629 points in 21 games, setting a city record with a 29.96 average. Ryzewicz was right there with him, scoring 649 points for a 29.5 average.

Payne finished with 1,358 points in 61 games, Ryzewicz with 1,606 in 77.

On Jan. 21, 1964, in the last game Payne would play in the old Commerce gym, he fired 64 points – a Western Mass. record which stood until Travis Best came along to score 81 for Central in 1991.

"We played St. Stephen's of Worcester that day, and they didn't have me scouted. Teams usually played box and one against me on that court, but St. Stephen's went man-for-man, so I just took off," Payne said.

"We both had great respect for each other, and we had different styles. And every time we met, it was special," Ryzewicz said.

Payne was noted for his speed and passing ability, Ryzewicz for his sweet jump shot.

"I've played against a lot of jump shooters, and I've seen a lot in college and the pros. I'll tell you, nobody had a better jump shot than Gene Ryzewicz," Payne said.

Ryzewicz also excelled in football and baseball, sports he played at Dartmouth College. He gave up basketball, simply because there was no time for it.

Payne went on to star at American International College, where his teammates included Chicopee star Moose Stronczek and a future UConn coaching giant – Hall of Famer Jim Calhoun.

"We went to the nationals, and came very close to winning it," Payne said.

Both Lahovich Award winners went on to careers in business and industry. Both are retired now. Payne lives in Springfield, Ryzewicz in Fort Myers, Fla.

"I came back to town on the way to my Dartmouth reunion (in Hanover, N.H.). I hate to mention the number – 45," Ryzewicz said.

Yes, and it's 49 since their favorite year – that year of the two Lahovich Awards.

Bruce Landon and the Heart of a Goaltender

Bruce Landon, a lifetime member of the goaltending fraternity, pondered the numbers, and said, "That's an amazing streak."

The president/general manager of the Springfield Falcons was talking about the scoreless string of 268 minutes and 17 seconds posted by goaltender Barry Brust of the Abbotsford Heat, a North Division member in the American Hockey League.

In that "amazing streak" which ended November 24, 2012, Brust shattered an AHL record that had stood for 55 years. Until Brust, the record belonged to Johnny Bower, a goaltender who has been elected to both the NHL and AHL Halls of Fame.

Landon has an abiding interest in the feats of goaltenders, because he played the position before going into the administrative end of the hockey business.

"Any time a goaltender does what Barry did, it means that he's not only playing solid, but the team in front of him is playing very strong as well," Landon said.

"I say kudos to Barry. Good for him, because his streak is remarkable. It's also remarkable that Bower's streak lasted so long, when you consider the offensive ability of today's players."

Landon broke into pro hockey in 1968–69 with coach Johnny Wilson's Springfield Kings of the AHL, at a time when the game was much different from what it is today.

"Back then, teams might have three guys who shot the puck exceptionally hard. Now, all the players shoot it like a rocket. Just watch them in warm-ups," Landon said.

The style of goaltending has changed completely since Landon's day. "Coaches wanted stand-up goaltenders when I was playing," he said. "Now, they all play on their knees, with the exception of Martin Brodeur (New Jersey Devils). He's basically a stand-up type, although he kind of blends both styles. Another factor is size – goaltenders are a lot bigger today than they used to be," he said.

Brust is an example – 6-2 and 215 pounds. Perhaps the most extreme in that department is Jason Missaen of the Connecticut Whale, an awesome target at 6-8, 220.

Another difference from Landon's day – every NHL organization has goaltending coaches. "They study the game, the styles. They watch videos. They tell the goaltenders to play on their knees, post to post. That forces the shooters to go high," he said.

The "go high" philosophy makes the goaltenders' masks all the more important. "Nowadays, they take a lot of pucks off the head," Landon said.

He remembers trying one game without a mask. "I got eight stitches, and that was the only time I didn't wear a mask," he said. "When you think of all the years goaltenders played without masks, it's hard to believe."

The goaltending mask was introduced in 1960, worn by Montreal Canadiens Hall of Famer Jacques Plante.

Johnny Bower played through both eras, masked and unmasked. He had 11 seasons in the AHL before making it to the NHL, where he played for 12 more. He retired in 1970 at the age of 45 with seven cups to his credit – three Calder Cups in the AHL, four Stanley Cups with Toronto.

Bower's record scoreless streak was established with the Cleveland Barons in late November and early December of 1957. It included three straight shutouts, the middle one of which came on Dec. 1 against the Springfield Indians.

Brust began his streak early in the first period of an Oct. 20 game against the Chicago Wolves. He followed that with three straight shutouts – Nov. 1 against Toronto, Nov. 13-14 against Lake Erie. His scoreless streak ended late in the first period last Saturday against San Antonio.

Brust, a 29-year-old journeyman, has a 5-0-0 record and 0.59 goals-against average with an Abbotsford club that has allowed only 32 goals in 18 games. Brust's backup is a former Falcons goaltender, Danny Taylor.

"The skill level in our league is fantastic, and that includes the goaltenders," Landon said. "One reason for our good start is the goaltending. Curtis McElhinney has four shutouts, and Paulie Dainton has been very strong as his backup."

By the way, today's goaltenders don't have to go through what Landon did in 1968, when he was a 19-year-old rookie. "Johnny Wilson wanted me to have a tutorial with (Hall of Famer) Eddie Shore, who was running the Eastern States Coliseum at the time. He worked with me on the ice for about 40 minutes, and when we finished, he said I'd better learn to tap-dance or I'd never make it as a goaltender. I think he wanted me to be lighter on my feet," Landon said.

In November of 2014, Landon was inducted into the Massachusetts Hockey Hall of Fame, in honor of his 35-year association with Springfield hockey, Most of that came as an executive after he opted for retirement as a player – at the early age of 28.

What caused that decision?

"It happened one morning in practice," he said. "George Leary (then owner of the Springfield franchise) brought in some new players for tryouts. One of them was Jeff Carlson, whose two brothers had been in the movie 'Slapshot.' The coaches set up a three-on-the-goaltender drill, and Carlson wound up running right over me. That tore my knee apart, and led to my decision to retire."

Leary told Landon that he could undergo surgery, or quit playing and take a job in the team's front office. "I already had a bad shoulder injury before the knee went, so I retired and took the job," he said.

Landon has been in the front office of Springfield hockey ever since. In 1994, when the Indians franchise went to Worcester, he kept the city in the AHL by joining partner Wayne LaChance to start the Falcons franchise.

In his heart, though, he's still a goaltender, That's why Barry Brust and Johnny Bower mean so much to him, He has been here and done that – going all the way back to his pond hockey days as a kid in Kingston, Ont.

A Christmas Rush To Remember

News item: U.S. Postal Service proposes closing five of Springfield's eight post office branches – Brightwood, Colonial Station, Mason Square, Tower Square and Indian Orchard.

Well, there goes a chunk of my life.

As a kid growing up on Myrtle Street, the Indian Orchard Post Office meant everything to me.

My father worked there for 40-something years, many of them as assistant postmaster. Our family lived one house away from his long-time boss, postmaster Armand Bengle.

Barring bad weather, dad would walk to work every morning – five, sometimes six days a week. He'd cut across Cottage Hill Park, head down Oak Street past the fire station, and be on the job in 10 minutes.

My uncle, John Crean, lived around the corner and two blocks down on Essex Street. He, too, was a Post Office guy. "Uncle Icha," as we lovingly knew him, not only walked to work, he walked all day as a letter carrier. At times, he would let me heft his mailbag. Unbelievable. I couldn't understand how he could lug that thing.

Ah, but its aroma was unforgettable. Something about leather, magazines, letters and sweat that stays with you for a lifetime.

So it was at the Post Office itself. Its rear area had eight huge mailbins, made of some kind of tough fabric – grey and black-stained, as I recall, and

they, too, had their special aroma.

The old Post Office, where a little parking lot now exists, had its own special décor – heavy wooden desks, strewn with paperwork; a metal counter, with a scale (for figuring postage costs), inky pads and wood-and-rubber stampers that imprinted messages like "First Class," "Special Delivery" and "Do Not Bend."

One of my earliest memories of being a "Post Office kid" was having one of my dad's co-workers pick me up and set me down on that metal scale. I couldn't have been more than four, but I can still recall the cold-yet-nice feeling I got when he plunked me there.

Ken Wallace, another Post Office lifer, and my dad often traveled around together. It was Ken's car that carried me to my first ballgame at Fenway Park. That was in 1946, a postwar year, and a pretty good one for my Red Sox heroes – until the World Series came along to spoil it.

Two years later, when I was 17, my dad deemed it time for me to experience something called "the Christmas rush." I had often heard him speak of it, but I never really understood what it meant until he conscripted me to work after school – and on Saturdays – in the days leading up to Christmas.

Yeah, it was a rush, all right. My job was to stand at a bench, and sort mail into those big bins. My shift would start with a huge pile of letters –

most of them "season's greetings" - and keep going. Just as I was getting near the bottom of the pile, someone would dump another in front of me. It's safe to say that I worked harder in three weeks as a part-time postal employee than I ever did in my 50-plus years as a sportswriter for the Springfield newspapers.

The "Christmas rush" was so real and relentless, it turned my dad into a zealous opponent of Christmas cards. He wouldn't send any such greetings, and he forbade my mother from doing so.

The Indian Orchard Post Office of today – the one they want to close down – stands on the lower part of Oak Street. The Post Office I first knew also was on Oak, but a couple of blocks further up. The move to the current address came in the last decade of my father's career.

Back in the day, the Post Office was just one of the many places that made the Orchard a town unto itself. Oh, we were part of Springfield – good old Ward 8 – but we had everything a small town could ever need.

The Orchard had five churches, three parochial schools, two public elementary schools, a junior high and a wonderful little library, across from the original P.O. We had our own police station with a staff that included an Essex Street neighbor known to us kids only as "Murphy the Cop." Yes, and we had the Oak Street fire station, the one that once had to undergo major repairs after a trolley car careened off its tracks and through the front door.

The trolley is long gone from the local scene, and so is much that I remember of Indian Orchard's vibrant Main Street – including my favorite stop, the Grand Theater.

Now, they say the Post Office must go, too.

They can close it, but they can't shut down my memories of a childhood in which "Neither rain, nor snow, nor gloom of night..." meant so much to so many.

Tracking Indoor Track

ON A DECEMBER MORN 45 YEARS AGO, twelve high school runners from the Pioneer Valley convened in Curry Hicks Cage at the University of Massachusetts. They answered a call sent out by Dick Atkinson, coach of track and cross country at Southwick High School.

"It was all informal. We didn't keep score. We just arranged races for kids who wanted to run in the winter," he said.

The first such "meet" took place December 7, 1968. Until then, there had been no such thing as indoor track competition for Western Massachusetts high school athletes.

That particular point bothered Atkinson, who attended Revere High in the Class of 1950 and had the opportunity to compete in indoor meets at the Newton Street Armory.

"I remembered how good indoor track was in Eastern Mass., and I felt the kids out here were being cheated by not having that opportunity to race in the winter," Atkinson said.

As a UMass graduate who ran for legendary coach Bill Footrick, Atkinson had connections there and at Amherst College.

"We had those Saturday sessions wherever we could – mostly at Curry Hicks, sometimes in the Boyden Building, sometimes on the dirt track at Amherst. We'd chip in to pay the janitor," Atkinson said.

After attracting a dozen athletes in the first week, Atkinson had 20 two weeks later, and the numbers just kept increasing. The first group of indoor runners included Bob Rosen, then an Amherst Regional senior, now a Springfield lawyer who volunteers as an assistant coach of the Amherst boys team.

"UMass had a board track, maybe 10½ laps to the mile," Rosen said. "Having that opportunity to run indoors really helped, and it was fun – a new thing for us."

With Atkinson as its guru, indoor track continued to grow over the years and really took off in 1986, when Smith College offered its sparkling indoor facility for use by the valley's high schools.

"It got to a point where I began to think that we should have a league," Atkinson said. "So I got together with Billy Kane of Holyoke and (the late) Ted Dutkiewicz of Springfield Central in 2001, and we formed the league you see on Friday nights at Smith," Atkinson said.

The Pioneer Valley Interscholastic Athletic Conference meets are directed by Kane, a retired 35-year coach of cross country and track at Holyoke High.

The numbers tell the story of how far indoor track has come. The PVIAC encompasses 21 schools, each with boys and girls teams. Kane said rosters of the 42 teams involve 1,670 athletes.

"They don't all compete every week, because some kids do more than one event, but altogether, it's a fantastic enrollment for track," Kane said.

Each boys and girls team competes in 21 events. Conducting a meet involving so many teams and athletes would appear to be a major undertaking, but the PVIAC handles it with precision.

"It may look that way from a distance, but it's really organized chaos," Kane said with a smile. "But we've had fourteen years to get it right, and things do go pretty well because we have great kids competing and a dedicated bunch of coaches and officials."

The field events come under the supervision of John Dias, Kevin Ferriter, Sue Petzold, Patrick Lavelle, Richard Clark, Lisa Helpa and Ralph Figa. In the running events, Tom Stewart serves as starter, assisted by Christina Crocker and Rick Lajoie. At the finish line, the competitors are taken care of by Elizabeth Haygood and Priscilla Chadwick.

Kane's wife, Eileen, and their son Christopher run the results table, and Wilbur Race Systems handles the electronic timing.

PVIACtrack.com, a website operated by Kane, posts the weekly re-sults each Saturday morning.

In the 1996 Summer Olympics at Atlanta, the PVIAC had three of its officials selected to work track events – Kane, Dutkiewicz and Lavelle.

Kane said he never ceases to be impressed by the sportsman-ship of the high school athletes.

"It seems to be greater among the indoor track kids. You see athletes from different schools cheering for each other. These kids see each other week after week, and they form friendly rivalries with mutual respect. When I see that, it keeps me going."

Along with learning to be good competitors and good sports, the athletes learn a lesson in public service. One meet each year is dedicated as a fund-raiser for the American Cancer Society.

As for Kane's "organized chaos," it works mainly because coach-es prepare their teams well.

"The kids know where they're supposed to be, and when they're supposed to be there. There is no wandering around. We run off the 21 events in the same order every week, and that helps. We do have to change the order for our championship meet, because state meets are run in a different order, and we want to mimic them to get our kids ready," Kane said.

The PVIAC will have its championships Friday. Since Berk-shire County schools don't have indoor track, this is the de facto Western Mass. championship meet. The scene switches to the Reg-gie Lewis Center in Boston for state divisional meets February 14–17. An all-state meet February 23 and the New Englands March 2 wrap up the indoor season.

"When you think about it, indoor track is a fantastic thing for the kids of our region," Kane said. "Eastern Mass. schools did it for-ever, and now we have a viable program that prevents them from getting the jump on Western Mass. teams when the outdoor season starts in the spring."

That's what Atkinson had in mind 45 years ago.

"You have to go back to him when you talk about indoor track around here," Kane said. "Dick helped so many kids at that time, mostly out of his own pocket. As for the meets we have now, a ton of credit must go to Smith College. They've been very generous to us, opening their indoor facility for our use. What we have now in the PVIAC wouldn't exist without the people at Smith. You might say indoor track started at UMass, then had a rebirth at Smith College."

Rosen, the lawyer-coach, has been involved in distance running since his high school years. He well knows the role Atkinson has played in the evolution of indoor track.

"There is no more significant person for the sport around here," he said. "I would call Dick Atkinson the George Washington of track and field in Western Massachusetts."

Atkinson, 80, had a teaching career that spanned 40 years. He retired in 2003 but continues to coach cross country and outdoor track at Southwick. Oddly enough, his school does not offer indoor track as a varsity sport, despite his many urgings in that regard. Still, he became a pioneer in the PVIAC league and has never lost his zeal. He often can be seen among the spectators at the weekly meets at Smith.

"A great place to go on a Friday night," he said.

Learning the City Game

Gary Mindell's career as a successful high school basketball coach actually began when he realized that he would have to leave his old neighborhood in the 16 Acres section of Springfield.

Oh, he continued to reside there with his family, but he knew that if he wanted to learn the "city game," he would have to go to the heart of it.

At the time – the late 1960s – that meant Winchester Square and its environs. It meant basketball courts at Buckingham Junior High, Dunbar Community Center, DeBerry Playground, the Family Center...anywhere the game was played by inner-city kids who knew all the moves.

"There I was – white and Jewish – playing basketball with and against African-American kids who really could handle the ball, drive to the hoop and play tough, aggressive defense. To play against them, you had to learn the moves – and how to deal with the banging under the backboards," he said.

So how could this "Jewish kid" – basically an outsider from an all-white neighborhood – blend into that inner-city scene?

"It helped that I had people like Ronnie Carroll and Jessie Spinks among my mentors," he said. "I first met Ronnie when he was an assistant coach under Red Downes at Kiley, but he also was a highly-respected and long-time coach at Buckingham and Dunbar. Jessie, one of the all-time

greats in city high school basketball, had charge of the gym at the Family Center. I think they both admired my fortitude and willingness to learn all that I could about the game. With them behind me, nobody ever bothered me. The other players came to accept the fact that I was going to be around, and they just let me play."

This remarkable lesson in racial tolerance had everything to do with Mindell becoming a highly-respected coach, first as a part-timer at Chestnut Junior High, then later as a 19-year head coach of boys basketball at the High School of Commerce.

After learning what it would take to play the "city game," Mindell became the only tenth-grader to make coach Dan Meder's Classical High varsity squad in December of 1970. In his junior year, Meder tabbed him as his starting point guard. As a senior, new coach Dave Stratton also had him in that role.

Mindell went on to Westfield State College, then returned to his home city, looking for a job. He had to settle for part-time work at first, but eventually landed the Granby job. He did that for eight seasons, all the time hoping that he could get into the Springfield school system.

"I was a city kid, and it was my dream to coach at one of the city high schools," he said. The dream came true in 1995, soon after Mindell completed requirements for a master's degree. He was hired as the Commerce coach – and won his first WMass title a year later.

Mindell retired after the 2013 season with a career victory total of 332. Sixty-eight of those came at Granby High School, 264 at Commerce. With the Red Raiders, Mindell won three Western Massachusetts Division I titles – in 1996, 2004 and 2005 – and a state title in '05. Perhaps his best coaching job came in a one-point loss to eventual state champion Springfield Central in the 2012 WMass final. Central had beaten Commerce by 35 points three weeks earlier, but was carried to the last possession by Mindell's valiant Commerce team.

Now, Mindell can look back on a career in which he coached four winners of the Lahovich Award, which goes to the top player in the Connecticut Valley. Mike Vaz won it in 2003, Will Dawkins in 2004, Josh Tate in 2005 and Alex Lopez in 2012.

He also can look with pride at two players he coached as a part-timer at Chestnut Junior High in 1983 – William Shepard and Gary Bestman. Shepard won the Lahovich Award three years later at Commerce, and both became successful coaches. In March of 2013, Shepard coached Putnam Vocational's first state championship team.

Manual Dexterity

After years of faithful service, our microwave oven finally toasted itself. Time for a new model, complete with all the latest features to make cooking so very simple.

Oh, yeah?

First let it be said that we had no trouble dealing with the old microwave. Just hit the right numbers, and away it would go. In precious little time, it would do whatever we wanted – defrosting chicken tenders, baking sweet potatoes, warming up leftovers. Yum.

The new model? Well, the first time I pressed a button marked start, I received a one-word message.

"Food," the oven panel said, leaving me completely baffled. I was just trying to help with breakfast by cooking a delicacy known as "turkey bacon." (By the way, my son the chef tells me that no part of the pig has turkey meat).

With "food" flashing at me, I panicked. What to do? The coffee, toast and scrambled eggs were ready, but the bacon was running woefully far behind.

Finally, in desperation, I opened the microwave door – simply because I didn't know what else to do. Then, I saw a little panel that said "add 30 sec." I closed the door, pressed that "add 30" button, and suddenly saw the microwave spring into action. So I pressed four more times, and hoped that would do it. Voila! The bacon came out nice and crispy.

After that harrowing experience, I decided that I really should take the time to read the microwave oven's manual – 32 pages of small print.

The first time through, I couldn't find anything that would explain the "food" warning. I did find a "time features" section that said my oven will allow me to cook up to 99 minutes and 99 seconds. My turkey bacon might get REALLY crisp at that point.

The second time through the manual, I finally spotted a reference to that dastardly "food" sign. It was included in a section ominously entitled, "Before You Call for Service."

Here's what I found about "food" – quoting verbatim from the manual:

"For safe cooking, food detection algorithm is added to prevent microwave cooking without first placing food in the cavity. Through monitor the door open/close switch, Food Detection Algorithm control the initiating a cooking sequence."

A bit garbled, wouldn't you say? But that's my manual, and I'm stuck with it.

Before I attempted to decide which words were missing from that poorly-edited set of directions, I needed to consult my Merriam-Webster to be sure about the definition of "algorithm." I had a vague idea, but the dictionary assured me that the word basically means "A set of rules that precisely defines a sequence of operations."

Beyond the algorithm, I was a bit taken aback to learn that the inside of a microwave oven is known in the trade as "the cavity." Sounds more like something out of a medical-school class in gross anatomy, eh?

By the way, I must protest all of the above instructions, because I absolutely did put the bacon in the cavity before I got that mysterious "food" signal.

Of course, our microwave manual isn't the only one guilty of fuzzy writing, with or without the missing words. It seems that everything new coming into the home is accompanied by pages and pages of baffling instructions.

Have you ever sat down and really studied the "owner's manual" for your automobile? Most of them are at least two inches thick – and that's enough to scare off any driver. I'm still trying to master all the intricacies of my vehicle's dashboard, but I can't seem to find an easy explanation for all the symbols. For instance, I'm not quite sure how to defrost the back window, or why the windshield fogs up when I least expect it.

And let's not get into problems with computers, tablets, iPhones and all the rest. In our house, we have come to realize that it's easier to have our teenage grand-daughters explain them to us, rather than try to follow the written instructions.

Anyway, I think I am now prepared for my next breakfast assignment. All I have to do is memorize my algorithm sequence, carefully examine "the cavity," then start pressing buttons frantically until something happens.

With any luck, we might have turkey bacon, nice and crisp. Or, we might be sending the oven and manual back to the factory, along with a nasty note – very easy to read.

Bertelli Recalls 'The Smell of Sulphur and Death'

He came out of "Little Italy," a Memorial Avenue neighborhood across from the Eastern States Exposition grounds in West Springfield. In an enclave which seemed to specialize in the raising of outstanding athletes, he became the best of 'em all.

He played football for Billy Wise, leading Cathedral to an undefeated season as a senior. He played T-formation quarterback for Frank Leahy, leading Notre Dame to a national championship. He became the only Western Massachusetts player to win the Heisman Trophy.

Angelo "Bert" Bertelli, now of Clifton, N.J., is well-known for all of the above. He is revered as a football hero and exemplary citizen. At 74, he still stands tall and lean, every inch the athlete.

In December of 1993, "Accurate Angelo" observed the 50th anniversary of his Heisman Trophy. Actually, others observed it for him. If it were up to him, he wouldn't have mentioned it. He remains that kind of guy, loyal to his West Springfield roots and totally unimpressed with himself.

It should not be surprising, then, that he wasn't about to bring up a 50th anniversary of a different sort. He is observing it right now, as quietly as possible.

No, Angelo Bertelli does not broadcast his football exploits, nor does he broadcast the fact that he served in the bloodiest campaign in the history of the United States Marine Corps.

That was the battle of Iwo Jima, which raged from Feb. 19 to March 26, 1945. Marine historians say this World War II campaign forever defined the Corps, both for its heroism and its terrible toll. Uncle Sam lost 6,821 men in that battle, some of them barely 17 years old. The Marine wounded amounted to 17,000, a casualty total just about equal to a full Marine division.

Bertelli entered the military in November of 1943. His call to war came after he had led Notre Dame to a 6-0 record, including a crushing victory over Michigan which just about clinched the national championship. When Bertelli heard about his Heisman, he was at boot camp.

"I guess it was a career thing. You don't win the Heisman for six games," he says. A career thing it was, because his remarkable passing had led Notre Dame to a 24-4-3 record before Uncle Sam needed him. Bertelli trained at Parris Island, then at Quantico, where he learned the rudiments of being a Marine officer. By the time he went overseas in 1944, he had earned the rank of second lieutenant. He arrived in Guam after it had been secured, and spent much of his time as a recreation instructor – "an easy job."

Then came Iwo, which brought this football hero face-to-face with the reality and horror of war. He landed on that strategic little island on February 22 – "D-Day Minus Three," as he calls it. A day later, six Marines planted Old Glory at the peak of Mt. Suribachi. A photograph of that flag-raising by Joe Rosenthal of the Associated Press became one of the most famous images of war ever captured on film. Lt. Bertelli was nowhere near Mt. Suribachi at the time. As he says, "I was busy on another part of the island" as a platoon leader.

A popular misconception is that the flag-raising signalled the fall of Iwo Jima. Actually, it signalled the beginning of a hellish struggle against a 21,000-man Japanese garrison entrenched in caves, tunnels and pillboxes.

"The way the Navy bombarded that island before we went in, it made you wonder how anybody could be left alive. It was the most awesome fireworks show I've ever seen," Bertelli recalls.

As he talks, grudgingly, about his time on Iwo, this old West Sider offers a reminder: "I was no hero. Don't make me out to be a hero. I was just there, doing what had to be done."

No hero, perhaps, but he does admit to two near-death experiences. The first occurred when a mortar exploded nearby, killing a corpsman who was attending to a fallen comrade. Another occurred when Bertelli threw a grenade into a foxhole. To his shock, the grenade came flying back out at him. "You never saw Bertelli move so fast," he says. He and his men finally did blow up that foxhole – "we threw five grenades at once."

The volcanic island had to be taken through slow advance at high cost. "The only way to move ahead," Bertelli says, "was by driving the enemy out of their tunnels with flamethrowers and tanks. And still they'd be shooting at us from every direction."

When he thinks about that campaign, "the smell of sulphur and death" remains with him to this day. "Life goes on. You learn to live with it. How do you get through a battle like that? You get through, because when you're young, you think you're going to make it. Other people get killed, but you think it won't happen to you."

So now he belongs to a select organization known as "The Survivors of Iwo Jima." They took an island that had to be taken, for its airfields and its proximity to Japan. They took it, but 50 years later, a football hero looks back and wonders.

"Maybe," he says, "we should have dropped The Bomb on Iwo, instead."

Angelo Bertelli passed away June 26, 1999, at the age of 79.

When Marbles Was the Game

HOW MANY PEOPLE IN GREATER SPRINGFIELD can say they won a national championship, bantered with Johnny Carson on the "Tonight" show and drew a crowd of 5,000 at Pynchon Park?

Well, Springfield's own Jimmy "Red" Donohue did all of that — at the tender age of 13.

Now, on the 50th anniversary of his victory in the United States Marbles Tournament at Wildwood, New Jersey, Donohue lives in West Springfield, goes about his daily routine and hears very little about his remarkable summer of 1963.

"Once in a while, somebody might say, 'Oh, yeah, you're the marbles champ,' but most people have no idea. Around here, marbles is a thing of the past. Nobody plays," he said.

Back in his day, though, marbles was still big nationwide.

"Just about any kid you'd see would have a bag of marbles. In Springfield, every playground had tournaments going," he said.

Even in that heady atmosphere, Donohue had no trouble handling the celebrity status that came with his national title. Sure, he won it. Sure, he appeared on the "Tonight" show. Sure, Pynchon Park was packed for "Jimmy Donohue Day," but as soon as all that subsided, he was a Hungry Hill kid again, getting on with his summer. "I was 13. I didn't know anything about being a celebrity. I got back to normal life immediately," he said..

For those few days at the end of June, though, Donohue captivated this region as he became the third Springfield marbles shooter to win a national championship.

The feat first was accomplished in 1925 by Howard "Dutch" Robbins, a 13-year-old Brightwood kid who would go on to become sports editor of *The Springfield Union*. In 1934, Cliff Seaver brought Springfield another title before he became an outstanding athlete at Classical High School.

As Springfield's first marbles king, Robbins made front-page headlines and was welcomed home with a gala parade along Main Street. Hy Neigher, the sports patriarch of Western Massachusetts, faced Robbins in the finals of a tournament that would lead to the nationals. "We played at Forest Park. Dutchie won the lag, and I never got a shot. He cleaned the ring three times, and that was it," Neigher recalled.

The lag is the first move in marbles, which is played in a 10-foot circle. The players toss or roll their shooters toward a line, and the closest "lag" gets the first shot.

The ring contains 13 marbles, set in the pattern of a cross. The first player to knock seven out of the ring without having his or her shooter go out, wins the game.

"I still have my 13 original marbles, and my shooter," Donohue said. He then proceeded to place the marbles on his living room carpet, and demonstrate his shooting style.

"Some kids put their thumb behind the shooter, but the only way to get real English on it was to curl your hand under and the thumb sort of on top of the shooter. Release it that way, and you get the kind of spin you need." Donohue said he so perfected his technique, he could shoot long, knock a marble out, and have his shooter come back to him with "reverse English."

"Marbles is like pool – it's all about plotting ahead, knowing where your shooter needs to be for your next shot," he said.

As for the rules of lagging, they were changed by the time Donohue met John Riccardi of Yonkers, New York, in the 1963 finals. "When we played, it was the best of 21 games, but we only lagged once. After that, we alternated. But when it got to be 10–10 with one game left, I got to go first because I had won the original lag. If the other guy had won it, we might not be talking about this now," Donohue said.

As the Springfield kid coolly won the deciding game, his father couldn't watch. "He was so nervous, he ducked behind the bleachers on the boardwalk until it was over," Donohue said.

Not so with Ed McMahon, Johnny Carson's sidekick. As celebrity host for the tournament, McMahon watched every shot leading to Donohue's championship. When it was over, McMahon congratulated him, then surprised him.

"I think he liked the way I looked – short, freckles, red hair, buck teeth – because he told me that he wanted me to be on the 'Tonight' show. And he meant right away," Donohue said.

After conferring with Donohue's parents, McMahon arranged a limousine for the trip from Wildwood to New York City.

"I rode in style with Ed McMahon and the champion of the girls tournament (Patsy Coon of Philadelphia). I wasn't nervous at all because I never heard of Johnny Carson – my mom would never let me stay up that late. I think the girl was too tensed up to say much, but I felt at ease when Johnny asked me to show what I can do. I cleaned the ring they set up, just like I did at Wildwood," Donohue.

After the show, McMahon arranged rooms at the Statler Hilton for the two champions. "Ed stayed with me, and at midnight, he woke me up so I could see myself on television," Donohue said.

The next morning, he put the champions on trains for home.

Over the next couple of days, Donohue received the key to the city from Mayor Charles V. Ryan, then rode in another limo from the Springfield Newspapers building (then on Cypress Street) to Pynchon Park, where he was honored before a Springfield Giants game that drew the top crowd of that Eastern League season.

"The newspaper sponsored the local tournament and my trip to Wildwood," Donohue recalled. "I liked that, because I was a newsboy for a long time, and later I worked in the mailing room at the paper after school."

Donohue's 1963 victory came in his fourth trip to the nationals. Through all those years, he came under the guidance of a caring coach, Gene Oberlander.

"He was so happy when I won – even happier than my father, I think," Donohue said.

In two of his previous trips to Wildwood, the celebrity hosts were retired NFL players, New York Giants end Andy Robustelli and Philadelphia Eagles quarterback Norm van Brocklin.

"After I won, out of the blue I got a Christmas card from van Brocklin, with a team picture of the Eagles. What a surprise," Donohue said.

Under national tournament rules, if a player wins the title, he or she cannot compete again. However, Donohue was invited back to Wildwood in 1964 as "celebrity champion."

"I brought my shooter, in case they wanted me to do an exhibition, or something. Well, halfway through the final game, one of the players, a kid named Pee Wee Bower of Wheeling, West Virginia, cracked his shooter. He didn't know what to do, so I offered to lend him mine. He used it, and he won. So my shooter actually won back-to-back tournaments."

In later years, Donohue attended Cathedral High School and St. Anselm College in Manchester, New Hampshire.

He worked 28 years at MassMutual, and played on its basketball team for all of that time.

"They say I'm the all-time leading scorer," he said.

At the age of 50, his job was eliminated. He recovered from that by finding a job at a Chicopee printing company, where he has worked for the last 13 years.

Now, as he looks back on that golden summer of '63, he remembers himself as a kid who never felt the pressure of tournament play. "I never thought about it. I just kept shooting, because to me, marbles was fun. I loved the competition," he said.

Metal Detection

Let's see...silver fillings in teeth, two titanium hip joints, five titanium screws and posts for dental implants, hearing aids with transmitters and tiny zinc batteries.

And now, let's add a pacemaker in a titanium casing, complete with titanium-covered wires leading into the heart.

Yes, all of the above has become an integral part of me. Egad, I used to think I was made of flesh, blood and bones, but over the years I have come to realize that staying alive often requires varying degrees of metallurgy.

That point was made crystal-clear to me recently by a surgeon at Baystate Medical Center. The day after he installed a pacemaker just below my left collarbone, he stopped by my room to see how I was doing. There I was, already up and around, and ready to walk the hospital halls (per orders from one of the many marvelous nurses I met during my hospital stay.)

"Basically," the surgeon said, "you had faulty wiring that needed to be replaced. The pacemaker takes care of that, and you're good to go."

I was hoping he would add "for another 200,000 miles or more," but he didn't. I couldn't complain, though. Rather, I could only be supremely grateful that I was again "good to go" after surviving two very scary blackout episodes caused by "faulty wiring" which seriously slowed the heartbeat.

The experience made me think about Elaine Stritch, the feisty singer/ actress who passed away in 2014 at the age of 89. In a New York cabaret act which she performed after a long career on Broadway, her signature song was Steven Sondheim's "I'm Still Here." As she often said, "You should be over 80 before you attempt to sing this."

Yes, still being here is quite a gift, not to be taken lightly.

However, when it comes to metal work for the body, age isn't always an issue. I know this only too well, because my first experience with it came when I was 14.

After a many a failed attempt to do the standing broad jump at Myrtle Street playground, I developed a limp which soon made my parents realize that it needed attention. An examination revealed that the repeated broad jumps had knocked my right hip out of its socket. It was repaired at Springfield's Wesson Memorial Hospital on High Street, where a surgeon used a silver pin to anchor the hip back into its socket.

Now, fast-forward to 1998, when I began limping again. That eventually led to a trip to New England Baptist Hospital in Boston for some complicated surgery – remove the worn-out, 51-year-old silver pin and install a whole new hip joint of titanium. Three years later, the right hip was replaced, as well. That made it a clean sweep for the Brown household, because my wife also has two hip replacements.

Two years ago, that feeling of being

a mechanical man struck again as a team of dental experts introduced me to the wonderful world of implants. By the way, there's nothing quite like sitting open-mouthed while a dentist uses a wrench to tighten a "tooth" into place.

"Just like one of your own," he told me as he returned the wrench to his tool kit.

Here again, a sweep for our household (my wife had implants done before mine).

In between our dental implant ventures, we had dual visits to an audiologist, who fitted us with hearing aids. After too many days of saying "what?" to each other, we finally faced the reality of diminished hearing. The aids

work really well. Just make sure you never run out of those little zinc batteries.

Now, I must make a major adjustment to life with a "mechanical heart." Hey, I'm not alone. Wikipedia says some 1.5 million Americans live with pacemakers.

It's no wonder that "I Robot" and "The Bionic Man" take on new meaning for the Browns. And it might explain my growing fascination for the band "Metallica."

Anyway, my wife knows how to handle it all – with good humor.

"Just think." she says, "When we go, our bodies can be used for scrap metal."

Funny, huh?

My Friend Lennie

May, 1964. I'm standing behind the screened backstop at Van Horn Park, watching Tech play Classical in Interschool League baseball. Next to me stands Lennie Merullo, an East Boston guy who was scouting for his old team, the Chicago Cubs.

I was there to watch Tech clinch the city title and report the game for The Springfield Union. Lenny was there to watch Kevin Collins, the smooth Tech shortstop he hoped to sign at season's end.

We both had pencils in hand. I held a scorebook, Lennie a pad for making notes on KC's play. Late in the game, I happened to drop my scorebook. As I quickly bent over to pick it up, I heard

something that sounded liked fabric tearing. I was right. The "rip" happened in the backside of my pants.

Lennie heard it, too, and immediately knew what to do about it.

"Don't worry, Brownie, I gotcha," he said.

For the rest of that game, he stood behind me, shielding the torn pants from public view. After it was over, he gingerly walked behind me to my car.

"See ya next week. Buy some new pants – and lose some weight," he said.

Luckily, I had time to go home and change before I headed to the newspaper office to write my game story. As I drove along, I thought about Lennie, just a great guy and a real baseball man.

My job as the main high school beat writer for The Union and Sunday Republican in the 1950s and '60s put me in contact with some unforgettable people – and Lennie certainly ranked high on my personal list.

He knew everything about baseball, and he would fill me in on what to watch for in a young player. Foremost for him was speed. If the kid didn't run well, he had slim-to-none chance of playing pro ball, Lennie would say.

He liked everything about Kevin Collins, but never got the chance sign him. The New York Mets got there first, in what proved to be the last season before baseball instituted its current system of drafting college and high school players.

Lennie himself was quite a shortstop. He came out of East Boston to play at St. John's Prep of Danvers in the '30s. From there, he went to Villanova University, where he drew the attention of baseball scouts. He made the big leagues with the Cubs, and blessed himself every time he got the opportunity to play in his favorite ballpark – Braves Field, that is.

I first came to know of him from afar, in the fall of 1945, when I was 14 years old and following the first post-World War II World Series. Just from listening to those games on radio, I began rooting for the Cubs against the Detroit Tigers. I got to know those Cubbies – Stan Hack (later a manager in Springfield) at third base, Lennie at short, Don Johnson at second, Phil Cavaretta at first. In the outfield, I rooted for Andy Pafko, Bill "Swish" Nicholson and my favorite Cub of all – Peanuts Lowery. The catcher? Mickey Livingston, who had played Eastern League ball in Springfield before making the majors. He caught a pitching staff featuring Claude Passeau, Hank Borowy, Paul Derringer, Hank Wyse and Bob Prim.

The Cubs lost that World Series in seven games, but I found a special place in my baseball heart for their '45 lineup.

Lennie's major league career didn't last long – 639 games over seven seasons – but he followed that by working as a New England scout for more than 50 years. Later in his career, he became head of the Major League Scouting Bureau.

Later in my own career, when covering the Boston Red Sox became my main journalistic role, I would often see Lennie in spring training. He would be in Florida, not to watch the major league teams, but to cover New England college players on their spring-break trips.

Mostly, though, he enjoyed going to high school games from Caribou, Maine, to Newport, Rhode Island – and all stops in between. He loved to see New England kids make good in professional ball. They just need a chance to play a lot of baseball, he would say.

Lennie Merullo passed away May 31, 2015 at the age of 98. To the baseball world, he's best remembered as the last surviving member of the last Chicago Cubs team to play in the World Series.

Certainly, I remember Lennie for that, but most of all, I remember him for the day in 1964 at Van Horn Park, when he saved me from sartorial embarrassment. He was a pretty good ballplayer, very good scout, and a friend you could count on in the clutch.

Cheering the Cheerleaders

"Don't feed the flyer."

That's a T-shirt inscription – a sly inside joke, reserved for members of the cheerleading community. Yes, there is such a thing, and "flyers" play a very important role in it.

You see, the term "flyer" refers to those lightweight girls who get lifted to dizzying heights by their cheerleader teammates as they perform daring and difficult routines.

Thus, the T-shirt joke means that flyers must not gain weight. If they do, they won't be flying anymore, because their teammates at ground level wouldn't be able to bear that burden. Not only do the flyers need the support of their teammates while in midair, they need to be caught by them when they come back to earth.

Gone are the days when cheerleaders would run onto the football field or basketball court and do a simple "go team, go" routine. Nowadays, pirouettes and handstands in midair – performed by those tiny flyers – are an everyday part of a cheerleading squad's routine. Oh, yes, and let's not forget the tumbling. A team needs expert tumblers, or its routine just doesn't make it.

How, you may ask, would an old fogey like Yours Truly know this? And why would he care?

Simple answer – we have a granddaughter who gives her all as a cheerleader for Minnechaug Regional High

School of Wilbraham, where she's a member of the junior class. And, boy, does she look spiffy in that green, gold and white cheerleading uniform.

Over the last two years, we watched in wonder as she worked, worked and worked some more to get ready for cheerleading. All that tumbling, all those cartwheels at home and in our front yard led to big family news in 2012, when she made the cheerleading varsity.

In the 2012–13 academic year, we often would venture out on a cold

Our granddaughter, Rayna Mary Brown, as tri-captain of the Minechaug Regional High School cheerleading team in her senior year, 2015

winter's night to attend a Minnechaug basketball game. To root for the Falcons? Well, yes, but mainly so we could cheer for the cheerleaders.

As we did so, we came to realize that cheerleading is as much a varsity sport as any of those that take place on fields and courts. Cheerleaders must be athletes – both gymnast and acrobat. They also must be good dancers, well-versed in all the steps that go into a successful performance. And they must have the strength and will to hold steady while the flyers do their stuff.

As grandparents, we have learned from the younger generation – and not just how to solve a computer problem, or send text on a telephone.

For instance, we never realized what a great sport volleyball is until our oldest grand-daughter began playing it at Amherst Regional High School. After four years of watching games – some of them very intense at tournament time – we came to appreciate the skill that volleyball requires, and the togetherness it builds among teammates.

Same with our other two Amherst grandkids. They have shown us the work ethic and focus that the sport of track requires. Going to meets, we also have come to appreciate the spirit of competition – and yes, friendship – that track builds among athletes from the various high schools.

So it is with cheerleading. This sport – yes, I will gladly call it that – has its own way of building character and forging a bond among teammates. The routines simply will not work unless each member fulfills her particular role.

Speaking of tournament intensity, it certainly exists in cheerleading. We learned all about that last spring, when we attended a day-long state championship competition at Tantasqua Regional High School of Fiskdale.

What most impressed us was the obvious camaraderie among the contestants. For instance, when the Ludlow High School girls did their routine, cheerleaders from Chicopee, Holyoke and Minnechaug sat along the sideline, rooting for them. It was thus throughout the day as team after team took the floor for its one shot at a state title. The competition was intense, the feeling of togetherness even moreso.

In district and state competition, cheerleading teams really put on a show, doing well-choreographed routines that feature their flyers.

Of course, cheerleading also has its "school spirit" aspect, which comes to the fore at football and basketball games. In that setting, the "flying" routines are seldom used. Rather, the cheerleading teams concentrate on boosting the home team through chants, dances and some tumbling.

In late August, we were reminded that another summer was slipping away when our Wilbraham granddaughter called to say, "Guess what happens tomorrow? First cheerleading practice."

We have come to know what that means – lots of time, lots of work, lots of tumbling and acrobatics. All performed with a sense of team spirit and school pride.

By the way, no snacks allowed at cheerleading practice. Don't feed the flyer, remember?

Sprinting Along with Dan Walsh

WHEN DAN WALSH OF SPRINGFIELD WAS A BOARDING STUDENT at St. John's Prep in Danvers, he came under the guidance of a tough teacher who also happened to be a successful track coach.

"Brother Patrician," Walsh said, thinking back to the man who helped him become part of the school's rich track history.

As a senior in 1959, Walsh ran the 600 and a relay leg on a St. John's team that went undefeated and won the state Class C indoor championship. There was nothing new about that – Brother Patrician's teams went from 1957 to 1962 without losing a meet, indoors or outdoors. That included New England Catholic meets and relay carnivals, as well.

Walsh relived the memories of that championship time of his life Wednesday night when the 1957–62 teams were honored as part of the St. John's Prep Athletic Hall of Fame enshrinement at the Danversport Yacht Club in Danvers. Special honors also went to the school's 1985 state championship hockey team.

The St. John's Hall of Fame's Class of 2010 consisted of 11 athletes, including Longmeadow resident Ted Fleming, 80, a member of the class of 1948.

Fleming grew up in Springfield and attended Cathedral High School until his father decided that he was having "too much sports and not enough books." So he enrolled him at St. John's.

Too much sports?

"At St. John's, I played football, hockey and baseball as sophomore and junior, and I added track as a senior," he said. Like Fleming, Walsh was enrolled at St. John's after beginning his secondary education at Cathedral. He didn't go out for Cathedral's track team, but when he got to St. John's, he followed an edict that "everybody was supposed to do something" in athletics. So he tried track.

"I always knew I was fast, and Brother Patrician taught me what I needed to know about running," he said. "The first time I ran for him, when I was on the junior varsity, I finished last in a 100-yard dash. He told me that I waddled – meaning I had too much movement from side to side and wasted a lot of energy. He said we had a lot of work to do."

Walsh learned to stop "waddling" by following a Brother Patrician regimen which included running in a couple of inches of water during his family's summer on the Connecticut shore. He made the varsity as a 142-pound senior in 1959. He lost only one race during that indoor season – the state 600 final at Boston Garden. On the first turn, he got accidentally spiked in the right shin. He scrambled up to finish the race despite the injury.

"I made up 40 yards. Another 10, and I would have won it," he said.

As it was, he finished only a shade behind Leon Waithe of Charlestown, who set a state record of 1:17.6.

Even after the injury, Walsh ran an important second leg of the final relay, making up 15 yards after the first runner got a bad start. Teammates Johnny Barrett and John Carroll took it from there as St. John's went on to win the race and the state Class C title.

"I still have the medals from that night – Feb. 9, 1959," he said.

High school indoor track was a major sport in Central and Eastern Mass. in those days. A total of 53 teams scored points in the four divisions of the '59 state indoor meet. Western Mass. schools did not have indoor teams in those days.

In the spring of 1959, Walsh incurred a hamstring injury which kept him out for the rest of the season. One of the meets he missed was the New England Catholic Championships, hosted by St. John's. He thus was deprived of an opportunity to run against a former Cathedral classmate, Jim Trelease.

Trelease, later to be widely celebrated as a *Springfield Daily News* illustrator and author of "The Read-Aloud Handbook," won New England titles that day in the 440 and high jump. With Trelease's teammate, George "Dizzy" Desnoyers, winning the shot put, Cathedral placed fourth with 18 points. St. John's won the meet with 34½.

"Jim was a real good track man. It would have been quite a race between us," Walsh said.

As for his St. John's teammates, he regards Barrett as one of the school's all-time great athletes. In 1960, Barrett played center field as St. John's lost 1–0 to Pittsfield High in the state championship baseball game at Wahconah Park, Pittsfield. He made the switch to baseball after completing the track season.

From St. John's, Walsh went to Providence College. After graduation in 1963, he joined the U.S. Marine Corps. By January of 1966, he was in Vietnam.

As a first lieutenant serving with the second platoon, Lima Company, First Marine Division, he incurred severe wounds from machine-gun fire during Operation Utah near Quang Ngai on March 5, 1966. He vividly recalls it as "a pitched battle" during which his platoon sergeant, Leonard Hultquist of Boys Town, Nebraska died in his arms.

For his action in continuing to lead his men throughout the battle despite his wounds, Walsh received the Bronze Star and Purple Heart. The Bronze Star also went to Patrick Barth, a lance corporal from Minnesota who attended to Walsh after he had been hit.

"We were the last two to leave the mountain that day," Walsh said. Forty-four years later, they met again on Veterans Day. Walsh was invited to Marietta, Georgia, to deliver a speech to Marine veterans. Barth, now a resident of the Atlanta area, was in the audience.

"That was an emotional time, for sure," Walsh said of their reunion.

Because of a snafu in military record-keeping, he did not receive his Bronze Star until 1998. In a ceremony at Springfield City Hall, the honor was pinned on him by his son, Bennett, a career Marine officer. Simon Gregory, commanding officer of Walsh's company during Operation Utah, spoke at the Bronze Star ceremony.

"In addition to his personal bravery and ability to function under fire, my most enduring memory of Dan that day was his complete dedication to his men. He understood the sacred trust required to be a Marine officer, and was willing to sacrifice himself in execution of that responsibility," Gregory said.

In later life, Walsh became a member, then president, of Springfield's City Council. His wife, Kateri, now serves as the council's senior member.

He also served the city on its Park Commission. In the late 1970s, he became a co-founder of the Basketball Hall of Fame Tip-Off Classic with Joe Auth of Longmeadow.

"It was being at Providence College that turned me into a rabid basketball fan," he said. "I was there when Joe Mullaney was the coach and we won the NIT twice, with Vinny Ernst in 1961 and Ray Flynn and John Thompson in 1963."

Ernst, the '61 MVP of that tourney, was Walsh's roommate during his junior year. Flynn, MVP of the '63 NIT, went on to become mayor of Boston. Thompson, after playing briefly for the Boston Celtics, embarked on what would be a Hall of Fame coaching career at Georgetown. Walsh, 68 is now close to retirement after 14 years as Springfield's director of veterans services.

He was out-of-the-blue surprised when he received a letter telling him that Brother Patrician's track teams would be honored by the St. John's Hall of Fame.

"It's really a great thrill, to look back and know that I helped one of those teams go undefeated," he said.

The Hockey Project

WEAVING THROUGH TRAFFIC WHILE STICKHANDLING THE PUCK, Gabriella Miranda finds open ice and puts a shot on goal.

As the puck dents the twine, she raises her stick in celebration.

Gabriella is 11 years old, a student at Springfield's Sabis International Charter School. Until two years ago, she had never skated, never held a hockey stick, never chased a puck.

Now, as she cruises across the MassMutual Center ice surface – enjoying every second of her new life on the blades – she symbolizes all that is good about an admirable endeavor known as "The Hockey Project."

It's been going for four years, under the direction of two former kid hockey coaches – Donnie Moorhouse and Bill Foley.

Moorhouse might be better known to readers of *The Republican* for his 20 years of columns and reviews covering the local music scene. Foley might be better known for his 14 years as head supervisor of Springfield's Sabis International Charter School.

Beyond all that, though, these two basically are blue-collar hockey guys. They love to be around the game. They love to work with young people. They are, in other words, ideally suited for The Hockey Project and its outreach to youngsters who otherwise might have no opportunity to try this sport.

The 2012 edition of The Hockey Project has fifty kids, ranging in age from 6 to 13. For each of them, their first day in The Hockey Project was their first day on skates.

The sessions take place on Monday afternoons. They'll carry into March. The capper will be a March 10 tournament in Milton, Massachusetts, where the Springfield kids will go against teams from IceHockey Harlem and ScoreBoston, which have programs similar to The Hockey Project.

It's all part of what Moorhouse calls "hockey immersion," which means the youngsters don't just learn to skate. They learn to do it with a stick and a puck. At the same time, they learn to compete.

"There's a theory that hockey is all about skating, but to me it's all about the puck," Moorhouse said. "We don't do drills. It's better for kids to start learning how to control the puck right from the start. We send them into two-on-two or three-on-three competition right away, tell them to put the puck in the net, and watch them learn."

Moorhouse knows the old saying that "hockey builds character."

He adds this: "Hockey also reveals character, and it's amazing to see kids go from a point where they're immediately humbled, to a point where their skill and self-esteem soar. You see kids who have never skated digging away at the puck as their competitiveness comes out."

It's clear, then, that there's more to The Hockey Project than the game itself. It is designed to teach life skills and promote academic achievement.

"We want these kids to be better citizens and better students through hockey. If they're not doing the first two, they can't do the third," Moorhouse said.

Most of The Hockey Project's pupils come from Sabis, but the program also has kids from Agawam, Westfield and the Springfield Renaissance School.

Walter Kroll, 12, a Renaissance student, is one of The Hockey Project's four-year "veterans." His sister Madelaine, 9, also takes part as a Sabis pupil.

"Learning how to play hockey is fun and helpful to me," Walter said.

Gabriella Miranda learned to skate in two weeks.

"I love this. It helps me improve my skating and keep my grades up. And it helps with other stuff in my life," she said.

"Our girls have a lot of grit," Bill Foley said. "They're not shy about competing, and they have a good nose for the puck. It's really something to see all these kids come out of their shells and engage in banter on the ice and in the locker room."

Ah, yes, the locker room. Moorhouse says it can be "chaos" as the 50 players get ready. Most of them need help with such necessities as putting their skates on properly.

The Hockey Project comes free to the youngsters. The Mass-Mutual Center donates ice time, and Moorhouse has a network of equipment donors.

Then there are the volunteers. Moorhouse's son Evan, a 17-year-old Westfield High School senior, basically has taken over as The Hockey Project's on-ice supervisor.

"I was late getting out onto the ice one day because I was lacing skates for kids, and when I showed up, Evan already was running things. So I just sat back and let him do it. He understands the concept, and he really has taken charge," Moorhouse said.

Each session with Evan ends with the players clustering at center ice and raising their sticks.

That "goal!" gesture says it all.

Evan's dad played goal for Cathedral and American International College. Now Evan plays the same position as a standout for the Springfield Pics of junior hockey.

"Our whole family loves the game," Donnie said. "I've had great opportunities to play since I was a kid, and now I enjoy helping kids who don't have the opportunities I had."

"It's a great feeling to see kids who couldn't skate, out here now having a blast. When they're old and skating around, they can look back and say, I learned it at The Hockey Project."

Donnie Moorhouse's wife, Kate, and sons Sean, 13, and Ryan, 10, also help out.

Kevin Collins of Springfield, a retired NHL linesman who serves as a supervisor of officials, has helped through the "Zebras Care" program.

Other volunteers include John Jacques of the Hampden County Sheriff's Dept.; Nick Catjakis, a Springfield Falcons intern; Cathedral High School grad Colin Fenton, and Tom Campagna, Sabis director of athletics and guidance.

Why do they all do it?

As Foley points out, it goes back to their roots in kid hockey programs.

"I played for Classical and led the Berry Division – in penalty minutes," Foley said. "Before that I was a Van Horn kid, growing up on that pond and playing for great coaches. Now it's all about giving back, giving back to these kids what was given to us."

Moorhouse started "on the duck ponds of Forest Park." He played for the Forest Park VFW and the Elks before going on to backstop Western Mass. championship teams at Cathedral in 1982 and '83.

He now works for the Springfield Falcons as director of strategic sales – just another way for him to be close to the game he loves.

"You could take away my music, but don't take away my hockey," he said. "I'm at rinks six days a week, and on the seventh day we do The Hockey Project. It's the most rewarding thing I've ever done."

Middle-Infield Warbler

Back in the late 1920s, sportswriter George Springer of The Springfield Republican loved to pin nicknames on some of the high school athletes he covered. Perhaps the most colorful of them all – "The Purple Meteor" – was reserved for Cathedral's Don Herlihy, one of the great all-around athletes in the history of Springfield sports.

Herlihy's middle infield mate on city championship teams of 1928 and '29 also earned a nickname from Springer – "The Singing Second Sacker."

That was Walter Sullivan, at 116 pounds a supremely confident competitor for teams coached by Billy Wise.

During lulls in the action on the diamond, Sullivan was noted for breaking into song – and once Springer heard that, the nickname soon followed.

Actually, it was the second nickname for this kid. When he was nine years old, he became a fan of "Tux" Clark, an outfielder for the Springfield Ponies of the Eastern League. He decided to adopt "Tux" for himself.

Tux Sullivan came out of "The Brickyard," a Springfield neighborhood off lower Carew Street, to live a full life devoted to family and the sport he loved so dearly – baseball.

He was so sure of his ability to play second base that, in 1931, he took a bus to Orlando, Fla., and tried to walk onto a Brooklyn Dodgers spring training workout. Manager Casey Stengel had him ejected, but Brooklyn catcher Al Lopez (later a Hall of Fame manager) was so amused and impressed by this 20-year-old kid's feistiness, that he told him to go across town and try out for the Triple A Montreal Royals.

Tux did so – and made the team. However, his dreamy spring ended when he incurred a double-hernia while trying a hook slide. He was forced to come back to Springfield, and that proved to be the end of his pro career.

Not the end of baseball for him, though. He settled into a home life that included many years of coaching sandlot teams, most of them sponsored by the Holy Cross and Sacred Heart parishes. He served in the Pacific with the Army in World War II, worked for the New Haven Railroad and the Post Office, and raised a family as a resident of East Forest Park.

"Tux loved coaching kids, and he also was dedicated to following what they did in later life. Every city should have a Tux Sullivan," said his cousin, former Springfield mayor Billy Sullivan.

Even as a senior citizen, Tux wanted to be out there, hitting infield practice and teaching the fundamentals. His last coaching job came at the age of 77, with Cathedral's freshman team. In 2003, he worked on a committee headed by one of his old Cathedral teammates, Dr. Martin "Tim" Murray, and his cousin Billy to get a memorial erected to the 1934 Post 21 American Legion team.

The "Brothers All Are We" monument in Forest Park honors the Post 21 players who withdrew from a sectional tournament in Gastonia, N.C., rather than play without Bunny Taliaferro, their African-American teammate who would have been barred from going onto the field. Tux served as master of ceremonies at the dedication, giving it his own brand of warmth and wit.

Those qualities came through when, in his late 70s, he turned his attention to the writing of three books. The first, "What Have They Done to My Game?" tells of his baseball life and his concerns about the state of major league baseball today. He also wrote "Baseball Makes Friends" and "Ireland Smiling Through Tears."

Walter Patrick "Tux" Sullivan, 99, died Tuesday in Thiensville, Wis., where he had been staying with his son, Patrick, and his daughter-in-law, Olga.

His funeral mass will be celebrated Tuesday at Sacred Heart Church, not far from "The Brickyard."

Instead of the traditional funeral processional music at the end of mass, the organist will play Tux's favorite, "Take Me Out to the Ballgame."

Senior Years

For those of us who know the joy of grandparenting, there's nothing quite like high school.

Yes, the years of watching grandkids undergo the transition from wide-eyed freshmen to sophisticated seniors are precious, indeed. So precious, in fact, that deep in our hearts, we almost hate to see them end.

Well, it's time for my wife and I to face reality – this is our last high school "senior year." And it comes to us in a dazzling double dose, with graduation day approaching all too rapidly.

Our line of four grandchildren ended in 1997. Now, the two close cousins born that year are deeply involved as seniors at separate high schools.

When our three children were of school age, we faithfully watched sports and attended concerts, plays, teacher conferences and other related functions. Then, in the fall of 2006, we were thrilled to see the cycle starting all over again when our first grandchild entered ninth grade. Now, she's already a college graduate.

Did somebody say time flies?

Our last senior year has been busy, all right, with one grandchild involved with cheerleading, the other with track.

We followed the cheerleaders through football and basketball seasons, then into regional and state team competitions. Meanwhile, we kept up with indoor and outdoor track. Some of those early-spring meets…brrrr.

On top of all that, we had to worry and wonder about college decisions, but they finally were settled after weeks of uncertainty.

Until our grandkids grew to teen-age, the last senior year in our immediate family came 33 years ago, at dear old Cathedral High School. What a difference the decades make – our son's senior class of 1982 had more than 600 members.

Now, as we follow our remaining two through the dwindling days of senior year, we know what's coming: a family dilemma, as of June 5.

Yes, both graduations are scheduled for the same Friday, an hour apart. My wife and I are pretty good at getting to as many grand-kid events as possible, but we still haven't figured out how to be in two places at the same time.

Obviously, some kind of decision must be made. Maybe a coin flip can settle who goes to which ceremony.

One of our seniors, realizing that we were baffled by the impending graduation conflict, offered soothing words of compromise.

"Don't worry, Grandpa," she said, "We can have a party together the next day."

Great idea, eh?

By the way, this discussion about our last high school senior year came about because of a family photograph I uncovered while rummaging around for something else. It shows Yours Truly with the toddlers, one on each knee. The photo was taken in May of 1999, in the middle of their "terrible twos."

When I look at them now…wow.

As my sainted Irish mother used to say, "The good Lord willin'," we could face another graduation conflict in 2019 at the college level, because most commencements take place on the third Saturday in May.

Oh, well, can't think about that right now. Rather, we must consider first things first, like the remaining meets on the Western Mass. outdoor schedule for high school track.

Ah, senior year…there's nothing quite like it. Especially for the grandparents.

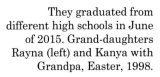

They graduated from different high schools in June of 2015. Grand-daughters Rayna (left) and Kanya with Grandpa, Easter, 1998.

A Farm Girl Remembers

A vast tract of land known to local folks as "Westover Field" has been an integral part of Connecticut Valley life for 75 years. Okay, but what was Westover before it became Westover?

My wife, the former Mary Helen Bukowski, knows the answer to that question, because she lived it.

Yes, as a child growing up in the middle of The Great Depression, she spent her early years on farm land that would be taken by eminent domain as part of America's military buildup leading to its inevitable involvement in World War II.

For a little girl, life on the farm created sweet memories. She must have been no more than four, she figures, when she was momentarily frightened by a cow, only to be swept up onto the shoulders of her tall daddy. She still remembers the uplifting feeling of being able to look DOWN at that huge cow.

She also has very pleasant memories of those cows that were cared for, day after day, by her parents. In the early mornings, her mama would take her to the barn where she milked the cows. Little Mary would bring her very own cup, and get to drink milk – straight from the cows...at its warmest, purest and sweetest. Nothing quite like that, she says. By the way, there was no worry about the health and cleanliness of the cows. Her daddy, a stickler for hygiene, saw to that.

The cows also brought a different kind of warmth to a little girl. She would lean against the huge expanse of the animal's side, soaking in its warmth and enjoying the particular sweet aroma that cows can have.

Pigs? Oh, yes, her daddy raised pigs, too, and sometimes he fed them Darcy's pies. With Mary and her cousin Lorraine Minkos as passengers, he would drive an old pickup truck to the bakery where his brother-in-law worked, and they would load that vehicle with pies which had to be discarded by the bakery because they were broken. The pigs would get most of those pies for dinner, but as the truck rattled back to the farm, the cousins would sit among the pies, snacking as they went. Mary remembers lemon as her favorite. Lorraine loved the French apple.

As hard as life was during The Great Depression, it got a bit easier for her family when the government established a CCC Camp (Civilian Conservation Corps) on property that was part of their farm.

Her mother then was able to earn some money by doing laundry for the men in the camp. Of course, that meant hauling water each day, but she long since had learned to live by the "work hard, it's good for you" mantra of her husband, who went out looking for work every day, sometimes landing odd jobs on adjacent farms "for $1 a day, and lunch," as Mary remembers him saying. The family also could count on him for meat on the table, because as a former Army sharpshooter, he excelled at hunting rabbit, squirrel and duck.

Meanwhile, his wife did laundry so long and so well, that she eventually was able to buy a precious device known as a washing machine.

The family also received medical care courtesy of the CCC Camp's resident physician, who was always close at hand. And the camp's cook often would drop by with food for the family. So appreciated was he, Mary's first dog was named "Cookie" in his honor.

By the way, Mary often could be seen wearing Paris fashions in the middle of the 1930s. How so? Because the wife of the CCC Camp's commanding officer had a daughter, and her grandmother lived in Paris as the wife of a State Department diplomat. She would buy Paris clothing and send it to her grand-daughter at the CCC camp. Thus, Mary would be second in line for some nice "hand-me-downs." A photo of her at age 5 shows her wearing a frilly white dress, straight from Paris.

All of that changed in the mid-1930s, when it became clear that the farmers who owned and worked the flatlands of Chicopee Falls and Ludlow soon would have no choice but to move. Uncle Sam had other plans for their property.

Thus, Mary would be transformed from country girl to city girl. When it finally happened, the Bukowskis relocated into a house in Chicopee center, on Springfield Street, across from the Assumption School, which since has been transformed into Holyoke Catholic High School. The new family home was fairly close to the drop-forging job her father would get as the nation went into war-production mode.

The bad news? She would never again drink a cup of that sweet, warm cow's milk. The good news? The Rivoli Theater was right down Springfield Street hill.

So it went in the 1930s, as that huge tract of Chicopee Falls/Ludlow farmland underwent a dramatic transformation, destined to become the site for hangars, barracks and runways. It has been that for 75 years.

Westover before it was Westover? An older generation does not forget.

Dolphin Butterfly Gold

WHEN BILL YORKZYK WAS A TEEN-AGER in his native Northampton, he tried several sports, but just couldn't make the high school varsity in any of them.

What he did show, though, was an admirable ability to put heart and soul into whatever he tried. That dedication to duty served him so well in his local Boy Scout troop, he reached its pinnacle – Eagle Scout.

His parents had his scouting achievements in mind when he was considering where he might go to college. Eventually, the family settled on Springfield College, because its mission seem to lend itself to all that Bill had learned as an Eagle Scout.

"When I got to Springfield, I didn't know how to swim. (Northampton High had neither a pool nor swim team in Yorzyk's time.) But I soon found out that I'd better learn, because you couldn't get out of freshman year without passing tests for swimming, diving and life-saving," he said.

So it was that Northampton Bill took the plunge – into little old McCurdy Natatorium, a 20-yard pool that has long since been transformed into a museum on the Springfield College campus. It was replaced by Linkletter Natatorium in 1968.

Soon, swimming became more than a necessity to Yorzyk. He quickly learned to love it, and his dedication to the sport eventually would enable him to complete a remarkable transition – from non-swimmer to Olympic gold medalist.

It happened for him in 1956, when he went to Melbourne, Australia, as part of a United States swimming team coached by Bob Muir of Williams College. Red Silvia, Yorzyk's mentor at Springfield College, served as Muir's assistant.

"We had a terrific team, but I was the only one to win a gold," Yorkzyk recalled.

Now 79 years old and living in quiet retirement in East Brookfield, Yorzyk does not have that gold medal in his possession.

"You'll find it nailed to the wall (at Linkletter Natatorium), he said. "I gave it to the college out of gratitude because Springfield, and Red Silvia, did so much for me. Besides, I feel that seeing the medal might inspire some of the young athletes on campus, show them that it can be done."

No question about it, Springfield College and coach Silvia meant everything to Yorzyk's life as a swimming champion. His talent in the dolphin butterfly stroke – taught to him from Day One by Silvia – stayed with him for years after, as he shattered records in the U.S. Masters Swimming Association.

"I think I held them all at one time, but they're being broken right and left now," he said.

Speaking of records, Yorzyk's victory in the 200-meter Olympic butterfly event was accomplished in an astounding time.

"He won in 2:19.3, and took 20 seconds off the world record. Can you imagine that?" said one of Yorzyk's long-time friends and coaches, Charlie Smith.

In winning the gold, Yorzyk trounced Takashi Ishimoto of Japan and Gyorgy Tumpek of Hungary, both of whom had been world record holders in the event.

"I have footage of Bill's race, and you can see the crowd exploding with cheers as he took off to win that race. With 50 meters to go, he just turned into a sprinter and left everybody way behind. It was as if he turned on the after-burners," Smith said.

As an SC swimming coach in the '60s and '70s, Smith worked with Yorzyk during his time as a Masters champion. But it is what Silvia and Yorzyk accomplished together at SC that makes Smith most proud.

"The dolphin butterfly stroke is, in a sense, comparable to basketball," Smith said. "Both basically were invented at Springfield College."

Actually, the dolphin butterfly stroke had been around for years before Silvia and Yorzyk became interested in it. Until then, many coaches shunned the event because it relied so heavily on upper body strength.

"Red Silvia was a remarkable guy, with expertise in mathematics and exercise science. He studied the dolphin butterfly stroke, and concluded that it could be done much more efficiently," Smith said.

Silvia brought about that efficiency by changing the method of kicking during the stroke. Simply put, he concluded that the swimmer should do two kicks within each arm cycle. That was vastly different from the accepted method, in which swimmers would do one arm cycle followed by five or six kicks.

"The thinking was that the shoulders couldn't take it unless there was kicking time in between," Smith said. "Red proved that by changing the kicks, the arm cycle became all the more efficient."

In effect, Yorzyk was the first swimmer in the world to be taught the proper dolphin butterfly stroke. He had never done it any other way, so adapting to Silvia's teaching was easy for him.

"We came together at the right time – serendipity," Yorzk said.

With the proper stroke in place, it now was Yorzyk's job to train for the Olympic Trials. And what a training regimen that was.

"I worked mainly in the college's 20-yard pool. I did 18 to 20 miles a day – morning, noon and night. I lived in that pool. It was I was like a ping-pong ball, bouncing back and forth," Yorzyk said.

Doing twenty miles day in a 20-yard pool?

"I think it comes out to 88 laps," Yorzyk said, and he is right.

Every so often, he would get a break from the 20-yard pool by driving to New Haven for his workouts.

"Yale had the only 50-meter pool in New England at that time, and I was able to use it now and then," he said.

In the Olympic Trials, and in the Olympic heats and final, Yorzyk never lost a race.

"That doesn't mean I wasn't scared," he said. "When you're up there, in the start position, it comes down to one race, one chance, so you'd better do it right."

What was it like when Yorzyk stepped onto the podium and heard "The Star Spangled Banner" playing?

"A feeling of exhilaration that I never had before, and haven't had since," he said. "I knew I was representing my team, my college, my sport and my country."

Homecoming didn't quite match that exhilaration, but it came close.

"They met me at Bradley Field, and I rode an open convertible through Springfield, up to the college campus, and then it was on to Northampton for a parade," he said.

Yorzyk's gold medal was the first for an American swimmer since 1932, when Buster Crabbe won one. Before him, Johnny Weissmuller won three golds in 1924, then two more in 1928.

Both Weissmuller and Crabbe went on to Hollywood to star in a series of "Tarzan" movies.

"I could have had the role, too," Yorzyk dead-panned, "but I couldn't do the Tarzan yell."

Bill Yorzyk (right) with one of his Springfield College coaches, Charlie Smith, at a reunion in 2012. (Photo by Mark Murray, *Springfield Republican*)

Dog Years

What? Venus the Labrador retriever is 11 years old?

When our son mentioned that fact to me, it came as a shock, although I should have known. After all, there's no denying that his family's beautiful black pet has gotten gray around the snout.

Still, it was kind of unsettling to realize that – in dog years – Venus is almost as old as I am. Oh, well, she's still in good shape, sleek and always ready for a walk around her Amherst neighborhood.

Because Venus makes a weekly appearance in my "Hitting to All Fields" column on the sports page, readers naturally assume she is our dog. No, she's our "grand-dog," and she's always flat-out happy to see us when arrive at her back door. Hmm. Could our pockets full of oyster cracker packets have something to do with that?

Anyway, the arrival of Venus in Amherst soon led to a return of "Labrador retriever" items in my column. And that's a good thing, because Venus draws more hits, e-mail and comments than anything else I might write about. (She also has more than 1,000 Facebook friends worldwide).

According to archival searches by my computer-savvy son, the first Labrador retriever reference in "Hitting" appeared Feb. 18, 1975, as follows:

"Mets pitcher Tom Seaver and I have something in common. He is rich, famous and owns a Labrador retriever. I, too, own a Labrador retriever."

The inspiration for that first reference came from a photo I saw of Seaver, hugging his black Lab. Only a few months earlier, in 1974, we had acquired a black Lab mix – and we soon came to realize why people love their dogs.

Sparky, our first one, came to us in a roundabout way. As my father-in-law was trying to deal with the death of his precious little dog, Chubby, good neighbor Ed Struzziero attempted to ease his pain by giving him a new dog. He thanked Ed profusely, but said he was too old to take on the care of another pet. So Ed passed Sparky on to us – and we're forever grateful to him.

We had her as a family member for 12 years. Our two teen-age sons adored her. She would croon along with one, when he would practice clarinet. She would let the other dress her in cutoff blue jeans, wrap an ace bandage around her tail, then walk her around the house like a wheelbarrow. She was a great ballplayer, too, running down every error in our pepper games. As for my wife, she treasured Sparky's comforting company at a time when I was working nights at The Springfield Union.

We finally had to put her down, and the pain of it made us vow never to have another dog. Wrong – a caring reader offered us a gorgeous chocolate

Lab pup, and we just couldn't resist her.

We named her Koko, and she was ours for 14 years. While Sparky had been serene and sedate – almost lady-like in her demeanor – Koko was just the opposite. We were warned that chocolate Labs tend to be hyper, and Koko certainly was all of that.

Yet, she also happened to be a great family dog (although a little on the stupid side). She loved playtime, even to the point of creating a game that we came to call "cellar ball." She would take a hard-rubber baseball to the top of the cellar stairs, give it a nudge with her nose, then watch it bounce down, step by step. When it reached bottom, she would tear down the stairs, retrieve the ball, bring it back to the landing – and do it all over again. Whenever we heard that "thump-thump-thump" of the hard rubber ball, we knew Koko was at the top of her game.

When she passed away, Labs disappeared from my column until the arrival of sweet Venus in 2003, another Lab mix (and one almost as lovably stupid as Koko). Venus is a Lab like no other – she doesn't retrieve, doesn't swim, hates snow. Hey, we love her, anyway.

Put the three of them together, and they add up to nearly 40 years of Labrador retrievers in our family. That's a whole lotta love and companionship.

Now, at age 11, Venus often reminds me of my favorite "Hitting" line:

Labrador retriever's theme song: "Ain't Too Proud to Beg."

Oyster crackers, anyone?

The Fading Face of Tech

On my way to a recent Springfield Falcons hockey game at the MassMutual Center, curiosity forced me to turn right off State Street and onto Elliot.

Spurred by a painful twinge of nostalgia, I had to take another look at my old high school – or, what's left of it.

All that remains of Springfield Technical High School is the frontal façade. Staring at it, I suddenly realized that behind those bricks once existed the second-floor room where Miss Kelly tried her best to teach me geometry.

The preservation of that façade is the city's way of remembering one of its great schools. The rest of the building? Demolished in 2011 as prelude to construction of a $110 million Springfield Data Center. Among the classrooms that no longer exist was 326 – left corner, Elliot Street side – which served as my home room for three years (city high schools at that time consisted of grades 10–12).

Our home room came under the supervision of the esteemed Charles Allen, who also happened to be our physics teacher. He spent more time than he should have trying to help certain baffled students, present company included, with the basics of a tough subject.

Of course, I probably was in the wrong high school. My junior high principal had urged me to go to Classical, but I wasn't listening. After all, my three older siblings had gone to Tech, so I would go there, too.

Well, let it be said that even though I lacked the natural bent toward science – not to mention wood shop and machine shop – I did manage to graduate in the Class of 1949.

At that time, Tech's student body came under the stewardship of M. Marcus Kiley, an educator so respected, they later named a city junior high school in his honor.

Tech's athletic department of that era included several successful coaches who doubled as gym teachers. In any given week, I might have a class in tumbling with Johnny Kalloch, a class in basketball with Bill Lawler, a class in vaulting with Milt Orcutt, a class in rope climbing with Vic Kodis (the toughest one).

As a kid, I dreamed of playing second base for the Tech Tigers. Actually, my dream was to succeed Bobby Doerr when he retired as captain and second baseman of the Red Sox, but I figured I might need some playing time at Tech before taking that next step into the big leagues.

Of course, the reality was that I never got to play varsity sports for any of those gym teachers. My second-base dream didn't make it past 10th grade.

To compensate for that disappointment, I took my father's advice and went looking for a spot with the Tech News. Lucky break there – my home room buddy, Don Campbell, was the school newspaper's editor-in-chief. He gladly allowed me to write about Tech's real athletes of the day – city stars like Jim Hamilton, Alex Korbut, John Jeffries, Lefty Ferrero, Elvin Eady, Al

Colonna, Joe Gulluni and a big pitcher named Red Stewart. Red was a giant among us, only to die young.

Editor Campbell also showed me what newspaper work was really about – getting the pages ready for print. We spent many an after-school afternoon downtown on Taylor Street at a little print shop where the Tech News pages came together. I watched, wide-eyed, at a process that would fascinate me for a lifetime.

Until Springfield College opened its Field House in 1948, Tech's gym served as the city's best basketball venue. And let's not forget the school's auditorium and stage, where "Tech Tantrums" would showcase the school's talent each spring. You want talent? The alto sax soloist in 1949 was a junior named Phil Woods, who went on to international renown in the jazz world.

What happened at Tech in the post-World War II '40s merely was a snapshot of what happened there every decade, from the school's opening in 1905 to its closing 81 years later. Tech's top students would win the Warner Achievement Medal. Tech's teams would win some and lose some, with any game against arch-rival Cathedral always the most important of any season. The Tech News would come out, year after year, even winning scholastic journalism awards now and then.

Yes, but buildings rise and fall – and that surely has been the story for Springfield's schools. Gone are the original homes of Tech, Cathedral and Trade. Classical? It still stands, but as living quarters rather than a high school. Only Commerce remains in its original building, in which major renovations were done some years back.

As the old buildings fade from memory, the newer ones take their place...Central, Sci-Tech and that state-of-the-art Putnam Vocational Technical Academy.

Meanwhile, if you're an old Tech Tiger, I would not recommend a trip down Elliot Street. It might be too painful. Then again, it might send you on a nostalgia trip, to a familiar tune...

"Cheer, cheer, cheer for Tech, with her royal banners flying ..."

Dinosaur On the Line

After watching Sonia, our oldest grandchild, give her all for Smith College in a varsity volleyball game, we stayed around to get some much-needed hugs.

As I embraced her in her sweat-soaked uniform, she whispered into my hearing aid.

"Grandpa, I can't believe you texted me."

That happened last October, which certainly would rank as a milestone month for me. Yes, as Sonia noted so sweetly, I completely surprised her by taking one more step into the 21st century. I finally had learned – after owning a cell phone for much longer than I care to admit – how to send a text message. My first one went to Sonia, telling her we would be at her volleyball game.

I also have made attempts at embracing other aspects of that new-fangled world known as "social media" but as I do so, I am reminded of the one time that New England Patriots coach Bill Belichick had something funny to say.

It was back there at training camp in 2011, when he said, "I don't Twitter. I don't do MyFace. I don't use Yearbook. I don't do any of those things..." Well, Coach Bill, I do some of those, but not very well.

My introduction to the world of cell phones actually came some time ago, when I was still working full-time as a sportswriter for the dear old Springfield Republican.

When I first started using the cell phone, people made calls, but didn't send messages. Back then, who would have dreamed that the noun "text" some day would be turned into a verb? As in, "Text me later." Ugh – an English major's nightmare.

When I got my first cell phone, another of our grand-daughters grabbed it and said, "Grandpa, I'll give you a special ringtone." In a matter of seconds, she had it done. When my phone rang, it would play music. I had no idea how she did it, or how to change it. So the music stayed.

I first brought the phone into the press box at Fenway Park, when I was covering a Boston Red Sox game. I had it in my jacket pocket as I attended one of manager Terry Francona's pre-game press briefings.

Going through the door to the briefing, I had neglected a sign which warned, "Turn off all cell phones." Halfway through Francona's briefing, mine rang – loud and clear. Music blared all over the room as I scrambled to find the phone and turn it off. Too late.

"What the hell was that?" Francona bellowed.

Talk about embarrassing moments in the big leagues.

Years later, just when I was learning how to send a text message, we made a decision to get new cell phones.

"We have instructional sessions here every week if you need them," our salesman said, giving me a sly, knowing look.

The fact that he appeared to be about 12 years old, and could manipulate any electronic device with blinding speed, only added to the uncomfortable feeling I had about my new "smartphone." Deep down, I knew it would be too smart for me.

How right I was. I not only have trouble texting on my new device, I'm not even sure about answering a call.

"Just sweep your finger across the screen, then say hello," our son the computer scientist advised me. Easy for him to say, but when I tried it, I found that my sweeping style wasn't what my phone wanted.

Well, I finally have mastered it – to a point. I do answer my calls, but sometimes it takes several sweeps before I get it right. More often than not, the caller gives up before I finish sweeping. Then I am forced to call back and say sheepishly, "Were you trying to reach me...?"

Oh, yes, I also have old-fogey problems with my phone. Lots of times, I can't find it. Sometimes, I forget to bring it with me. Sometimes, I forget to put it on the charger, which is a major no-no.

And then there are those frustrating times when it rings but I don't hear it because it's buried in my coat pocket. Aarrgh.

As for the texting (there's that verb again), I'm doing better, thanks to our grandchildren. They giggle when my wife tells them that we are "techno-stupid," but they ignore the generation gap and do provide lots of valuable help.

For instance, they have taught us the shorthand of texting, designed to save time and typing mistakes. Last week, when our son came home from a doctor's appointment, we sought information on how he was doing.

"R U OK?" my wife texted like an old pro.

Of course, he had to be a wiseguy in return.

"What's RUOK?" he asked.

No doubt about it, senior citizens take a beating as they try to adjust to all the new technology. Heck, it wasn't until a few months ago that I came to understand the true meaning of "app."

Back at the telephone store, as I attempted to grasp what the salesman was telling me, I stammered, "I'm trying hard, but I come from back there in the last century."

"Don't worry," he said. "You're doing better than a lot of people your age."

I tried to take that as a compliment.

Music For The Love of It

FIVE SAXOPHONES, FOUR TRUMPETS, THREE TROMBONES and a rhythm section.

That's the lineup for the usual high school jazz band, but it doesn't come close to matching the musical ensemble at Springfield's High School of Science & Technology.

Sci-Tech's jazz band, directed by a 29-year-old bundle of energy named Gary Bernice, has 51 players in its alto sax section alone. Altogether, this band consists of 100 members – and that's only part of the total package in the school's music program.

"Altogether, we have 300 students involved. The jazz band represents just a part of what we do," Bernice said.

Sci-Tech's music program begins with Symphonic Band, as an introductory course. Concert Band, Jazz Band and Advance Percussion Ensemble and Chamber Ensembles also are offered.

The Jazz Band recently played at the Springfield Public Schools Athletic Hall of Fame's induction ceremony, and drew round after round of applause from the crowd.

The band's rendition of John Lennon-Paul McCartney's "Yesterday" was a highlight of the night.

The most recent appearance by Sci-Tech musicians came at a Dec. 13 WinterFest, subtitled "Celebrating Student Success in the Arts," at Chestnut Middle School. In recent years, they have played at the inauguration of Mayor Domenic J. Sarno, at fireworks displays, area college events, community music festivals, pancake breakfasts and school graduations.

In spring, the band's growth over the school year is measured, in an "Arts Alive" concert.

Bernice, the maestro of all this, sees much more to his role than merely teaching students how to play instruments and advance their musical skills. Rather, he sees the band as a way of helping them learn the value of teamwork and leadership.

"I consider this a student-led program," he said. "Every day they mentor each other, and from this process they can become leaders in whatever path they may choose. The band is an extremely effective teaching tool."

Stepping to the forefront of band leadership in the current school year are its president, Antonio Narvaez, and vice-president, Carlos Cintron Torres.

Narvaez ranks among the 99 percent of Sci-Tech band members who came to the music program with no prior experience in playing an instrument.

"The theory is that music education should start early, in the lower grades," Bernice said. "That's not how it is with our school population, so we have to make up all that time and still become a performing band. To do that, we don't spend the school year working on "Mary Had a Little Lamb." They grow and learn with the music. They prove what's possible when you have high expectations for them. I believe and they believe, and together we carry on with what I would call relentless persistence. The fact that all of this happens, merely shows what students are capable of," Bernice said.

Narvaez first had to pick an instrument, and he chose a dazzling white sousaphone (tuba).

"My father was afraid that I'd break my instrument, or lose it, and he would have to pay for it. So I chose the biggest instrument I could find. My father accepted what I wanted to do when he saw the passion I have for music, and how I was getting better at it."

Cintron Torres plays the baritone sax – a hefty instrument that stands nearly as tall as he is. Unlike most of his bandmates, he came to the program with some musical background.

"We lived in Virginia before we moved here, and I had some

music education there. They wanted me to play the alto sax, but it just felt too small for me. So I picked the 'barry.' I love playing jazz, but I'm also interested in other genres of music," he said.

Both band officers extol the 'family' feeling they get from playing music with their fellow students. And both plan to pursue careers in music.

"I'll be going into the Navy after I graduate, and I hope to play in the Navy band," Narvaez said. "Ultimately, my hope is to be the director of a symphony orchestra."

Cintron Torres said his dream is to compose and conduct.

"The feeling I get from interpreting music is amazing," he said.

Although Bernice says "our focus not on developing music majors," he does take pride in having one of his former students, Jeremy Turgeon, studying at Berklee School of Music in Boston, and another, Alton Skinner, studying music performance at Holyoke Community College.

"Our main goal is to give our students something they can share with their families forever," Bernice said.

An undertaking as large as Sci-Tech's band program can only work if it really is a labor of love. And so it is with Bernice and his students.

"They know I care about them, and in turn they care about me and each other. We call ourselves 'The Pride of Springfield' because we want our students to take pride in their city," Bernice said.

The Sci-Tech job is the first of his teaching career. He calls it "the most challenging thing I have done, and the most meaningful." He came to the school on January 27, 2007, after earning undergraduate and graduate degrees in music education at the University of Massachusetts.

In his first class, he had twenty students. Now, he teaches six classes involving 300.

"Actually, it could have been more. Something like 500 kids applied at the beginning of the year, but we just couldn't handle that," he said.

As it is, Bernice's program encompasses one-fourth of Sci-Tech's total enrollment.

"The six classes become a unified band, and our goal is to be growing together at the end of the year," he said.

Handling such large music classes and holding the attention of a 100-piece band would seem to be an awesome task for any leader.

Not so for Bernice, because he has a lot of help.

"I don't have to control the band. The students take care of that. They take ownership of their program, and control it because they are so invested in it. They choose the music we will be playing," he said.

"Some of these students have seen a lack of success in their lives. So if they see that this (the music program) works, it gets into their hearts and helps them grow."

Bernice grew up in Ridgefield, N.J., which he describes as "an affluent community." He followed the lead of his grandfather, who was a well-known trumpet player in his home state.

"In my town, if you wanted to play a trumpet, the school gave you a trumpet. In some schools, if students want to be in a band, they have to own their instruments. We don't do that. We provide our students with the instruments, getting them through support of sponsors, the school and the city," Bernice said.

Sci-Tech has been successful in musical productions even though the school does not have an auditorium. Its building on upper State Street formerly housed the Springfield Fire & Marine Insurance Company.

"When they were remodeling it for school purposes, they had to make a choice – auditorium or swimming pool. They picked the pool," Bernice said.

So it is that every "gig" for the school's band requires a major moving job. A large van transports all the equipment and instruments that go with a 100-piece musical ensemble.

Who pays for the van? Bernice admitted that he and his wife take care of that.

His stress on having students learn to be leaders resulted in a heartwarming experience for him and his family last June.

"The band was scheduled to play at Symphony Hall for our school graduation," Bernice said. "The date was June 12 – and that just happened to be the day my wife, Elise, gave birth to twin girls, Lily and Hannah. I didn't make the graduation because I wanted to be with my wife and our new daughters. So the students took charge of the band's performance at graduation. From the start, my dream has been that the band should be student-led – and it came true on a very special day."

Good Old Junior Hockey Days

Junior hockey programs still thrive in Western Massachusetts, but they can never be quite what they were in the good old days of the Eastern States Exposition Coliseum in West Springfield.

That was the arena's official name, but most people lovingly referred to it simply as "The Old Barn."

For decades, it was the only hockey arena in the Pioneer Valley. And for years, it served as home to the Greater Springfield Junior Amateur Hockey League. By the way, I always wondered why they felt the need to designate kids in the 10 to 16 age group as "amateurs," but that's a minor point in a very big picture.

Yes, the GSJAHL was big, all right. Every Saturday morning from December to March, teams in the 10–12, 12–14 and 14–16 age groups would get the wondrous opportunity of skating on the same ice used by the Springfield Indians of the American Hockey League.

It was all done under the good works of Eddie Shore, a Pro Hockey Hall of Famer who owned the Springfield franchise. He didn't own the Coliseum, but you'd never know it. He ruled the building year 'round – except for Eastern States Exposition time.

Soon after he became owner of the Springfield hockey club in 1939, Big Ed reached out to youngsters. He and Exposition management not only made Coliseum ice available to them, they did so at no charge.

The only thing was, those junior players had to know the rules. If they broke them, they would face the wrath of Eddie, and nobody wanted The Man in the Hat coming at them.

First rule, teams had to be on time. This was an especially tough one for the 10–12 division, which always took the ice first. That meant the puck would drop for Game One at 8 a.m. Be there, or forfeit.

Second rule, each team had to have a designated minimum number of players. Show up a man short, and Eddie would send the rest of the team home.

Hey, it had to be that way. When games were being played like clockwork from 8 a.m. to 2 in the afternoon, there was no time for glitches.

"Eddie's way or the highway" paid off. Coaches and players learned to be on time and at full strength. Do that, and they'd get to skate and play. What could be better on a wintry Saturday?

Shore's top GSJAHL aide was Jack Butterfield, who would somehow do his real job as general manager of the Indians and still find countless hours to devote to the kids. Jack made the schedules, kept the league standings and had key people at rinkside, supervising play and keeping track of goals, penalties and all the rest.

In a way, Jack's junior hockey role was a proper precursor for the job he later would do so well for 28 years – president of the American Hockey League.

His No. 1 assistant on junior hockey day, Ted Shore, officiated many of the games. He had lots of on-ice help, all of it from volunteers, of course. One such was Charlie Ghedi, a full-time AHL linesman who gladly spent part of his Saturdays officiating junior games.

For Yours Truly, being assigned to cover junior hockey for The Sunday Republican was a joy, indeed. There was nothing quite like watching game after game, then going into the newspaper office and writing a story about them.

Of course, being a young writer at the Coliseum meant being a "gopher," as well. Ted Shore, Eddie's son, was just about my age, but he felt empowered to order me to go across Memorial Avenue to get coffee for the volunteers on duty.

Coverage of junior hockey gave me an early look at some local stars of the future. Many of the kids I watched in 10–12 hockey would go on to play for the high school and college teams that I also covered.

Case in point would be a Cathedral team which won the Western Mass. championship in 1954. Every player on that team grew up in the junior leagues.

One of them, Dave Keaney, cherishes his Coliseum days – and he has a special memory of life with Eddie Shore.

"One week, after one of our games, I was out in the Coliseum corridor and I found a used soda cup," he said. "I stamped on it, and began using it as a puck, firing it against the wall. I was flirting with trouble, because we all knew that Eddie didn't want anybody playing in the hallways. Well, he caught me, and threw me out. There I am, 10 years old, and I'm suspended for two weeks."

Yes, but Keaney also will tell you that Shore's junior hockey program changed his life. He went on to become an All-Western Mass. player at Cathedral and earned a hockey scholarship to American International College.

Saturday mornings at the Coliseum. If you ever experienced them, you know how absolutely precious they were to all concerned.

Gerry Finn – An Appreciation

Winter, 1950. I hurried up the stairs to the second floor of Stryker Hall, where a small room served as headquarters for "The Yellow Jacket," American International College's campus weekly newspaper.

My new boss, a World War II vet named Gerry Finn, gave me a gruff welcome, then cut right to it.

"I liked some of the stuff you wrote on freshman football, except for one thing – your stories go too long. For me, you'll have to write shorter," he said.

Gerry Finn, you see, was part of a second-semester change of command at the dear old YJ. A senior, Norm Staats, had been my first sports editor, but I hardly ever saw him and never heard any criticism from him. Now, with Gerry becoming sports ed, I could see that things would be different, and better. I hoped.

I was right. He let me cover the hockey team, which was a special favorite of mine because its stars, Joe Buchholz and Fred Zanetti, were in a couple of my classes. So I wrote hockey all winter – and yes, I kept the stories short and to the point, as ordered by You Know Who.

Not too many years later, Gerry and I again became members of the same staff, at The Springfield Union. The Union's sports department of the early '50s included five AIC people: Joe Napolitan, Gene McCormick, Jerry Radding, Gerry Finn and me.

Joe Nap soon left for political reporting and consulting, but the rest of us worked together in that sports department for fortysomething years. An experience for a lifetime.

It soon became clear that Gerry was a rising star. Because he wrote with such knowledge and insight, he soon began covering major events. He was there at Boston Garden when Ron Delaney became a sensation of the indoor mile. He was there when Bob Cousy broke in with the Celtics. A few years later, he covered the Masters during the height of the Arnold Palmer-Jack Nicklaus rivalry.

Then came the columns. Gerry's "Loud and Clear" and "Finn-ish Line" efforts became staples of the sports section. His readers always knew where he stood on issues of the day.

For a time, he left Springfield to become sports editor of The Hartford Times. When that paper folded, we were lucky – we got him back for the rest of his career.

I had the pleasure of covering three World Series with him, involving the Red Sox of 1967, 1975 and '86. We both learned how tough it is to write a losing Game 7 story and/or column on deadline.

In his later years, Gerry concentrated on columns and also served as our Boston Celtics beat writer. His work during the Larry Bird era gave readers an inside look at a legend.

In 1993, the Western Mass. Golf Hall of Fame enshrined him in honor of his years of outstanding coverage of local tournaments. Recognition well deserved, starting with his riveting stories about junior phenom Ronnie Mattson in the '50s.

A little-known fact about Gerry Finn: He was an outstanding basketball player at Arlington High. In the early '60s, when our staff organized a "Springfield Sportswriters" hoop team to play games for charity, he and Ray Fitzgerald were our top threats. We were so good, we actually beat a Smith Academy alumni team on its home court – the old Hatfield Town Hall.

After that game, Gerry called me aside and gave me a compliment I shall never forget: "Only two guys on this team know how to play defense – you and me," he said.

That was Gerry. Always right to the point.

He passed away June 30, 2014, and I shall miss him. In my heart, he's unforgettable – going all the way back to our dear old Yellow Jacket days.

Ralphie and the Falcons

As equipment manager for the Springfield Falcons of the American Hockey League, Ralph Calvanese works out of a small office near the team's locker room.

Next to his own modest desk, a small sewing machine sits on a table. Behind the sewing machine? A pile of nameplates, ready to be sewn onto game jerseys of Falcons players.

"Dansk" – a uniform nameplate reserved for one of the Springfield club's likely goaltenders – rests at the top of the pile. It is one of 32 that Calvanese has, at the ready, as he waits to see what the opening-night roster will be.

Not too far away, on a workbench, stands – as Calvanese calls it – "an industrial strength" sewing machine. He needs this heavy-metal device to handle such problems as torn skates or damaged gloves and pads.

"Sometimes, I put that one to work while a game's going on, as needed," Calvanese said.

Sewing uniform numbers and repairing equipment comes with a labor of love that has been Calvanese's life for 41 years. It's safe to say that there may not be another person in North America who has seen as many AHL games as he has, being with the team both home and away for one season after another.

Calvanese's number, by the way, approaches 3,000. He has kept careful track of his career, so he can say with authority that he will work his AHL Game 3,000 November 8, when the Falcons play at Manchester.

"Actually, it's pretty easy to know the number. I know how many games we had in each season, and I know how many I've missed when I was sick or had a bad back," he said.

Bruce Landon, director of hockey operations for the Falcons, has had a 45-year career locally as player and executive. He has known Calvanese for most of that time.

"I can flat out say that Ralphie is the best in the business. For one thing, he's an expert skate-sharpener, and a lot of people don't realize how important that is to hockey players," Landon said. "He's the best, simply because he cares about everything related to his job and the team. He puts in long hours, and does whatever it takes. The players know that, and year after year they come to know him and respect him."

In January of 2011, the AHL recognized Calvanese's long-time devotion to the league by naming him equipment manager for the midseason All-Star Classic in Hershey, Pa.

Regarding his 3,000 AHL games, Calvanese said he knows of two with similar longevity – equipment manager Skip Cunningham of the Carolina Hurricanes and retired trainer Pete Demers.

Cunningham has been with the Carolina franchise since its birth in the World Hockey Association as the Hartford Whalers. Demers worked 34 years and nearly 2,700 games in the NHL with the Los Angeles Kings.

"What makes Ralphie unique is that he's done it all in the AHL and in the same city," Landon said.

At times, Calvanese's office can take on a "bless this mess" look, but he keeps the Falcons locker room, showers and bathrooms in tip-top shape.

"No question, Ralphie's meticulous about that locker room and how the players look in their uniforms," Landon said.

The Falcons equipment manager cares so much because he has loved the hockey since his boyhood years in Springfield.

"I was 19 when I started as a stickboy in the visitors locker room. Coach Ron Stewart (of the Springfield Kings) liked me, and pretty soon I was doing equipment work," Calvanese said.

"That was the 1974–75 season, and it was scary for a time because there were a couple of months when everybody thought the franchise might fold. Instead, Eddie Shore kept it going and we wound up winning the Calder Cup."

Calvanese, a 1972 graduate of The High School of Commerce, says he doesn't just work for the Falcons – he roots hard for them, as well.

"Sure, I'm a big fan. I want to see them win, and it hurts when they lose. I want to see the team make it to the postseason. The playoffs? That's the best time of any hockey season," he said.

Ted Dunn's Magical Season

WHEN TED DUNN OF HAMILTON, NEW YORK, entered the Army Air Corps in 1942, he hoped to become a pilot, but color blindness grounded him. Instead, as a former football player at Colgate University, he drew duty to train cadets.

His job – get them in shape through a regimen of calisthenics, and teach them the survival swimming techniques they would need if they had to ditch an aircraft in the ocean.

One of his training colleagues was an officer named Ken Landon, who had played football at Springfield College.

"At Colgate, the athletic department had three head coaches who were Springfield graduates. Meeting Ken Landon reminded me of that, and got me thinking that Springfield might be the place I was looking for to get a master's after the war," Dunn said.

So it was that he arrived on the Alden Street campus in the fall of 1946 after 39 months of wartime service. When he learned that Ossie Solem was starting his first season as SC's head football coach, he went straight to his office and volunteered to help the coaching staff.

"Ossie was at Syracuse when I played for Colgate. We went 1-1-1 against his teams in my three varsity years at a time when Syracuse-Colgate was one of the big rivalries in college football."

In his Red Raider days, Dunn played quarterback – that is, blocking back – in the single and double-wing formations used by coach Andy Kerr.

Dunn grew up five minutes away from coach Kerr's home in Hamilton.

"In 1932, when I was twelve about 1,000 people gathered at Colgate to await big news that the football team would be going to the Rose Bowl. Big disappointment. Coach Kerr came out and announced, 'Pittsburgh is going to the Rose Bowl. Colgate is undefeated, untied, unscored upon – and uninvited.'

"That's the kind of atmosphere I grew up in, and that's why I wanted to play for coach Kerr," Dunn said.

"Ossie Solem remembered me, and took me on as a volunteer assistant. When I went to the first practice, he had 120 players out for the team. It seemed like every GI on campus wanted to play football."

The next year, Solem recommended Dunn to be his graduate assistant. Then, after he completed his master's requirements, Solem recommended him for a full-time job as an assistant coach.

Thus began what would be a 37-year career for Ted Dunn at Springfield College. He served as an assistant for 12 years, then took over as head coach when Solem retired in 1958.

The Dunn coaching era at SC lasted for 18 years. After he stepped down in 1975, he continued as a faculty member until his retirement in 1983.

Only one man has coached football at Springfield College longer than Dunn – the current head man, Mike DeLong, who is in his 27th season. DeLong played for Dunn. So did the current Harvard coach, Tim Murphy.

Why do SC coaches stay at the school for long careers?

"When you coach football at Springfield, you generally deal with a fine young man, and the facilities are great – getting better all the time," Dunn said.

A gathering of Dunn's fine young men – now in their 60s – will be on campus this weekend for the annual homecoming. It's a special year for them – the 45th anniversary of a 1965 season when they posted a 9-0-0 record. That's the only unbeaten-untied season in the college's football history.

The '65 co-captains – defensive end Scott Taylor and offensive guard Gary Wilcox – put the reunion together. They'll hark back to a season in which their football team scored 252 points and allowed 87.

"What makes this reunion extra special is that all three of our coaches will be there," Taylor said. "Coach Dunn is 90, and defensive co-ordinator Dave Auxter and offensive co-ordinator Jack Newmann are in their 80s. The more I speak with teammates from across the country, the more I realize that this kind of thing does not occur very often."

The '65 team will be publicly saluted at halftime of Springfield's Saturday afternoon game against Utica College.

Auxter played for Springfield in the '50s. He was coaching high school football in New Hartford, N.Y., when Dunn persuaded him to come back to SC as one of his assistants.

"Dave had a great love for the game, and he was a terrific defensive coach. Jack Newmann (another SC grad) came back after coaching for a time at Cal-Berkeley. He took care of the offensive line. I worked with the backs and ends. It was a great treat having them on our staff," Dunn recalled.

His '65 offense was led by Dave Bennett, a 6-foot-4 quarterback with a live arm. He still holds SC records for passing attempts (568) and completions (280).

"We had a couple of 6-foot-5 receivers on that team, Jay Hansen and George Wolfort. Dave being so tall himself, he had no trouble finding those targets," Dunn said. "He came to us from Holyoke. I remember getting a call from Archie Roberts (long-time Holyoke High School coach) telling me about his quarterback. We were grateful to get him."

Bennett ran an offense that featured quick slants and sideline passes.

"We weren't a throw-it-downfield kind of team. We were just a bunch of over-achievers. I think our defensive line averaged only 177 pounds, but they had speed. They flew to the ball, and they liked to hit," Bennett said.

Like many Springfield grads, Bennett went into a career of coaching. He got a late start, at age 30, because he played several seasons of professional football with the Hartford Knights and Holyoke Bombers. He coached locally at West Springfield High and Minnechaug Regional (where he won two Super Bowls), and on the west coast at Harvard-Westlake School of Hollywood, Calif.

"I had 26 kids go from there to play in the Ivy League," Bennett said.

The '65 Springfield team had four other players from the Pioneer Valley – linebacker Tom Sawyer of East Longmeadow, linebacker Steve Parker of Chicopee, quarterback John Mikzewski of Agawam and defensive back Chet Hawrylciw of Ludlow.

"We had a strong nucleus of seniors who had played together for four years," cocaptain Taylor recalled. "I don't think we were on too many radar screens (after going 3-6-0 in 1964) but we were determined and confident from the beginning of the season."

The team finished strong, whipping New Hampshire and Wagner in its eighth and ninth games. That led to Springfield being considered for a bid to the Tangerine Bowl, but Maine wound up getting it.

Now, it's time to look back on that once-in-a-lifetime season at a reunion that will carry through the weekend.

"It's kind of sweet to have this happen to an old coach," Dunn said. He lost his wife, Ann, in 2001. He still lives in the house they bought in 1968, in a Springfield neighborhood not far from the campus he loves so dearly.

When he was awaiting his 90th birthday on Jan. 15, the cards and letters started coming. "I have a clothes basket full of the birthday mail I received from my former players," he said.

A fitting testimony to a dedicated coach, one who made a lasting difference in so many young lives.

Ted Dunn, 96, passed away April, 25, 2016.

Winning One for Piotr

Note: This column ran in The Springfield Republican Oct. 28., 2004 – two days after the Red Sox won the World Series.

At this glorious time in Boston Red Sox history, I must tell you about Piotr I. Bukowski, the most loyal fan I have ever known.

He was born in Galicia, a town in southern Poland near the Austrian border. He came to America as a teenager, settling with relatives in Three Rivers. All too soon came the clouds of war. He responded by enlisting in the United States Army, a decision which would lead him back to Europe to fight the forces of Kaiser Wilhelm.

He served his new country in World War I with distinction, earning medals including a Purple Heart.

Despite his haunting experiences in the trenches, he took great pride in the fact that he had fought in what he called "the last gentleman's war."

He always stood straight and tall, a military man for life. When his children were young, he would take them on a "forced march" every Saturday morning, across the old Chicopee-West Springfield bridge and back to the family home on Springfield Street, Chicopee. An up-tempo march, an Army man's march.

Before he had to go to war, he became enamored of a sport he had never seen. The beauty of baseball entranced him, especially as it was played by the Boston Red Sox in their new green cathedral called Fenway. He was 16 years old when he saw Smoky Joe Wood, 18 when he saw Babe Ruth.

By the time he left for France, his favorite baseball team had won the World Series three times since his arrival at Ellis Island.

When a blessed armistice brought cessation to hostilities in "the war to end all wars" in November of 1918, he knew he would be coming home to Massachusetts and his Red Sox. He had missed their latest World Series victory, but he knew there would be more.

So began for him years of hoping, yearning, rooting for a team that went from consistent winner to annual loser. He lamented the sale of a favorite player, the one he always referred to as "Baby Ruth," but he never lost faith in his Sox.

When I married his beautiful daughter in 1952, I had no idea what a true-blue fan this man was. On Sunday afternoons, when relatives would gather for picnics in his big backyard, he had to have his portable radio at his side.

"Ball game," he would say, and his wife would mutter, "Crazy damn fool..."

Remember, those were the days of

Don Buddin and the bad Schilling – Chuck. Those were the days of Rudy Minarcin, Murray Wall and bonus baby Frank Baumann. Terrible Red Sox days, but he didn't care. They were his team, and he would not leave them. He could always find hope in the promising rookies of springtime. Watch those "young fellas," he would say.

So it went for the rest of his life, rooting just as hard for 90-game losers as he did for 90-game winners. Ball game every night and every weekend – he preferred radio, didn't like the TV broadcasts.

This was "Dziadzu" (pronounced Jaju), beloved grandfather to our children. In his company, they knew they would have love, laughter and baseball.

Peter I. Bukowski died in 1984 at 87, never having seen his beloved Red Sox win another World Series.

This one's for him.

Indian Orchard's French Connection

On one corner of Oak and Main streets in Indian Orchard stood Bissonette's Package Store. Diagonally across the way, Noe Flebotte and his family operated a busy "Mom and Pop" market.

Next to Bissonette's, Bengle's shoe store. Then came Madame Porcheron's, a boutique specializing in women's clothing. Two doors down, at Teddy Montcalm's drug store, you could get a dynamite strawberry ice cream soda. Further up the street stood Mongeau's, yet another drug store.

Hamel's OK Lunch on lower Main Street specialized in out-of-this-world jelly doughnuts – sweet strawberry on the inside, powdered sugar on the outside. Around the corner, Red Morrissette's barbershop offered service at 25 cents a head.

A little farther up Main Street stood the quarters for Gaudreau Insurance. Then came Chez Madame, another boutique, and Chouinard's Restaurant, a popular place for parties.

On the corner of Main and Pinevale streets, the Ratell family operated a funeral home that later was owned and run by brothers Maurice and Levis St. Pierre. Another St. Pierre brother, Fred, often assisted them at funerals.

Maybe a half-mile away, at Bolduc's, you could have gas pumped into your car, and get the oil checked and the windshield/back window cleaned.

The Orchard also was home to a thriving lumber and hardware business, run by Adelard Boilard. It is still going today.

The Orchard's medical community included Drs. Meunier, Genest and Roy.

Yes, the Orchard of my youth in the '30s and '40s had a distinct French-Canadian connection.

My dad worked fortysomething years at the Indian Orchard Post Office, most of that time as the assistant postmaster. His co-workers included Amos Ouellette and George Coupal, both of whom belonged to the Orchard's very active Franco-American Club.

In the Fourth of July parade, the line of march would include the Franco-American Drum and Bugle Corps, complete with gleaming silver helmets.

A majority of the kids who grew up in Indian Orchard at that time attended parochial schools – St. Matthew's for the Irish families; St. Mary's for the Polish and St. Aloysius for the French.

Up the hill at 154 Myrtle Street, a family named Brown lived one house away from Armand Bengle, postmaster of the Indian Orchard branch, and my dad's boss. In that neighborhood, my boyhood buddies included Junior Noel, Francis LaPierre and Marty Rickson (French on his mother's side). Sometimes, we would be joined by Mr. Bengle's daughter, Adele.

One might wonder what the Brown family had to do with all those French folks in the Orchard.

Well, it so happens that the Browns had French-Canadian roots, too. How they came to carry their non-French name remains a family mystery that may never be solved.

A couple of industrious genealogy trackers in our family have gotten all the way back to Quebec in 1770.

My paternal grandmother, Angele Lizotte, was born in 1849 in St. Nicolet, a Quebec town near the Nicolet and St. Lawrence rivers.

Her husband, Joseph, born in St. Leonard, Quebec, was the son of Louis-Paschal Provencher-dit Villebrun and Sophie Lampron. A little digging reveals that Villebrun was a "dit nomme," that is, a nickname used to differentiate people either by occupation or place of their family's birth. Villebrun is a very old dit nomme, with roots in France.

Despite having parents with obvious French-Canadian names, my grandfather Joseph's name turned out to be Brown.

How could that happen? Nobody in the family can explain it, and it was never a topic of discussion when I was growing up. The only conclusion we can draw is that Joseph's name was changed from Provencher-dit Villebrun when he came to the United States to begin a new job as a stationary engineer. That was in 1877, when he settled in Haydenville with Angele and their three children. There would be eight more – with my father, Jeremiah James, the youngest.

Why the name change? The most likely explanation is that a customs officer took one look at the name "Provencher-dit Villebrun" and decided to simplify it into "Brown." (The mangling and changing of names at the Canadian border was said to be common in those days).

So don't let the name fool you. The Browns of Indian Orchard really do have French-Canadian roots on my father's side.

Just call me Garry Provencher-dit Villebrun Brown.

Softball, Anyone?

As an enthusiastic crowd gathers, the Cardinals take the field, and the Blue Jays get ready to hit.

An interleague matchup at Busch Stadium in St. Louis? Nope, a rec league beginners softball matchup at Soule Road School in Wilbraham.

This is softball at its fundamental best. Watch the World Series of NCAA Division I softball on television, and it's likely that most, if not all, of the players involved got started in a rec league program much like this one.

In Wilbraham, the Cardinals and Blue Jays are just getting the hang of hitting, running the bases, catching the ball, throwing to the right base. Hey, they're all first- or second-graders, 6 or 7 year olds eager to learn. As one coach said, "Wait'll you see 'em a year from now."

If you think you know the rules of softball, forget about them when watching one of these games. There's no such thing as three outs in an inning. In fact, there are no outs at all. No strikeouts, no walks, no foul balls. What a concept.

In the three innings these girls play, each one is guaranteed three at-bats. When a girl steps to the plate, she stays there until she puts bat on ball. Never mind if it happens to go foul. As long as she hits it somewhere, that's definitely a good thing.

The side is "out" only after each player on the team gets a chance to hit.

Pitching? That's handled by the coaches. With a pile of softballs on the ground beside them, the pitchers – and the other coaches – encourage each hitter until bat meets ball. If somebody hits one back to the pitcher, she steps aside and lets the infielders do the work.

As for the outfielders, well, they're more like extra infielders. Nobody plays deep in this league.

An ingenious system between the pitchers and catchers keeps the game moving at an acceptable pace. Instead of throwing the ball back to the pitchers, the catchers drop it into a large white bucket nearby. When the supply of softballs is used up, one of the coaches dumps the bucket of balls back beside the pitcher, and the beat goes on.

In addition to teaching softball, the coaches must deal with a cross-section of personalities in any given rec league lineup.

Case in point: One of the Blue Jays chastised her coach – a 17-year-old Minnechaug Regional senior – for wearing what she deemed to be too much makeup on game nights. She also accused her of wearing false eyelashes.

"These eyelashes are not false," the coach insisted.

"Oh, they're false," the player said, then turning on her heel and racing out to her position on defense before the coach could get another word out.

At one practice, a coach happened to plunk a player in the ribs with a pitch. It was a very soft toss, with no harm done, but the player said she could not forgive her coach for hitting her.

A few nights later, when the Blue Jays assembled for their next game, the player approached her coach and said, "I do forgive you, but I didn't until just now."

The coach smiled and said, "That girl's a handful."

It was no surprise, then, when that little "handful" approached one of the assistant coaches. It seems that she wasn't at all happy hitting last in the order.

"Coach made out the lineup for this game, and that's the way it has to stay," the assistant said, patting her on the top of her batting helmet.

From that vignette, we can see that grumbling about lineups really is woven into the fabric of baseball, softball and just about any sport at any level. No surprise, then, to see it in a 6–7 rec league.

As the game unfolded, one of the coaches drew an X in the front of the batter's box.

"Step on the X and you'll step into the pitch," the coach said.

For some of the batters, that helpful hint paid off. For others, well...

As the red-clad Cardinals took their final turn at bat, the leadoff hitter smacked one down the first base line, way foul. No problem. She still had the right to run it out, and she never stopped 'til she scored. The defense threw to all four bases, late every time.

"We have to work on learning to tag the runners," one coach said.

Actually, it doesn't matter, because in this league, nobody's out, everybody plays, nobody loses and nobody keeps score.

Instead, everybody gets a lot of swings, a lot of baserunning, and that precious feeling of being part of a team.

No doubt about it, this Wilbraham Recreation Department league is a winner – even if one of its coaches happens to wear too much makeup.

Franconia at 85

IT HAPPENED JULY 2, 1929. FRANCONIA GOLF COURSE, Springfield's first public links, opened on a sunny Tuesday morning as four local pros played an exhibition.

Franconia's newly-appointed pro, 22-year-old Henry Bontempo, teamed with Eric Edwards of Oxford for a four-ball match against Victor East of Longmeadow Country Club and Walter Denning of Springfield CC. The East-Denning team won, one up, thereby christening a golf course that has served the city well for 85 years.

After that first match ended, Edwards gave a critique of the Franconia layout, calling it "unusually good for a municipal course."

At the time, Franconia had only nine holes open. By April of 1930, the other nine went into play.

The Springfield Daily Republican also gave Franconia a favorable first-day review. Don Bagg, the paper's esteemed golf writer, noted that the course's well-placed rough and sandtraps would assure that "poor shots to the green will be properly penalized."

For forty years, Franconia came under the stewardship of Henry Bontempo, one of the most accomplished and respected golf pros ever to grace the Western Massachusetts sports scene.

Currently, Kevin Kennedy's Kennedy Golf Management team operates Franconia and Veterans, Springfield's other municipal course. Kennedy said he plans to mark Franconia's 85th year with a special tournament in August, dates to be determined.

"We will invite a small group, including members of the Bontempo family," Kennedy said.

Henry's sons, Robert and David, had the rare good fortune of growing up on a golf course. When they were kids, they caddied for some of the region's leading amateur players, along with the "weekend warriors" who enjoyed their opportunities to play a beautiful public course.

"Henry was one of the area's top players, a great chipper and putter. From 50 yards in, he was untouchable," son Robert said.

The Bontempo brothers learned to play by watching their dad – and blue-chip amateurs like Walter Kupiec.

"Thirteen-time city champion, three-time New England public links champion. That was Walter," Robert Bontempo recalled.

Said David: "One year, when Walter played 36 holes in a New England Public Links Tournament, he came out for the afternoon round and shot a 30 on the front nine. 30 – can you believe it? 30 – after already playing 18 holes in July heat."

That happened in 1954, when the Publinx event was played at Memorial, Springfield's other public course.

"Franconia finished second to New Haven that year, but Walter was the medalist with 72-69-141. The thing about Walter was, his demeanor never changed, whether he was three up or three down," David Bontempo said.

In Franconia's early years, caddies would get anywhere from 65 cents to $1.25 per round.

"In 1950, a regular named Don Strong started paying $2. We would wait in the bushes until he showed up, then everybody would run to try to get his bag," Robert Bontempo recalled.

The Bontempo boys received a great golf education, getting lessons from their dad and his assistant, John Raimondi, then caddying for players like Kupiec and Jim Barry. They also grew up working in the pro shop.

Raimondi served as Bontempo's assistant for eight years, then took over as pro at Memorial in 1948. Today, four-ball tournaments are played in memory of them. This season, the Raimondi is scheduled July 19–20 at Veterans, the Bontempo on Labor Day weekend at Franconia.

Many a young golfing star emerged from the caddy ranks at Springfield's municipal courses. One of them, Jimmy McDonald, started at Franconia at the age of 4 when his parents began running the food concession. In 1960, he became part of a Franconia team that won the New England Public Links Tournament at Memorial. Two years later, Memorial was closed, with Veterans soon to replace it.

On the Western Mass. four-ball scene, Franconia produced Dick Murphy, a Cathedral High School basketball player of the '60s who went on to win more than fifty golf tournaments.

Murphy has been elected to the Western Mass. Golf Hall of Fame, along with Henry Bontempo, Barry and Kupiec.

"By the way, it was Barry who thought of the name 'Tee Party' for the spring celebration that marks the start of the golf season in Western Mass.," David Bontempo said.

In 2000, the brothers returned to Franconia for the dedication of the renovated course.

"It was a great honor that day to play in a foursome with Jim Barry, my brother David and Ed Montovani, who had been our baby-sitter back in the day," Robert Bontempo said.

Robert won the city championship when he was 17 years old. A year later, in 1957, he won the state high school championship on the day of his graduation from Classical High School.

Robert went on to a career in golf, which included 26 years as head pro at The Orchards in South Hadley and 39 years as golf coach at Mount Holyoke College. David took a different path, choosing a career in teaching and social service.

The brothers will never forget the special childhood they had, much of it spent on the golf course run by their dad.

"Franconia is one of the great municipal courses in all of New England, with a wonderful heritage. It's known as the country club of public golf. For us, it was such a great place to be. We knew it, and we appreciated every day of it," Robert Bontempo said.

Playing the Name Game

As I walked around the MassMutual Concourse between periods of a Springfield Falcons hockey game, a fellow senior citizen stopped me.

"You know what? You should compile a list of your all-time favorite sports names," the gentleman said.

He was referring to one of the staple lines in "Hitting to All Fields," a column I have been writing in this newspaper's sports section for so long, I can't remember when I started it.

The column line in question goes something like this: "Add (fill in the blank) to my list of all-time favorite sports names." For some reason, that resonates with readers, to the point of having them do a lot of my work for me, sending great names to my email box, with regularity.

The column's favorite name line is almost as popular as Venus the Labrador retriever. As in, "Venus the Labrador retriever will steal your lunch." She's actually our grand-dog, and she happens to receive more mail and shout-outs than anything else I write about. Heck, old ladies who say they know nothing about sports tell me they read the column just to find out what kind of mischief Venus is creating from week to week.

Venus rules our son's household in Amherst, which happens to be the hometown of my latest favorite in the name game – a high school athlete named Jazzy Moonstone.

Yes, she really exists. She plays for coach Kacey Schmitt's Amherst Regional softball team.

It's amazing to me that, after all these years, the great sports names just keep coming. Matter of fact, some of the most memorable are local athletes of today. For instance, American International College has a volleyball star with a fabulous name...are you ready?...Kervelle Redhead.

There was a time when I thought no sports name could be better than Keyburn McCusker, a Pittsfield High School basketball player who in 1986 won the Vi Goodnow Award as the best in Western Mass. Keyburn McCusker ...there's something about the lilt of her name that makes it unforgettable.

Before Keyburn, my favorite had been Muffin Spencer-Devlin, a Ohio native who played on the LPGA Tour from 1979 through 2000. I also ran across her playing a Starfleet medical staff member in the 1994 film, "Star Trek Generations." Yes, some of these favorite-name people are versatile, indeed.

Digging into the email box during the football season of 2012, I found a note from Bill Postel, a Springfield native who went to elementary school with our two sons. He's now an administrator at Valdosta, Ga., State University. Sometimes, when he has nothing better to do, he reads "Hitting to All Fields" on MassLive and is prompted to send me a name for consideration.

In this particular instance, he sent two, both linebackers – Barkevious Mingo and Bull Barge.

Was he kidding this time? Nope, those fellows really were playing football, Mr. Mingo for Louisiana State and Mr. Barge for a Georgia high school. In April, Barkevious Mingo became a first-round draft pick of the Cleveland Browns – six months after Bill Postel had "scouted" him for me. As for Bull Barge, with a name like that, he's destined to be a college star somewhere.

Yes, the names just keep coming. How about a New York Yankees farmhand, Graham Stoneburner? Or an NBA player, Zaza Pachulia? Or another NFL player, Derek Domino?

And those are from recent times. If you want to dig back through the years, you'll find my all-time favorite baseball name – Urbane Pickering. He played third base for the Boston Red Sox of 1932 (No, I wasn't covering the team at that time, as some wiseacre colleagues suggest).

Right now, the Springfield Falcons of the American Hockey League have a forward named Cody Bass. Somehow, that name sounds just right for his sport. So did Tyler Bodie, who played for the Falcons of a few years back. In hockey, though, my all-time favorite name has to be Metro Prystai, a center who skated on three Stanley Cup champions with the Detroit Red Wings of the 1950s.

Yes, the list goes on. And just when you think it can't get any better, along comes a gem like Jazzy Moonstone.

Compile an all-time list? Sorry, that can't be done. Too many great names over too many years. We'll just have to settle for doing it week by week.

Grand Old Days

If I could get my hands on 30 cents, I was set for the weekend.

That would mean two afternoons in my favorite place of refuge, the Grand Theater on Main St., Indian Orchard.

Thirty cents? Yes, that would do it – 12 cents for admission to the movies, three cents for the wonderfully sticky "penny candy" available in a little shop right next to the theater's front door.

Both the theater and the candy store were operated by John and Apolonia Kamuda, along with members of their hard-working Orchard family.

For us kids waiting in line on the sidewalk, the thrill of a Saturday or Sunday afternoon would come when Mr. and Mrs. Kamuda would arrive at the theater in their big black automobile. They would park right in front, in a space no one else dared touch. Then, they would stride up to the front door, unlock it and signal to us that it was time to go to the movies.

Ah, the movies. What better place for a kid to escape from real life?

Obviously, I'm talking about a different time – that is, the dark days just before and during World War II. Not exactly the greatest time to be growing up.

So it was that our little group from the Myrtle Street neighborhood would march to the Grand each weekend. The Kamudas helped our great escape by showing westerns like "The Adventures of the Durango Kid" on Saturdays and the big-time stuff like "Casablanca" on Sundays.

For 12 cents, remember, an afternoon at the Grand would consist of previews, a newsreel ("The Eyes and Ears of the World"), a cartoon and a double feature.

Sometimes, I would get a bonus treat. That usually would happen midweek, when my mother would decide she wanted a night out. My dad didn't like going to the movies, so she would take me.

Together, we could sit back and put the war out of mind, if only for a few hours.

The dear old Grand ran like clockwork because of those dedicated Kamudas, who spanned three generations. One of the grandchildren, Eddie, had a shock of the blondest hair you could imagine in a kid. He was younger than us moviegoers from Myrtle Street, but he already knew how to do a day's work. Yes, the Kamuda family members did it all – working in the candy store, working at Henry's Jewelry (another part of the family conglomerate), working in the theater itself as hawkers and cleanup crew.

It was while Eddie was on the job at the Grand that he first saw a movie with a one-word title: "Titanic." It was released in 1953, starring Barbara Stanwyck and Clifton Webb.

As a seventh-grader at Myrtle Street School, Eddie first became aware of the sinking of the Titanic (April 15, 1912) when he read "A Great Ship Goes Down," by New York Times reporter Hanson Baldwin.

The movie so revived his interest in that disaster at sea, he began a quest which years later led him to organize the Titanic Historical Society. An offshoot of the society is a Kamuda-run museum loaded with all things Titanic. It is based in Henry's Jewelry Store, now relocated across from the old Grand.

Edward Kamuda today ranks as one of the world's leading authorities on Titanic lore. When director James Cameron was making his 1997 Academy Award-winning "Titanic" (starring Kate Winslet and Leonardo DiCaprio), he called upon Kamuda's expertise for technical assistance.

Cameron then talked Kamuda and his wife, Karen, into making a brief walk-on appearance in the movie, strolling the deck.

"Having swept the floor of the Grand Theater after shows, and seeing great stars on the screen," Kamuda said, "how could I know that one day, I would be up there in James Cameron's movie many years later? And now I'm able to see all the actions and players again, (including my wife and myself), this time in 3-D!"

With the death of John Kamuda in 1948, the Grand Theater was carried on by his son Henry, Edward's father.

"It closed in the 1960s," Edward Kamuda said. "The combination of television and a lack of parking killed it."

So it went with neighborhood theaters – the Rivoli in Chicopee, the Burr in Ludlow, the Liberty, Strand and Jefferson in Springfield, the Victory in Holyoke, the Star in Palmer, the Wernick in Chicopee Falls and so many others.

They are long gone, but in their day, they were the place to be for mov-ie-goers of all ages. For the young ones, it was a case of "growing up in the dark" – some riding into an adventure with The Durango Kid, some sailing into history aboard the Titanic.

The Stooges and Me

A huge black-and-white photograph graces one of our walls at home.

There's Curly, lying flat on the ground, head raised. There's Larry, kneeling close by as he uses his right hand to tee up a football on the peak of Curly's head. There's Moe, one leg back, looking ready to kick a field goal – if he doesn't kick Curly in the head, instead.

The photograph was used as a promo poster for "The Three Little Pig-skins," one of the 190 movie shorts that The Three Stooges – America's slap-stick comedy team – made for Colum-bia Pictures from 1934 to 1959. (Alto-gether, The Stooges performed, with varying lineups, from 1921 to 1970).

Why, you might ask, would any self-respecting senior citizen clutter up a wall with such an outdated pho-tograph?

Why? Because I became hopeless-ly hooked on the Stooges when I was a kid, growing up in the dark at the Grand Theater in Indian Orchard.

All of their moves cracked me up – the eye pokes, the face slaps, the two-by-fours to the back of the head. And then there were priceless moments like pies-in-the-faces of society folks, or Curly the "plumber" getting hope-lessly entangled, and drenched, as he attempts to connect a maze of water pipes. (His older brother, Shemp, also did that routine in a remake of "A Plumbing We Will Go.")

I often wondered...why is all of that so funny? Well, maybe because it's happening to somebody else. That twisted sense of funny would explain why slapstick has been so popular for so long. Anyway, I readily admit it – I loved all the craziness and physical farce that The Stooges brought to film.

I wasn't that proud of my low-brow taste in comedy, so I made no attempt to pass it on to our children. As it turned out, our old black-and-white television set made that happen, anyway.

Our daughter showed no interest in The Stooges, but her two younger broth-ers got hooked early in life. They would watch The Stooges on Saturday morn-ings when they were in grade school. Then, when they reached high school, they locked onto superstation Channel 38, which carried three episodes a day after school, five days a week. For our guys, that was a great gift, courtesy of the cable TV revolution.

Of course, we weren't exactly "watch-dog" parents about it. We just let it hap-pen. Oh boy.

To this very day, our two grown sons can remember Stooges lines and scenes from back in the day.

Timeless comedy? In our family, it looks that way, because we have grandchildren who have been well indoctrinated in Stooges classics. All of which seems to prove that slapstick is funny, no matter what century it is.

My wife and I sometimes wonder, where did we go wrong? How could we expose our children to such zany, low-brow stuff?

Oh, well, our family can take solace in the fact that we're not alone when it comes to being hooked on The Stooges.

My late dear friend, Carl Beane, was such a "Stoogephile" that the message on his answering machine began with their theme music, and ended with Carl saying, "Will I call you back? Soy-tenly!" (If you know your Stooges, you know how funny that is).

Carl later gained celebrity as public-address announcer at Fenway Park, home of the Boston Red Sox. For years before that, he worked as a radio reporter, covering all the Boston pro teams. In that role, he often would break up the Fenway press box by doing a Curly imitation – "woo-woo-woo-woo-woo" – when a Red Sox outfielder would give chase after letting a ball get past him.

As for Carl's family, I'm sure they carry on his love for all things Stooges, just as many American families do.

Yes, but how many have an over-size poster of Moe, about to kick a field goal? In our family, that ranks as an "heirloom."

Now, after all these years, would I still love to see one of those old Stooges movie shorts?

Would I? Why, soy-tenly!

Tommy's Museum

IN THE FINISHED BASEMENT OF TOMMY THOMPSON'S East Longmeadow home, hundreds of photographs, posters, clippings and plaques adorn the walls.

"This isn't a museum, it just looks like one," he said.

The wall hangings all have to do with sports – mainly, Cathedral High School football and baseball and Florida State University football.

Oh, yes, there's also a poster-size photograph of Ted Williams and Mickey Mantle, taken at Fenway Park.

Of all the items on display in this Thompson sports shrine, one serves as a real attention-grabber.

Entitled "The Cosmopolitan Man," the 30-inch by 10-inch photograph shows actor Burt Reynolds languishing naked on a bearskin rug. Only a strategically-placed left arm prevents this photo from being triple-X-rated.

"You have no idea how much it cost me to have that darn thing framed," Thompson said. "Hey, I had to do it, because Burt sent it to my wife as a joke."

Why, one might ask, would a movie star of Reynolds' magnitude send an in-the-buff-photo of himself to a woman in East Longmeadow?

For the answer, you have to go back to the fall of 1954, when Thompson started his freshman year at Florida State. He was there on football scholarship after a solid career at Cathedral.

As such, he was assigned to room with another newcomer to the football squad. That happened to be Burt Reynolds, an all-state halfback from Rivera Beach, Florida.

"The first day of practice, it's 100 degrees and we're having double sessions. Hitting, nothing but hitting. When we lined up, it turned out that I was across from Burt. He said, 'I got to hit you?' I said, yeah, and I'm coming right at you.'"

From such confrontations are lifetime friendships made. Thompson and Reynolds played together in the same backfield for only one season, including a trip to the Sun Bowl in El Paso, Texas. Thompson left school after spring practice in 1955, and Reynolds' football career was impaired by injuries in an auto accident. Only one season together, yet Thompson and Reynolds remain friends to this day.

"After the auto accident and he couldn't play for a while, he decided to try acting. He called me one day and said, I might not see you for a while. They want me to go to Hollywood."

Reynolds had his breakthrough with *Deliverance* in 1972 (after which Cosmo wanted him).

"I haven't seen Burt for a while, but every so often he pops up in my life. He never forgets. Burt was a great football player – tough as nails. Oh, yeah, he was always the ladies man, too," Thompson said.

All of which might explain why Reynolds couldn't resist sending his Cosmo photo to Thompson's wife, the former Pat Rainville.

"She was a cheerleader when I was playing ball. I came home from Florida State because I missed her. The coach (Tom Nugent) told me I could have been team captain if I stayed, but, hey, that's life."

Pat Thompson died in October of 2007. After fighting back from the loss of his wife, Thompson married again last January, picking another Cathedral graduate, Fran Barney.

Now, at the age of 76, Thompson fights a battle against pancreatic cancer. He had surgery in October of 2010, and approaches each day with a positive attitude.

"I'm fighting it and holding my own," he said. "Since the surgery, I just ignore it (the cancer). It's not slowing me down a bit. I have a lot to be thankful for. I've had two marvelous women in my life. Pat and I raised four children, and we have six wonderful grandchildren."

Thompson's lifetime devotion to sports began at Blunt Park, where he played sandlot football and baseball on teams directed by two Springfield icons of youth sports, Romeo Cyr and Bill Oates.

"They were like fathers to me," he said.

It was because of Cyr and Oates that Thompson in later life devoted a lot of time to coaching junior teams.

"I figured I should give something back," he said.

Thompson grew up on College Street, near American International College. Many of his boyhood friends went to Tech, but he had a special reason for picking Cathedral.

"When I was at Buckingham Junior High, my father took me to a testimonial for Billy Wise. Frank Leahy (then the Notre Dame coach) was the main speaker. I mean, that was big stuff. I watched what was going on and I said, 'Cathedral's the place for me.'"

At his first football practice, Thompson almost was completely ignored by Wise. He didn't even get issued full equipment on that first day.

"If there was a depth chart, I probably would have been the fifth fullback," Thompson recalled. "But one time, Wise said, 'I need a fullback on this play.' I stepped up, took the ball, went off tackle 50 yards for a touchdown. Wise said, 'Who the hell are you? What grade are you in?'"

Thompson went on from there to become Wise's starting fullback for four years. As a senior, he was selected to the Catholic School All-America team.

Although football was his primary sport, Thompson also did all right as a baseball catcher.

"I played on two teams that won Western Mass.," he said.

As a freshman, Thompson backed up catcher Corky Czelusniak on a 1951 team that featured lefty pitcher Bobby Laporte. As a senior, Thompson did the catching for a 1954 team which had Al Hedin as its side-arming ace.

In 2005, Thompson was enshrined in the Cathedral Hall of Fame.

He admits to having a temper, and it cost him an opportunity to play on another Cathedral championship team. In the '54 hockey season, he was barred from the Coliseum by Springfield Indians owner Eddie Shore, who ran the building, for going off the ice and into the crowd to fight with hecklers. As a result, Thompson missed being part of a Cathedral team which upset perennial power West Springfield to win the WMass crown.

After his return from Florida State, Thompson played one year of football at AIC, but didn't stay.

"My wife was having babies, and I figured it was time for me to get a job," he said.

An AIC classmate, Bart Shea, got him an interview with Kemper Insurance. He got the job, and 29 years later, he was managing three branches before he retired.

"I did all right for someone without a college degree," he said.

Thompson had a long career as a football official, handling high school and college games around New England.

He also played several seasons with the Manchester, Connecticut, Merchants in a backfield that featured former AIC star Gayton Salvucci.

Now, as he looks back on a lifetime devoted to family and sports, he treasures friendships – and not just that of Burt Reynolds.

"All the touchdowns and home runs, they don't matter," he said. "To me, life boils down to loyalty, and the friends you make and keep over the years."

Editor's note: This story ran in The Springfield Sunday Republican in May of 2011. Tommy Thompson passed away four months later.

Curtain-Cutting Days

From my vantage point as a wide-eyed new employee, the table looked to be about three feet wide, and as long as a city block.

On its left end, mounted on a spool of steel, a huge roll of seemingly-endless fabric, white and sheer, awaited the day's work. The idea was to begin unrolling the fabric until it covered the length of that awfully-long table.

Then came the hard part. Armed with a pair of oversized shears, I would take a few steps to the right, looking for a carefully-marked spot on the table. Oh, yes, that table had such spots all along its edge.

At each spot, my job was to cut the fabric carefully, keeping as straight a line as possible. Cut, walk, cut again, walk, cut again. So it went until I finally reached the table's other end. Then, it was time to stack my carefully-cut pieces into a bin, which then would be carted to another area of the building, where the fabric would be turned into curtains.

While that was going on, I'd be back to the beginning of my table, for another unrolling and more cutting. Oh, the boredom of it all. Not to mention the wrist soreness.

Such was my life in the summer of 1949. I spent it doing eight-hour days in a curtain shop on the third floor of a building that was part of a historic complex known as the Indian Orchard Mills. Oh, and did I mention that there was no air-conditioning?

I was 17 years old, just out of high school and looking forward to starting the next phase of my education as a freshman at American International College in Springfield. However, there would be no hanging around my old hometown during the summer, enjoying life on the Knights of Columbus beach at Lake Lorraine.

At the time, my dad worked as assistant postmaster at the Indian Orchard post office, and part-time reporter for The Springfield Daily News. In those roles, he knew everybody in town – including the owner of the curtain shop.

"You should work this summer. Make a little money and not waste your time," he said while informing me that I already had been hired. His curtain-shop friend had agreed to give me a job, June through August.

Hey, how could I argue with my dad when he was doing two jobs himself?

By the way, the curtain-shop job was the second one he arranged for me. During Christmas break of my senior year in high school, he had me do a 10-day stint at the post office. There, I learned – the hard way – why they call that time of year "the Christmas Rush." As soon as I would sort one pile of mail, someone would du another one in front of me. Oh, begone, endless Christmas cards.

The curtain shop job was much like

the post office job, but it lasted a lot longer. By early August, I was yearning to hit the books at AIC.

I might not have made it through that summer if not for the friendship I developed with one of my co-workers. His name, appropriately enough, was Dave Cartmill. From my teen-age perspective, he seemed like an "old guy." Actually, he probably was in his mid-40s, a kind-hearted laborer with lots of mill experience. He knew I was a raw rookie, so he willingly showed me the best way to handle the daily workload. and at the same time became my lunch buddy.

By mid-August, my curtain-cutting days were coming an end. Although I felt elated about getting away from the boredom of that job, I also felt a touch of sadness, knowing that I'd be losing the friendship of my man Dave. When we walked together across that mill bridge after my last day of work, I wondered if I would ever see him again. (I never did).

Well, let it be said that the Indian Orchard of today looks nothing like the village that I knew and loved in my growing up years. No more strawberry ice cream sodas at Montcalm's Drug Store. No more new shoes at Kitchener's. No more jelly doughnuts at Hamel's OK lunch. No more comic books at Joe Riordan's variety store. No more bowling at Stanley Makuch's Or-chard Alleys. No more double-features at the Grand Theater. Worst of all, no more baseball at Goodwin Park (it's now covered by JFK Middle School).

Ah, but some Orchard standbys from my youth do remain in place, like The National House, still there next to my dad's Post Office; and the public library, still standing on lower Oak Street.

The Indian Orchard mills? Yes, those buildings also remain (although one was ravaged by fire in August of 2011). Built along the Chicopee River in the early 1800s, the mills handled cotton and linen manufacturing. The mills of today include some industry, plus considerable space for artists and artisans, with the Dane Gallery as their centerpiece.

My wife and I toured that art enclave a few times when our son had a glass-blowing studio on an upper floor. As we would slowly ascend the stairway, we could feel the old "déjà vu." Was this the building in which I cut curtains in 1949? Was this the mill where teen-age Mary spent the summers of 1948 and '49 (before I knew her) working for the Latrique Brassiere Company?

Yes, that mill building seemed almost ghostly to both of us, and way too familiar, stirring memories of those "endless summers" and our first ventures into the workaday world.

Keeping Score with Dad

My late father-in-law, Peter Bukowski of Chicopee, knew the value of work. He spent 40 years in front of a blast furnace as a drop-forger, so he wasn't about to sympathize with anyone who complained about the daily grind.

"Work hard, it's good for you," he would say, and there was no arguing with that.

My father, Jeremiah James Brown of Haydenville, qualified for a place in the "work hard" category. No, he didn't have a strength-sapping job like my father-in-law's, but he certainly wasn't afraid of work.

Fortysomething years at the Indian Orchard Post Office would have been enough. Ah, but there was more. He also happened to be a reporter, covering Indian Orchard for The Springfield Daily News. That meant writing stories at home every evening, then driving downtown to the newspaper office to drop them on his editor's desk.

Even that wasn't all of it. Somehow, he also found time for his real labor of love – serving as secretary of the Indian Orchard Twilight Baseball League. This one required lots of paper work, like making out the season schedule, taking care of umpiring assignments, and keeping the standings, batting averages and pitching records up to date.

Of course, to stay on top of it all, his presence was required at most of the games. No problem there, because he basically was a "baseball junkie" – in love with The Grande Olde Game since his time as a pitcher for his hometown Haydenville Cubs.

Growing up under the care of a dynamo like my dad, I learned a lot. For one thing, he taught me how to type on his old Underwood, while at the same time teaching me how to write a basic news story. Keep it simple, he would say.

For another, he taught me to love baseball, which he called "the greatest game ever invented." The Orchard Twilight League played its games at Goodwin Park, just across Sullivan's Pond from our house. We could circle the pond and walk to the games – and that in itself was fun, going hand in hand with my dad.

Those Twilight League games proved to be the ideal "classroom" for me as I learned to watch baseball from a scorekeeper's viewpoint. While my dad was keeping score of the games in his own scorebook, he was teaching me to do the same. By the time I began covering games for The Springfield Union, I knew exactly how to keep score of a game – batter by batter, inning by inning.

He also taught me the symmetry of baseball. It's a perfectly-constructed game, in which everything must add up. That's known as "proving" your box score. Each batter must be accounted for – either scoring a run, making an out or being left on base.

One night, when I tried to prove my box score, it just wouldn't add up. My dad quickly found the mistake.

"Your left on base total is off," he said.

As he pointed out, if a batter hits

into a force play for the final out of an inning, he is, in effect, "left on base." If you miss even one of those, your box score will not prove. Symmetry, remember?

Trivial as it may seem now, that "left on base" lesson was like a revelation to me. From then on, I knew that my box score would always be correct. Just keep an eye on that LOB total, and everything else will fall into place.

Of course, before you can do anything in a baseball scorebook, you must understand the symbolism involved. Who's on first? No, 3 is on first. That's part of a numbering system designed to help the scorekeeper track the players. It goes from 1 through 9, starting with the pitcher and ending with the right fielder.

On the night I saw the only game in major league history with two triple plays, they went into the scorebook this way: 5-4-3. Those "around the horn" plays were pulled by the 1990 Minne-

sota Twins – Gary Gaetti to Al Newman to Kent Hrbek. None of that would fit into a scorebook, hence the value of the very cool numbering system.

I never understood why "K" stands for strikeout, but why worry about it? Just put 'em in the book. I did a lot of that on a June night at Holyoke's Mackenzie Stadium, when Chicopee's Al Stanek struck out 25 and Amherst's Cliff Allen struck out 16. Stanek won it 1–0 in a quarterfinal game of the 1960 Western Mass. Tournament – 54 years ago, but unforgettable.

By the way, three years later as a member of the San Francisco Giants, Stanek watched from the bullpen at Candlestick Park when Juan Marchial beat Warren Spahn 1–0 in 16 innings. Try to put that one into a scorebook.

Yes, it can be done. No matter how tidy or messy a baseball game may get, it all fits into the scorebook.

Just watch out for those guys left on base. I learned that from my dad.

Tony Pena, Boston Red Sox catcher, was a fun guy to interview. This is from spring training, 1990. Photo by Dave Roback, Springfield Republican

A Tip of the Caps

Halfway through lunch at a Springfield restaurant, a gentleman in a booth across the way leaned toward me and asked, "What year did YOU graduate from Smith?"

Wise guy, eh?

Actually, the question arose because of the baseball cap I happened to be wearing that day. It says "Smith College," and I wear it proudly. It's a gift from our oldest grand-child, who graduated in Smith's Class of 2014.

The guy's question dripped with sarcasm, because he obviously knew that Smith is a women's college – world-renowned, I might add.

I shrugged off his wiseacre attitude and proceeded to brag about our Smithie grand-daughter. Grandparents love to do that, you know.

I didn't bother to tell the guy the rest of the story, which is that the Smith cap is merely part of a closetful of headwear that I have collected over the years. The collection is so precious, it even survived a recent round of "decluttering" as we tried to rid our house of accumulated junk.

In this case, cleaning a closet merely led me astray. Instead of concentrating on sorting out junk to be dumped, I paused to look through my collection of caps, each of which serves as a gentle reminder of days gone by.

In the back of the closet, I found one that I knew to be 20 years old. It's a cute little cream-colored cap bear-

ing this inscription, in green lettering: Universite de Sherbrooke. How do I know its age? Because I acquired it in December of 1994, when we traveled to Sherbrooke, P.Q., to be on scene for the birth of our grandson. (We made it a day ahead of his arrival). He was born in Canada while our son was working as a teaching fellow at...Universite de Sherbrooke, of course.

Three caps in my collection have to do with waterfowl.

One serves as a reminder of my time as a baseball beat writer for this newspaper, covering the Boston Red Sox spring training camp in Fort Myers, Fla. On an off day, we took a ride to Captiva, a beautiful nearby island, and stopped for lunch at a quaint spot known as "The Mucky Duck." Yes, they also sold caps bearing the restaurant's logo – and Ye Olde Collector couldn't leave without one.

Another bears the name of my favorite minor league team, the Toledo Mud Hens of the Class AAA International League. I've never seen them play, but I had to have their hat, so I sent away to their memorabilia department. Also got a great Mud Hens sweatshirt for my wife.

The other waterfowl cap came from our daughter, Melissa, who picked it up last summer in Madison, Wisconsin, where she played in the Word Cup scrabble tournament. While there, the competitors had the opportunity to attend a Northwoods Collegiate League baseball game. The home team's name? The Madison Mallards. She knew right away that I would want to add them to my collection.

Of course, if you love baseball caps, you have to love those with an old-time flavor. I picked up three of them on one of our family trips to Cooperstown, N.Y., home of the Baseball Hall of Fame.

How could I resist the St. Louis Browns? They not only bear my family name, they represent baseball as it used to be in a simpler time when the major leagues had 16 teams and nobody played night games. The Browns ceased to exist when the franchise was moved to Baltimore after the 1953 season. Yes, but their caps remain quite an item in the world of baseball memorabilia.

My old-timey caps represent two other franchises that left their National League homes in the '50s – the Brooklyn Dodgers and Boston Braves. I always liked the Dodgers, who had some great World Series duels with the New York Yankees in the '40s and '50s, so I cherish their deep blue cap with its distinctive white "B." I always liked the Braves, too. Their caps were

done in navy blue with a red bill, red button on top and another distinctive white "B."

Of course, my collection features several Boston Red Sox caps. I even have one done in beige with a white letter. I also have three caps of the Eastern League's New Britain Rock Cats, courtesy of their now-retired owner, Bill Dowling of Holyoke.

While the Madison Mallards cap remains as my favorite because of its ducky logo, our daughter's travels have yielded other noteworthy additions to the collection, including a Golden Gopher cap from the University of Minnesota, and a "TC" cap which she obtained at a Minnesota Twins gift shop. Oh, yes, I also have the Triple A Iowa Cubs from dear old Des Moines.

Locally, I'm especially proud to own American Legion baseball caps presented by East Springfield Post 420 and Springfield's historic Post 21. The Post 21 cap honors its "Brothers All Are We" team of 1934. You'll find their story on a monument in Forest Park.

Am I done with collecting? Nope. Not with teams like the Mankato Moon Dogs, Kenosha Kingsfish and Traverse City Beach Bums out there, just waiting to sell me a cap.

Dusty League Days

ON AN AUGUST NIGHT AT PYNCHON PARK, a smallish right-hander with a baffling curveball pitched his team to a championship.

His victory over an old rival came in the deciding game of a tough postseason series. The finalists had jockeyed all year long, going in and out of first place in a race that went to the wire.

Was the smallish right-hander – a great city athlete named Ray Fitzgerald – pitching for the Springfield Giants of the Eastern League? The Springfield Cubs of the International League? The Springfield Ponies of the Roaring Twenties?

Nope. This was 1949, and Ol' Fitz (age 42), was pitching for a team sponsored by American Bosch, a thriving manufacturer with huge quarters on north Main Street, straddling the Springfield-Chicopee line.

Fitzie's challenge in that series came from a team sponsored by Chapman Valve Manufacturing Company, a plant that anchored the economy of a thriving little section of Springfield known as Indian Orchard.

Like Bosch, Chapman had been part of Springfield's industrial scene for much of the twentieth century. Both plants peaked in workforce when they were called upon to play major production roles in Uncle Sam's military effort during World War II.

In the 1930s and '40s, Bosch and Chapman joined other local companies in an organization known as the Triple A Industrial League. Along with baseball, Triple A offered competition in basketball, tennis, softball and golf. Some of the factories also sponsored teams in the Connecticut Valley Hockey League.

The term "Triple A" had nothing to do with professional baseball. Rather, it stood for Amateur Athletic Association – and it produced many a top local team in each of its sports.

Baseball ranked as the most popular sport in what was commonly referred to as the "Dusty League."

Chapman Valve's baseball team had a loyal following, mainly from Indian Orchard and Ludlow. For its games at Goodwin Park – where John F. Kennedy Middle School now stands – fans would sit in an old wooden grandstand (complete with a refreshment booth), or in parked cars that ringed the outfield. Many a Chapman rally would be accompanied by a loud honking of automobile horns.

"It was such a good league back then," said Dave Garrow, a Ludlow resident who grew up in the Orchard. He well remembers the era when Tom "Mac" McCarthy served as supervisor of Goodwin Park and mentor to budding young ballplayers.

"I started playing in the league when I was just a kid, still at Tech," he said. "When I first went into the Triple A, I was in awe, because the players were older and so good. But I gradually worked my way into it."

Garrow played shortstop for Chapman Valve, coming under the tutelage of team managers Benny Benoit and Russ Hughes.

"There were so many good, solid players. Every team had them," Garrow said.

Garrow's infield mates in that 1949 championship series included Stan Zarod (later a state senator) at third base, team captain Bob LaMothe at second and Don Crean at first. Doug Falconer, a Garrow teammate at Tech, did the catching. The outfield was manned by Caz Obrzut, Bill Avezzie and Joe Paquette. Chapman's deep pitching staff featured Roger Bourgelas, Baldy Walczak, Frank Worthington and Cliff Seaver.

They played against the teams that had such local stars as Bob Findlater, Bob Silk, Bobby Senk, Joe Morrisino, Teddy Stanek, Johnny Urban, Happy Symanczyk, Chet Grondalski, Joe Dombrowski, Hooks Cournoyer, Bruno Chistolini and Buck DeSorcy.

"The list could go on and on," he said.

The Bosch-Chapman championship final of 1949 drew a crowd of 1,990 (tickets went for 50 cents).

The finale to the best-in-three series was switched from Blunt Park to Pynchon after the teams played a 1–1 tie in what was supposed to be the series clincher. It had to be called after eight innings because of darkness.

Thus, for the first time, Triple A League teams played a game under lights – and it was a masterpiece. Bosch won it 2–1 on a two-run, bases-loaded single by team captain Danny Sullivan in the bottom of the seventh (all Triple A games were seven innings).

"We had quite a team, and a tough manager in George Kane," said Tony King, who worked at Bosch for 45 years. He's now 93 and living in his hometown of West Springfield.

"I played third base, but toward the end of my career, I told George to put me in right field, because I was too fat to bend over for ground balls," King said.

Tony was in right field for that 1949 series with Chapman, playing in a veteran lineup that included first baseman Mike Raffaele, second baseman Frosh Lizak, shortstop Danny Sullivan, third baseman Bob Seaver, catcher Werner Kuhn and outfielders Jerry Mercier and Paul Lussier. Fitzgerald and Fritz Jezouit were the team's top pitchers.

"We had good clubs before that, too," King recalled.

King played for Bosch before and after World War II. At various times, he had Art Murphy, Lou Shapiro, Dom Ruby and a couple of West Springfield greats – Betts Bessone and Angelo Bertelli – among his teammates.

Bessone went on to the U.S. Hockey Hall of Fame as a coach at Michigan State. Bertelli went on to win the Heisman Trophy as a quarterback for Notre Dame.

Before World War II, the Triple A League also served as training ground for a future New York Yankees star, Vic Raschi.

In 1937 and '38, when he was a teenager out of Springfield Tech, Raschi pitched for the New York, New Haven and Hartford Railroad club, which led the league.

He went from there into minor league ball. Then, after service in World War II, he reached the Yankees in 1947 and pitched on six world championship clubs.

For sheer iron-man efforts, though, no Dusty League pitcher could top Ray Fitz.

In the '49 championship series, he started and finished every game, at one point pitching on one day's rest.

"I never saw a playoff pitcher like him," King said. "When we beat Chapman, he pitched all those games only two weeks after having an appendectomy. He was very competitive."

In 2000, Fitzgerald was selected as one of *The Republican*'s Top 50 Greater Springfield athletes of the 20th century.

Like local industry, the Triple A League was undergoing gradual changes at that time. By the early 1950s, the Triple A was fading away and Tri-County League was emerging as a force in local baseball.

For the period from 1950 to 1953, Bosch and Chapman played in both leagues. By 1954, the Triple A League had become local history as three of its remnants – Bosch, Chapman and Spalding – moved into the Tri-County League.

By the 1960s, local "Dusty" baseball was no more.

That happened because of gradual loss of industry in the Connecticut Valley.

The area was much different, for instance, in 1939 when the Triple A Industrial League had a six-team baseball membership made up of teams representing Westinghouse, Fisk Tire, Bigelow-Sanford, Bosch, Somersville, Connecticut, and the New York, New Haven and Hartford Railroad. At that time, thirteen teams played Triple A tennis, and twelve played Triple A golf.

In the 1940s, Bosch and Chapman Valve were playing in a baseball league whose membership included, at various times, Smith & Wesson, Spalding, Stanley Products, Monsanto, Bigelow-Sanford, Gilbert & Barker, the Springfield Armory, Pratt & Whitney, Indian Motocycle and Van Norman.

Those old rivals, Bosch and Chapman Valve, stand as prime examples of what happened to local industries and their teams.

In 1986, the Chapman Valve complex along Indian Orchard's Pinevale and Goodwins streets were closed. In 2009, the plant was demolished. In 2004, the Bosch building burned to the ground, also long after its closing in the 1980s.

So now we have an entirely different era for local baseball. The Tri-County League goes on, but without any of those dear old "factory" teams.

They played at a time when industry boomed in Greater Springfield – and interest in local baseball boomed along with it.

The Call of the Y

I had a nice chat recently with Jim Smith, who serves as head football coach at Mohawk Trail Regional High School in Buckland.

By the way, he's not your everyday football coach. Rather, he's a working wonder, 81 years old and still out there, running practices and walking sidelines on game days.

He could have quit years ago – in fact, he did, in 1995. But soon after his retirement from a 35-year career at Deerfield Academy, an old friend called him from Franklin County Tech, of Montague. The new school needed somebody to jump-start its football program.

Smith lived nearby, so he answered the call. He figured it would be temporary, but he has been coaching high-school teams ever since.

"I'm going to keep doing this until I get it right," he says, showing a sense of humor that would serve any senior citizen well.

From my perspective, though, the most telling comment came at the end of our telephone conversation.

"Keep writing – and keep moving," he said, in a fatherly advice tone that I could not ignore. The writing part I can handle, even though Jim and I are the same age (actually, he's four months older). It's the "keep moving" part that hit me hard.

Lord knows, I've tried. Way back in the 1970s, when the jogging craze took hold in Western Massachusetts, I got out there and ran on the roads. Usually, I would do one to three miles. Ah, but when my 50th birthday came around, I decided to celebrate by seeing if I could do five miles. I did it, counting lap by lap on the little outdoor track that was behind the Springfield Y in those days.

Five miles may not seem like much for a true jogger, but for me it was a milestone that led me to consider entering some real road races.

I did so with one goal in mind – don't worry about where you finish, just finish the darn thing. I met that goal, all right.

In a Longmeadow Father's Day race, I finished in a tie for last place, only because the guy just ahead of me suggested that we cross the line together. Yes, there is a special bond among the running set.

I ran in 10K (6.2 miles) races for the next couple of years, even though it was a real struggle. Some people are naturally built for running. Others, like me, have to work at it with bodies more suited for sitting and typing.

Some "nerds" can handle the relentless pounding of road running. Others, like me, eventually pay a price. Mine was two hip replacements, one in 1998 the other in 2007.

When I finally finished the required rehabilitation process after my second new hip was securely in place, I heard familiar words from Andy, a physical therapist with an attitude.

"Get out there and keep moving," he said. "I don't want to see you back here."

I think he was trying to be nice, but with Andy, you could never tell.

Actually, I had been trying to keep moving, off and on, since the first hip job. For me, the workout advice translated into time on the treadmill at Wilbraham's Scantic Valley YMCA. Ah, but when the other hip developed an all-too-familiar ache, I let up on the walking, hoping the hip would feel better. It never did, so there I was on my way to surgery again.

After Andy and his gruff advice, I did get back to the treadmill, trying to hit the Y three days a week. Gradually, something happened. As the weeks went along, I found more and more reasons to skip my workouts. They dwindled to twice a week, then once a week, then...

Yes, I must admit that after all those sporadic attempts, I sank into my desk chair at home, there to stay even on those mornings when I was supposed to hitting that treadmill. I got a lot of writing done, but not much moving.

One morning, two key things occurred in concert. First, my wife gently suggested that it might be best to drop my Y membership instead of paying to stay away. Second, I made my call to Jim Smith for a little football chat.

His "keep moving" comment really hit home, because it was obvious to me that he continues to function as a coach because he's in as good physical condition as one could ever expect from an 81-year-old male.

If it was working for Jim, I knew it should work for me. Suddenly, his words – and Andy's harangue from 2007 – thundered in my ears and I just could not ignore the sound. Nor could I ignore my wife's bottom-line message.

So, I have returned yet again to the Scantic Valley treadmill, sheepish but with a new outlook. Finally, 10 months late, I am fulfilling my New Year's resolution.

When I went back, the first guy I saw in the locker room was an old friend, Ed Matulewicz. He's a Chicopee Hall of Famer, a guy I wrote about when he played the back court for a Chicopee Comprehensive High School basketball team that won Western Massachusetts in 1965. Looking at him, I just knew "Steady Eddie" had been doing his workouts all the time I had been away.

"Back at the Y?" he said with a knowing little smile.

Yes, back at the Y. And this time, I mean it.

Move That Type

On a recent afternoon, I received an ominous e-mail from one of the editors at The Springfield Republican.

"You're due for a lesson in Movable Type. Everybody else is using it, and now it's your turn."

To me, that sounded very much like a letter to a dinosaur.

Yes, I know what I am. I'm the old guy. The throwback to the 20th century. The retiree who doesn't know how to retire.

The hard fact is, I began working for The Springfield Newspapers 64 years ago. Now, in retirement, I still do a lot of writing for The Republican, mainly because I love it – and it's really all I know.

I must admit that the "movable type" email worried me. It didn't say "or else," but I understood the tone.

Of course, there was a lot I did NOT understand. Mainly, I had no idea what the true meaning of "movable type" is. So, I had no recourse except to Google it and hope for the best.

Here's what I found – and it did nothing to ease my mind:

"Movable Type was created by a husband and wife team with a single purpose: to establish a powerful solution for the creation and management of web content. An originator of the blogging field, Movable Type offers stability, a user-friendly interface, and beautifully extensive visual customization for websites and blogs."

Clear? Maybe not.

Luckily, one of our sons happened to drop by while I was struggling to cope with this new-fangled phase in my long life as a journalist.

"Oh, yeah. It's just a form of blogging," he said. "You won't have any trouble with it."

Easy for him to say, eh? Like I was a blogger from way back? Not.

Actually, I did make it through the transition, and it took only three lessons from my stern-faced editor. Now, I can turn everything I write into "movable type," and it miraculously winds up in print and on the MassLive web site.

The young whippersnappers working in journalism today think they have something new with their danged "Movable Type." Well, I've got news.

In the long ago, newspaper composing room workers would "move type" around every day and night of the week. That was when they worked with hot lead and linotype machines. Operators who were very good at it, would take our stories and turn them into "movable type" – that is, lines of lead that would be used to put together the daily newspaper pages, getting them ready for print.

That kind of newspapering was known as "hot type." Then came another revolution called "cold type." Instead of linotype machines and lead, we came to learn how to do stories in a computer system, readying them for print in an entirely different way.

Yes, over the years, I have gone from struggling with inky typewriter ribbons to struggling with my laptop. Typewriters could be ornery at times, but they never sent scary messages like "your computer may be at risk."

So I deal with computer glitches, just as I dealt in the old days with trying to send game stories from remote locations by Western Union. Most of the time, they made it. Sometimes... well, let me tell you about the WU printer that got stuck in one spot and shredded its paper as it was printing what should have been my column about Yogi Berra from the 1973 World Series at Shea Stadium. Sorry, no column that night.

As for that laptop, I'll gladly take it over the clunky Teleram, a mid-'70s device which was supposed to be a major technological advance in the transmitting of stories. Trouble was, it not only weighed too much, it could be very sensitive to noise. At the 1982 All-Star Game, hosted by the dearly departed Montreal Expos in Olympic Stadium, I had just completed a pregame column for use in our early editions when the Canadian National Anthem began blaring. As "O Canada" reached a crescendo...whoosh – my words flew off the Teleram screen, never to be seen again. I had to do a quick rewrite, and

hope for a little less background noise.

After the dreaded Teleram came a wondrous invention called the Radio Shack TRS-80. This little workhorse had limited storage space, so stories could not be saved over the long haul. But for day-to-day use – like covering major league baseball – this minicomputer was as dependable as you could get. It actually was a telephone of sorts. Plug your "Shack" into a telephone line, and your stories got to the paper in a matter of seconds.

The next step brought me to several generations of laptops. The first time I sent a story to the paper by e-mail, I was shocked at how easy and fast the process was.

Long before all of this, I worked in a different age of "movable typing." That is, typing stories while riding from Boston to Springfield on the Mass Pike. Soon after our marriage, my bride bought me a present – an Olivetti portable typewriter. On Sunday afternoons, I would cover a Red Sox game at Fenway Park. Then, with her serving as "designated driver," I would perch the Olivetti on my lap, and have my game story done by the time we got back to the newspaper office.

Movable type, movable typing...it's all part of my life as a newspaper guy. Yes, I'm an old dog who has learned some new tricks, but I still have a way to go.

Twitter, anyone?

She Was So Raven

Every so often, life delivers a jolting reminder that it is, indeed, later than we think.

Example: As I scanned one of the too-many magazines that come into our house, I came across a full-page advertisement for "Sister Act," a Broadway musical based on the 1992 movie that starred Whoopi Goldberg.

With my wife sitting across from me at the breakfast table, I suddenly blurted out, "That's So Raven!"

"Are you talking about the new John Cusack movie?" my wife said. (She knows Poe, all right).

So I showed her the ad, featuring an actress named Raven-Symone Christina Pearlman. She's a very familiar face, because she used to come into our living room on weekday afternoons as the star of a Disney Channel hit called…you guessed it, "That's So Raven."

The jolt was this: Raven-Symone is now 26 years old. Come on, that can't be true. It doesn't seem that long ago that I would be laughing at her teenage TV show with our youngest grandchild at my side. She would drop by after school – and soon talk me into watching the tube with her.

"Just for a while, Grandpa. OK?"

Hey, I loved it. The shows sometimes were simpy, but there was just enough good stuff – and hearty laughs – to make those TV interludes with her something to remember and cherish.

As for Raven, she wasn't just a teen-ager. She also happened to be a psychic who never quite knew when her powers would be there. Of course, they usually would kick in at times that could be funny, awkward – or both.

Raven wasn't the only star in this particular Disney firmament. In my granddaughter's younger years, I also got to know "Even Stevens" (teen-age siblings who argued a lot), "Kim Possible" (a teen-age crime fighter) and "Phil of the Future" (a time-traveling teen from the year 2121).

Then we moved on to my personal favorite, "Lizzie McGuire," an honor-student leader of her high school pack with an All-American mom, clueless dad and obligatory smarty-pants little brother.

Still later came the adventures of "Hannah Montana," with episodes that also featured Billy Ray Cyrus, her dad on TV and in real life. (The "Achy-Breaky Heart" singer, remember?)

Yes, with my perky granddaughter as my guide, I would drift into "Disneyworld" and, to my surprise, actually came to enjoy some of those shows. Of course, her sweet company had a lot to do with it.

The trouble is, Disney kids grow up. Hillary Duff stopped being Lizzie McGuire and became a singer and movie star. She's now 25, married and a mother.

Miley Cyrus has gone from playing Hannah Montana to playing solo concerts and doing movies. I don't know what happened to some of the others, but I can only assume that Phil of the Future time-traveled back to where he belongs.

Our granddaughter still drops by a couple of times a week, but these days she's a very cool 14-year-old into math, French, cheerleading, volleyball and I-Phones.

We still watch TV together, but no more Disney Channel afternoons for us. We both move on – and as we do, Raven-Symone moves on, too, dazzling 'em on Broadway.

She's 26 years old? C'mon. That can't be true.

Peanut Bowl Memories

QUICK NOW, NAME THE LAST WESTERN MASSACHUSETTS high school football team to play in an intersectional bowl game.

Only those who were around in the 1950s would know the answer – the West Springfield Terriers. They did it on January 1, 1953, when they lost 28–26 to Valdosta, Georgia, in a north-south rivalry known as the Peanut Bowl.

It's 60th anniversary time (2013) for those Terriers, many of whom remember that New Year's Day very well.

"I'll never forget it, because I got hurt carrying the ball on the first play, and had to sit out the rest of game," said Ernie LaBranche, a sophomore who started at halfback for that undefeated West Side team coached by Ed Mason, a former Agawam High and Springfield College quarterback.

The '52 season and the ensuing New Year's Day game would prove to be the end of a memorable five-year period in local high school football. In June of 1953, the Massachusetts Headmasters Association voted to ban Intersectional bowl games for high school teams.

The headmasters (school principals) frowned upon such games because they used proceeds only for local charities while at the same time forcing northern schools and their towns to raise money to finance the trips.

They also had misgivings about sending teams from the north into the segregated south, as it existed at that time. No team with an African-American player ever was invited to the Peanut Bowl. In 1951, undefeated Greenfield High made it clear that it did not want to be considered because it had an African-American in its backfield.

How did WMass involvement in the game come about? It started in 1946 with Lon Gammage, president of the Exchange Club of Columbus, Georgia, who envisioned it as a way to raise money for Georgia charities, including a hospital for crippled children. He patterned it after the big bowl games of the day – Rose, Sugar, Cotton and Orange – with the big difference being that it would involve high school teams.

Atlanta Tech defeated St. Joseph's, Missouri, 34–0 in the first Peanut Bowl on January 1, 1947. In the second game, North Charleston, South Carolina, beat Lanier of Macon, Georgia, 34–6.

Dismayed by the one-sided scores, the Peanut Bowl committee began looking for better matchups. Its attention turned to Western Massachusetts because of Harold Jambon, a Columbus Exchange Club member who had been impressed with high school football in this area when he was stationed at Westover Field in Chicopee near the end of World War II.

At Jambon's suggestion, Gammage contacted school officials in the Connecticut Valley about a possible Peanut Bowl matchup.

That led to 1948 Western Mass. champion Westfield, coached by Bill Moge, becoming the first area team to play in the game on New Year's Day, 1949. Westfield represented Western Mass. well, beating Fitzgerald, Georgia, 25–7.

Westfield went 9-0-0 in 1949 and made its second trip to Columbus. Again the Bombers prevailed, this time beating Glynn Academy of Brunswick, Georgia, 26–20.

Vinny Ciancotti played on both Peanut Bowl teams as an outstanding two-way lineman. He went on to become a Hall of Fame player at American International College, then into a long and successful career in business.

"I could be elected president of the United States, and Westfield people still would think of me as playing for those Peanut Bowl teams. That's how much they meant to the city," he said.

Westfield's postseason success turned coach Moge into a celebrity. In 1950, Chicopee succeeded in hiring him away from

Westfield, and he had a long career as a three-sport coach of Chicopee High School teams.

Holyoke, coached by Archie Roberts, lost to Rockmart, Georgia, 19-14, in the third Peanut Bowl involving Western Mass. teams. The fourth saw Harmon Smith's Agawam Brownies turn back Richmond Academy of August, Georgia, 25–12.

Then it was West Side's turn. Coach Mason's Terriers established themselves as Peanut Bowl material when they rallied from a 7–6 halftime deficit to hammer Cathedral 33–7 on Hallowe'en Night before 6,000 at Pynchon Park.

From there, West Side went on to win the Western Mass. title with a 8-0-0 record, ending its regular season in a hard-earned 13–7 victory over arch-rival Agawam. A late pass interception by defensive back Joe Harrington clinched it.

Those Terriers were the first in Western Mass. to operate out of the split-T, a formation which worked well because they had the right guy at quarterback – Les "Porky" Plumb.

His passing and shifty running carried West Side into the Peanut Bowl, and very nearly to victory. The Terriers were down 21–0 in the second quarter before Plumb rallied them.

As LaBranche said, "Valdosta had a real good team, but we did ourselves proud, and I think we made a good impression for Western Mass."

That they did. Tall end Newt Blanchard caught two touchdown passes – one on a trick play with his opposite end, Kenny Mattoon, doing the throwing; and the other from Plumb. Fullback Al Klein scored West Side's third touchdown on a five-yard plunge and Mattoon scored the last one on a pass from Plumb.

Valdosta scored its fourth TD after Klein's to make it 28–20, and seemed on its way to a clinching score when Blanchard recovered a fumble at the 10-yard line.

Plumb then whipped his team 90 yards for a fourth-quarter touchdown, capping the drive with a 36-yard pass to Mattoon. He got loose for the TD when Blanchard delivered a key block.

Time ran out with the Terriers driving at Valdosta's 30.

"They didn't beat us – the clock beat us," coach Mason said after the game.

Plumb went on to quarterback an undefeated team at Springfield College in 1956, with future UMass, Syracuse and New England Patriots coach Dick MacPherson as his center. One of their teammates, Dick Shields, played a backup backfield role as a junior on West Side's Peanut Bowl team.

"Our high school team had a great coaching staff – Eddie Mason, Gordie Vye, my older brother (Bob Shields), Bob Ryan and Sahler Smith. They were all young, about the same age, and they were all from Springfield College," Dick Shields recalled.

After SC, Plumb coached at the college and high school levels, including a 32-year stint at Westwood, New Jersey. He now lives in retirement in Fort Pierce, Fla.

Plumb, who served as West Springfield co-captain with guard Art Pernice, has fond memories of his West Side days.

"Eddie Mason had a phenomenal way of approaching everything. He treated every player the same, and we all respected him," Plumb said.

LaBranche remembered his coach as "the fairest man I ever met. With him, there was no baloney."

Mason left West Springfield after the 1958 season for a job at Springfield Tech, where he coached football and hockey. In November of 2012, he was enshrined posthumously in the Springfield Public Schools Athletic Hall of Fame.

Peanut Bowl memories? LaBranche, 75, still has a scrapbook that his family put together, covering the entire '52 season.

"I thought the Peanut Bowl was something special for Western Mass.," he said. "I think the teams that went got a lot out of the trip, and were treated very well. Actually, I was kind of sad to see it go. After our team, there were a lot of good ones in Western Mass. that could have had the experience. Just look at West Side. Coach Mason had another great team in 1956."

Ken Kindig, who started at guard on offense, called the Peanut Bowl "the most exciting thing that ever happened to me in sports." Shields said his memories of the trip include sights seen from the train – it was the first Pullman ride for most of the players.

"I can still remember going through the south and seeing houses on stilts," he said.

French Fadeaway

Smith, Johnson, Williams and... Brown.

Yes, according to the U.S. Census Bureau, our family's surname ranks No. 4 on the "most common" list. We even beat out Jones, which was kind of a surprise.

In our case, though, Brown has been our family name only since the late 1800s. That much has been established by a couple of genealogy buffs in the family, whose due diligence has traced my father's side back through Quebec, then to France of the early 1500s.

Quebec and France. Hmmm. That means Brown actually is a French name, right? Wrong – it means that somebody changed it at some point, probably when my grandfather Joseph left the Quebec village of St. Leonard in 1877 on his way to a job as a mill-worker in Haydenville, Mass.

Obviously, some U.S. customs officer wrote "Brown" on my grandpa's papers before allowing him to cross the border. Now, why would a customs officer do that? Probably because he didn't want to deal with writing Joseph's real surname, which was Provencher-dit-Villebrun. Instead, he took one look at the "brun" part and deftly turned it into Brown.

Given all that, wouldn't it be safe for our family to assume that we had French roots in Canada – and back to the "old country"? After all, with ancestors named Lizotte, Lampron, Gaudet, Lajeunesse, Osins, Lemire, Lebeau and Bretonnet how could we be anything but French on my father's side?

He certainly believed. My dad was so sure of his French roots, he lovingly would call me "m'enfant" (my child) when I would be hanging out with him in his garden, at the Post Office where he worked, or at a local baseball game.

Well, guess what? Our family history – murky, at best, because of that Brown-Provencher mixup - has taken a new and even stranger twist.

It happened when our favorite (and only) daughter suggested that we take part in an ancestry search on a website that offered DNA testing. We decided to give it a try, and after a few weeks, we received the results.

What a surprise. According to my DNA testing, I am 67 percent Irish, 14 per cent Iberian Peninsula (Spain and Portugal) and 19 percent "trace regions." Those include Eastern Europe, Italy-Greece, Finland-Northwest Russia and Western Europe. The Western Europe trace accounts for 2 percent – and that means the French part, which I had expected to be up around 50 percent. Hey, DNA does not lie.

The "67 percent Irish" finding really baffled me. I had assumed that it would be no more than 50 percent, given that my mother was 100 percent Irish (Connell on her father's side, Larkin on her mother's).

Obviously, the rest of the Irish finding – 17 percent – had to come from somewhere on my father's side. As for that 14 percent Iberian, my wife says to chalk it up to those Spanish and Portuguese explorers who sailed the world in the 1500s.

By the way, back before my DNA testing, I received an interesting writing assignment from Wayne Phaneuf, executive-editor of The Republican. He knew of my family background, and asked me to submit articles for use in a book that The Republican plans to publish on the history of the French-Canadian culture in Western Massachusetts.

I submitted four articles, including one about the changing of our family name. Little did I know at the time that my "French-Canadian heritage" amounted to a mere 2 percent on the DNA scale.

One of our sons has done his best to keep our family's French-Canadian feeling alive. Each of his children has a French middle name – Marie, Pierre and Michelle. On top of that, our favorite (and only) grandson was born in Sherbrooke, Province of Quebec, while his dad was serving as a teaching fellow at Universite de Sherbrooke. Now 20 years old, our grandson still holds dual citizenship.

Despite all that, one fact remains perfectly clear – I'm far more Irish than French.

C'est la vie.

Baldy Lee – An Appreciation

December, 1951. Baldy Lee, an energetic young man with a crew cut and a beautiful Boston accent, stood behind one of the benches at the Eastern States Coliseum's hockey rink, talking to his team, the Longmeadow Tinkers.

It was 8 a.m. – faceoff time for the first 10–12 division game on the day's schedule in Eddie Shore's Greater Springfield Junior Hockey League.

The energetic guy counted heads, assuring himself that the required number of players were in uniform and ready to skate. That, by the way, was rule No. 1 with the iron-handed Shore. He had plenty to do as owner of the Springfield Indians professional team, but he always took time on Saturday mornings to watch over his junior

league. And watch he did – if a coach came up one short of the required roster number, his team did not play that day.

Well, on this particular morning, all went right for Baldy and his Tinkers. They skated pretty well, considering their age, and came away with a victory. After the game, Baldy had more to do – he also worked with the 12–14 Longmeadow Jugglers and the 14–16 Longmeadow Squires.

That meant a pretty full day at the old hockey rink, and Baldy loved it. After all, he had grown up in hockey-mad Walpole, and skated for Walpole High in the tough Greater Boston Interscholastic League (better known as the GBI). No doubt about it, he was born to be on skates

In the early '50s, he was a student at Springfield College, where he led a campaign to have hockey instituted as a varsity sport. That never happened, but it didn't stop Lee and his hockey-playing pals from organizing a Springfield College club team that would play on Thursday nights at the Coliseum against opponents from around New England.

While he was still a college student, Lee's natural bent for leadership brought him to Longmeadow, where he worked with the Tinkers-Jugglers-Squires organization. I never found out why those names from old England were selected for the Longmeadow teams, but I soon found out what a good coach, organizer and all-around great guy Baldy was.

In March of 1952, Shore assembled an all-star team to represent Springfield in an Eastern Pee Wee Hockey Tournament at New Haven Arena. Baldy liked the idea so much, he entered his Longmeadow Jugglers. He also found time to work with Romeo Cyr – the man for whom Cyr Arena is named – as his assistant coach. That dynamic duo came up with a winner. Mike Kober's dramatic goal, on an assist from Karl Balland, gave Springfield a 3–2 overtime victory against host New Haven in the championship game.

Baldy never lost his love for hockey – he spent many a night officiating high school and college games – but as an SC grad with a master's degree in sports management and recreation, his career path took him into recreational work.

He held jobs in Ludlow and West Springfield before becoming Spring-field's superintendent of parks and recreation. That role reunited him with Cyr, who was a member of the Park Commission.

Baldy had an eventful career, all right. It included an unforgettable night in April of 1967, when Jiggs, a 19-year-old chimpanzee housed in the Forest Park zoo, escaped and was roaming the Trafton Road neighborhood adjacent to the park.

At one point, he made his way back into Forest Park, and knocked over a man as he was digging for nightcrawlers on the baseball fields. Lee and Springfield police went into the night, hoping to track down the fast-moving primate before he injured someone, or himself. Springfield Daily News photographer Ed Malley happened upon Jiggs, catching him in his headlights as he was coming up an access road near Cyr Arena. He alerted Lee and the 10 police officers who were in pursuit. Finally, with public safety in mind and no recourse, one of the officers shot Jiggs dead. Thus ended the most bizarre night of Lee's tenure as superintendent in Springfield.

Yes, Baldy had a very interesting life, but my memories of him always race back to the Coliseum. There, he was in his element – a down-to-earth hockey guy who loved the game and the kids he helped on the ice. It was my privilege in those days to cover the junior leagues, a assignment which enabled me to meet a colorful cast of Coliseum characters. Baldy fit right in with them.

Baldwin Barker Lee, 86, passed away April 11, 2015. A generation of Tinkers, Jugglers and Squires will never forget him. Nor will I.

Watching Baseball

On a sunny Friday afternoon in Manhattan, I boarded the Boston Red Sox team bus, bound for Yankee Stadium. (Yes, those were the days when writers covering the team could ride with players).

I took a seat near the front, next to Joe Castiglione, the team's long-time radio broadcaster. At that point of his illustrious career, Joe C already had worked more than 2,500 Red Sox games.

"How do you do it, Joe?" I asked. "Don't you ever grow tired of watching game after game?"

"Absolutely not," he said, "because there's always the chance I'll see something I've never seen before. That's the beauty of baseball. Every game is different."

Well, that night – Sept. 10, 1999 – Joe and I had the privilege of witnessing one of the great pitching performances in baseball history. It certainly was something we had never seen before – a 17-strikeout one-hitter by Pedro Martinez which he won 3–1. The one hit was a second-inning homer by Chili Davis (currently the Red Sox' hitting coach).

After Chili's homer, Pedro retired 22 in a row, 15 on strikes. His 17-K total is still the most ever against a Yankee ball club. He absolutely dominated a first-place team that would go on to win the World Series.

Yes, the grande olde game can be full of surprises, even to folks who have watched it for a long time.

Have you ever seen a triple play? In all my years of covering high school, college and professional baseball, I had never seen one – until the night of July 17, 1990, at Fenway Park, when the Red Sox were playing the Minnesota Twins.

In the fourth inning, the Sox loaded the bases with nobody out. Tom Brunansky then rapped a hot one-hopper to third baseman Gary Gaetti, who was guarding the line. He stepped on third, then went around the horn – triple play.

It seemed so easy, but such a play can happen only if the third baseman is playing close to the bag.

In the eighth inning, the same bases-loaded scenario produced the same result, with Jody Reed grounding to Gaetti for a triple play. So there I was, never having seen a TP and suddenly seeing two in one game.

By the way, in all of baseball history, that's the only game with two triple plays. And get this – the Red Sox still won it, 1–0.

Here's another "first" for Yours Truly – an unassisted triple play. Yes, I saw that July 8, 1994, when Red Sox shortstop John Valentin caught a line drive near second, stepped on the base to double off a runner, then tagged a runner coming down the line from first. It happened so fast, Valentin didn't quite realize what he had done until his teammates began running to the dugout.

Home runs? I've seen a ton of those, but I had never seen an inside-the-park grand slam until June 2, 1989. That stunning blow was delivered by Junior Felix, a speed-to-burn outfielder for the Toronto Blue Jays. His drive to right-center took a crazy bounce off the bullpen wall as desperate Sox outfielders gave chase. Too late. Felix scored standing up. Amazing.

A 14-run first inning? I'd never seen such a thing until June 27, 2003, when the Red Sox had one against the Florida Marlins. Imagine this – the Sox scored 11 runs before they made an out. For the inning, they had 13 hits, including a double and triple by leadoff man Johnny Damon and a three-run homer by Manny Ramirez. (Final score, 25–8).

Little things can surprise you in baseball, too. For instance: I once saw Baltimore lefty Erik Bedard field a one-hopper with two outs and the bases full. Instead of throwing to first, he charged the ball, fielded it, and just kept coming, stepping on home plate for the third out. Very cool – and I'd never seen a pitcher do that before.

Baseball produced another of its "wow" moments on April 19 of this year. Chicago Cubs pitcher John Lester fielded a comebacker, but couldn't get the ball out of his glove. So he improvised, throwing the glove-and-ball to first base. Anthony Rizzo dropped his first baseman's glove and made the catch for the out. (Yes, that's a legal play). The video of it went viral.

No doubt about it, Joe C was exactly right when he talked about "the beauty of baseball." It really is the greatest game ever invented – as my dad used to tell me – and it can surprise you any day of the week.

Reading the Boston Globe to find out what's really happening with the Red Sox. Summer, 1988, when short-shorts were in vogue.

Maris and the Sandlotters

BARRY METAYER REMEMBERS IT AS "MORE LIKE A POP FLY."

Norm Burgess remembers it as "looking like a checked swing."

Whatever their perspective as Greater Springfield sandlot kids sitting in the stands at Yankee Stadium, Metayer and Burgess witnessed baseball history – home run No. 61 for Roger Maris.

Maris topped the season record of 60 homers, which had been in place since Babe Ruth did it in 1927.

It happened on Sunday, October 1, the last day of the 1961 season.

That also happened to be the day on which winning teams in the 35th annual *Springfield Daily News* Sandlot Tournament were rewarded with a trip to New York. Today (October 1, 2011) marks the 50th anniversary of their unforgettable ride.

Aboard "The Sandlot Special" as it rolled into Grand Central Station were players and coaches from the Holy Name Aces, 10–12 division champions; Monson Aces (12–14) and Fairview Boys Club (14–16).

"It was a very big deal for us. Hey, just being able to see a Red Sox-Yankees game at the stadium was great," said Metayer, who was twelve years old at the time. "I was a kid, but I knew about Maris and the 60 home runs, and I knew he would be going for the record."

As Metayer remembers it, the sandlot champs had seats about halfway out toward right field. From that vantage point, he had a clear view of No. 61, when Maris knocked it into the right field seats.

"To me, it seemed more like a pop fly when it left the bat, but it made it into the stands, and when it did, I saw a guy jump up like he was on a trampoline and catch the ball. He turned and ran for his life with people after him. They were trying to get the ball away from him, but security guards came along to protect him."

The "trampoline man" was Sal Durante, a 19-year-old truck driver from Coney Island. Rather than keep the ball, he returned it to Maris and received a $5,000 reward from Yankee management.

Durante was one of the invited guests last Saturday at the new Yankee Stadium when the Yankees gave a 50th anniversary salute to the Maris family.

"I saved the ticket stub from that game," Metayer said. "I still have it somewhere at home."

The Maris homer off Red Sox right-hander Tracy Stallard not only set the record, it won the ball game 1–0 as Bill Stafford, Hal Reniff and Luis Arroyo combined on a four-hitter.

The game took an hour and 57 minutes. Metayer now lives in Wilbraham and works at Quinsigamond Community College in Worcester as director of public grants development. He is a graduate of Middlebury College

As a sandlotter, Metayer played on Holy Name teams that also won titles in the 8–10 and 12–14 divisions.

His 10–12 teammates on the sandlot trip included pitchers Jim Stebbins and Steve LaPerle; infielders Jim McGrath, Steve Lotterman, Bob LaPerle and Bob McLaughlin; catcher Pete Lalli and outfielders Phil Ward, Steve Gerrold and George Ashwell.

McLaughlin went on to win the Lahovich Award of high school basketball at Cathedral in 1966. Metayer and Ward became football and baseball teammates at Classical. In 2007, Metayer was elected as part of the Springfield Public Schools Athletic Hall of Fame's first class.

The Monson Aces contingent included its star pitcher, Ronnie Constantino. He went on to become an All-Western Mass. ace at Monson High School before going into professional baseball as the No. 3 pick of the Cleveland Indians in 1965, year of the first baseball draft.

He spent six seasons in the minor leagues before moving on to a career as a director of recreation, first in Monson and later in Belchertown. He died in July of 1998 at the age of 51. A baseball field in Belchertown bears his name.

Burgess, now in his 27th year as principal of Bowie Memorial Elementary School in Chicopee, well remembers the reaction when Maris connected.

"Being there that day was a really big deal, especially after reading about all the highlights (of Maris chasing Ruth). The fans went nuts, and people were scrambling to get the ball."

The sandlotters had assigned seats, but Burgess and some of his Fairview buddies began moving around, from level to level, because there were a lot of empty seats. It might be hard to believe now, but that game, even with Maris going for the record, drew only 23,154.

"We went up to other levels of the stadium, then back down. When Maris hit the homer, I was in a perfect spot in the stands to see it. But from where I was, it almost looked like a checked swing," Burgess said.

In that magical baseball season, Burgess played on a Fairview team stacked with talent that later would help Chicopee High School set a record by winning three consecutive state baseball titles (1961–63).

Burgess played shortstop on all three of those teams. His Fairview teammates who helped Chicopee during its streak included George Leocopoulos, Leo O'Neill, Joe Viamari, Bob Suchecki, Ron Wysk and ace pitcher Billy Davis.

Burgess and Davis went on to become baseball teammates at American International College.

On the train trip back to Springfield after their big day at Yankee Stadium, the sandlotters took part in a raffle conducted by their chaperones from *The Daily News* – Sam Pompei, John Sears,

Dick Maroney, Ed Malley, Bill Powers and Jack Chevalier.

"They raffled off a baseball autographed by the Yankees. I won it, and I still have it," Burgess said. "Everybody's on there…Roger Maris, Mickey Mantle, Yogi Berra, Whitey Ford, Elston Howard, all the Yankees."

It wasn't until years later, when Burgess was showing the baseball to family members, that he realized it also contained the autograph of Art Ditmar, his baseball coach at AIC.

Ditmar, a Pittsfield native, pitched for the Yankees from 1957 until June of '61, when he was traded to Kansas City. His name was on the baseball, because it was signed early in the season and later given to the *Springfield Daily News* in advance of the sandlot trip.

Ditmar left pro ball after the '62 season. He coached at AIC from 1965-72.

The '61 Yankees, regarded as one of the all-time great teams, beat the Cincinnati Reds 4–1 in the World Series.

"I've been a Red Sox fan my whole life, but looking back, I'd have to say, that was quite a Yankee ball club," Burgess said.

And that was quite a trip aboard "The Sandlot Special," which took three kid teams on a ride into baseball history.

Tech-Cathedral Revisited

In the long history of Springfield high school sports, one football game stands far above the rest.

It was played on Tuesday, Nov. 11, 1941 – Armistice Day, celebrating the end of World War I in 1918. We now know it as Veterans Day.

It turned out to be a duel in which Tech defeated Cathedral 6–0 before a crowd of 12,000 at Pynchon Park.

Tech and Cathedral became natural rivals simply because they stood across from each other on Elliott Street. Their rivalry began when Cathedral started football in 1926, and lasted until Tech closed in 1986. At that time, the city school system also shut down Classical. The student bodies were melded into a new school, Springfield Central.

Tech and Cathedral came into their momentous matchup undefeated. Tech stood 6-0, having outscored its opponents 163–13. Cathedral also entered the game at 6-0, having allowed only one touchdown all season.

Although the rivals still would have one more game on their schedules after this, they were so dominant, it was clear that the winner would be on its way to the regional title. Unlike school football of today, schedules back then were limited to eight or nine games.

This matchup marked the second such between the schools over a three-year span. As was the case again in 1941, both teams went into the 1939 game unbeaten. Before a crowd of 10,000, Cathedral won 19–7 on the passing and running of Angelo Bertelli, a West Springfield "rink rat" who went on to win the Heisman Trophy at Notre Dame in 1943.

In the days leading up to the 1941 game, Cathedral coach Billy Wise received a telegram from Bertelli, who then was a sophomore star in coach Frank Leahy's T-formation offense.

"I'm here at South Bend, but my heart will be with Cathedral at Pynchon Park," Bertelli's message said.

The heat of this rivalry, the importance of the matchup and the holiday setting stirred so much interest that The Springfield Republican reported "a brisk advance sale" of tickets.

Brisk, indeed. The advance sale, plus a walkup business that began early in the morning, led to the crowd of 12,000 – the largest ever to see a high school sporting event in Springfield.

How to explain such a crowd? Well, for the fans who were there that day, it actually was an exercise in escapism. The United States stood on the brink of war as Nazi Germany blitzed its way across Europe, so who could blame local folks if they looked upon a big football game as a way to forget the bad news and war clouds for a couple of hours?

The game was played four weeks before Imperial Japan bombed Pearl Harbor, plunging the U.S. into global war.

Indeed, most of the players who performed at Pynchon Park that day went on to serve in the military during World War II.

The Tech-Cathedral game of '41 could have drawn even more fans, but an estimated 3,000 had to be turned away at the gate.

As sportswriter Harold Wade of The Springfield Union reported, "Fans were lined six deep along the sidelines and in the end zones. Many of them had to crane their necks as they tried to get a glimpse of what was happening."

Those who did "get a glimpse" saw a grinding game which was settled by one spectacular play – a 88-yard kickoff return for a touchdown, delivered by Ken Beausoleil, Tech's quarterback and captain.

Billy Carroll of Cathedral nailed the second-half kickoff, sending it fast and low into Beausoleil's arms. He went straight up the middle behind a wedge of blocking, broke free at midfield and could not be caught.

Tech's extra point attempt was blocked, but its defense held fast for the 6–0 victory.

Cathedral did make one threat in the fourth quarter, but Tech held on fourth down at its own 12.

Tech's starting lineup had Bob Frappier and Sherrod Shaw at ends, Clarence Linville and Ollie Rickson at tackles, Fred Miller and Roland "Truck" Berard at guards, Crain Wright at center and a backfield of Beausoleil, Eddie Dobiecki, Gene Papineau and Bob Jennings.

Cathedral's starters were ends Bill "Bull" Martin and John Kenney, tackles Ted Budynkiewicz and Izzy Yer-

geau, guards John Houlihan and John Dwyer, center Carmelo DeCosmo, and a backfield of Fran "Lefty" Keough, Don Evans, Bob Sullivan and Gerry O'Connor.

The victory gave the Orange and Black the Interschool League championship, ending a four-year run for Cathedral.

At a celebration back at the Tech gym, Walmer said Beausoleil's touchdown came on a play his team had been practicing for two weeks.

"I had the first six men cross-blocking through the middle. It just happened that every one of them carried out his assignment, and Kenny ran right through a gaping hole. Plays like that need perfect execution, and we were fortunate to have it in such an important game," Walmer told The Republican.

The big game had an all-star set of officials: Jimmy Sullivan as referee, Gus Winters as umpire, Gerald Fitzgerald as head linesman and Henry Batt as field judge.

Tech went on to cap its first and only perfect season by beating a tough Holyoke team, 12–6. Cathedral closed at 7-1, defeating Archbishop Coyle of Taunton 20–0 in its finale.

When school sports editor George Springer picked his 1941 All-Western Mass. football honor roll for The Sunday Republican, it included four Tech players – Dobiecki, Frappier, Rickson and Berard. O'Connor, Budynkiewicz and Yergeau made it for Cathedral.

Walmer coached football at Tech from 1924 to 1947, posting a career record of 98-59-11. Wise coached Cathedral football for 35 years, amassing a record of 161-92-23 with six undefeated seasons. His 1955 team won the championship in the first year of the AA Conference.

Walmer and Wise both have been elected to the Massachusetts Football Coaches Hall of Fame.

Those dedicated coaches symbolized the heat of the Tech-Cathedral rivalry. The fierce competition they fostered carried on, even after Cathedral moved from Elliott Street into new quarters on Surrey Road in the fall of 1959.

Now, Cathedral tries to recover from damage which forced the closing of its tornado-scarred building. As for Tech, the city closed it in 1986, along with Classical as Central replaced both of them. Now, only a facade of its Tech's former structure can be seen on a site being used for a new state computer data center.

When that opened, all vestiges of those Elliott Street days were gone. Tech-Cathedral, a rabid rivalry in all sports, now becomes a distant, fading memory.

The greatest memory of all? No doubt about it - Armistice Day, 1941.

1941 football season scores for Tech and Cathedral:

TECH

19	Greenfield	13
19	Hartford	0
12	Pittsfield	0
26	Trade	0
61	Commerce	0
26	Classical	10
6	Cathedral	10
12	Holyoke	6
181		19

Record: 8-0-0

CATHEDRAL

27	Adams	0
12	St. Bernard's	0
19	Trade	7
13	St. John's	0
32	Classical	0
28	Commerce	0
0	Tech	6
20	Bishop Coyle	0
151		13

Record: 7-1-0

The Carla Coffey Way

For coach Carla Coffey of Smith College, her love of track began on a television set.

"My father didn't want television, so if I wanted to watch something, I had to go up the street to a friend's house," she said, harking back to her growing-up years in Somerset, Kentucky.

On one unforgettable day in the summer of 1960, she went "up the street" to watch the Olympic Games, being broadcast from Rome. She sat transfixed as she saw Wilma Rudolph of the Tennessee State Tigerbelles win the 200-meter dash – one of the three gold medals she reaped for Team USA.

Italian newspapers nicknamed Rudolph "La Gazella Negra" (the Black Gazelle) after she also won the 100-meter dash, and anchored a gold medal-winning relay team.

On that day, Carla was only 11 years old, but she suddenly knew what she wanted to do. She wanted to be Wilma Rudolph.

Well, Coffey never made it to the Olympics, but she did have her shot at the Olympic Trials of 1972. Beyond all that, though, having Rudolph as a role model inspired her to excel in three sports in college, and follow with an exemplary coaching career that is still going strong. Along the way, she became the first woman athlete enshrined in the Murray State University Athletic Hall of Fame. She's also a Hall of Famer at her high school and in the Kentucky Track and Cross Country Coaches Association.

Internationally, she has served five times as manager and coach of USA Track and Field junior teams. In 1995, she managed Team USA for the world indoor championships in Barcelona. Within the NCAA, she has served on its track and field rules committee.

This marks her 21st year at Smith, and her 42nd as a head coach.

When she got to Somerset High School, she found that tennis was the only sport offered for girls.

"In my senior year, we finally got a girls track team," she recalled. "I went around and recruited who I thought were some of the best girl athletes in the school prior to talking to my phys-ed teacher about it. She became our sponsor.

"Our school's first outdoor track team competed that spring. I read books by Dr. Nell Jackson (a pioneer of women's track) and I watched the boys track training methods. I learned to hurdle from one of the boys. That year, we won the regional championship. I qualified for the state meet in the 70-yard hurdles and finished third."

Going into high school, Coffey had never played organized basketball, but she did play a lot of "unorganized" games with her four older brothers. With that background, she made the high school varsity. She also played volleyball.

"I never played volleyball until high school, but it was in my gene pool, I guess," she said.

Then it was on to Murray State, where she co-captained the volleyball, basketball and track teams as a senior in 1971–72.

She then took high school coaching jobs in Louisville and Bowling Green, Ky. In 1976, she moved into the college ranks as head coach of women's track and cross country at Western Kentucky University.

Her career then led her to coaching jobs at Cal-Davis, the University of Kansas and Dartmouth College. At Dartmouth, she not only coached women's track, she had charge of hurdlers and sprinters on the men's team.

In July of 1992, Smith College hired her as head coach of track and cross country, and lecturer in the Department of Exercise and Sports Studies.

Over the years, Smithies have learned to love her dedication to the sport, and her always-candid approach with them.

"Coaching at Smith is a challenge, because we get all different types of student/athletes here, but coaching has always been a passion with me, and it helps me remember how hard my parents worked when I was growing up," she said.

In the late 1970s, when she was coaching at Western Kentucky, she had a chance to meet Wilma Rudolph.

"It was so exciting, talking with the person who had inspired me to pursue track as my career path," she said.

A Home Run at 4:30 in the Morning

IT WAS 4 A.M. FRIDAY, BUT BILL AND PEGGY CLARK of Springfield couldn't think about sleep.

Instead, they sat transfixed before their television screen, watching the Caribbean World Series championship baseball game, with their son, Doug, playing left field for Mexico's entry, Yaquis de Obregon. Their opponent: Leones del Escogido, a powerful team representing the Dominican Republic.

Would this game ever end? The Clarks had been watching ESPN Desportes for more than seven hours, and still the teams battled on, tied at 3–3.

"Something's got to happen. Somebody's gotta make a miscue," Peggy said to her husband.

Well, something finally did happen. In the top of the 18th inning, the Clarks broke into a whoop of joy as Doug sent a high drive to right field. It just barely made it over the wall – a home run to give Mexico the lead. It was a great moment in the career of their son, a former Springfield Central High School and University of Massachusetts athlete.

"I was praying that they could score more, because the Dominican Republic was the home team in that game, so we still had to get through the last of the 18th," Peggy Clark said.

The Dominicans put the leadoff man on base in the 18th, but the next three batters went out. The game ended at 4:30 a.m. (EST). It lasted seven hours and 28 minutes, with 21 pitchers throwing a total of 507 pitches. All of that set records for the 55 years of Caribbean World Series play.

Then came the celebration, and presentation of the tournament's Most Valuable Player Award. Fittingly, it went to Clark

— not just for his game-deciding home run, but for his all-round outstanding play throughout the seven-game series.

"This was a game for the ages," Clark told MLB.com while trying to muster his best Spanish. "This is like three or four games in one. We had the game in our hands twice and they came back. But they're a very dangerous team, and we had to maintain our focus every inning."

The Dominicans twice tied the game, scoring in the last of the ninth to make it 2–2, and in the 14th to make it 3–3.

In that tense finale, Clark went 2 for 7. For the entire series, he hit .393. In helping Obregon win the Mexican winter playoffs, he hit .492 over 16 games covering three rounds.

Clark's teammates included seven with current or past major league experience – Rodrigo Lopez, Luis Mendoza, Luis Ayala, Alfredo Amezaga, Dennys Rys, Karim Garcia and Marlon Byrd. It was Byrd who caught a line drive to right field to end the game.

The Dominican squad, which had been favored to win the championship, included big leaguers Hanley Ramirez, Miguel Tejada, Fernando Rodney, Julio Lugo and Fernando Tatis.

The Caribbean World Series involves the champions of winter leagues in Mexico, Puerto Rico, Venezuela and the Dominican.

Garcia, who played ten years in the major leagues, is considered as a Mexican Pacific League legend. He led off the top of the 14th with a go-ahead homer, but another long-time big leaguer, Tejada, tied it again with a two-out RBI single in the bottom of the 14th.

Four innings later, the lefty-swinging Clark jumped on a breaking ball out over the plate for his clutch homer.

The final game, played in Hermosillo, Mexico, at Estadio Sonora, drew a capacity crowd of 16,000. Most of them were still in the stands when the game ended.

Mendoza, a Kansas City Royals right-hander, told MLB.com that the fans kept the team going.

"They were here the whole game. Nobody ever left. That's why we're here. This championship is for them," Mendoza said.

"It's Mexico, man, they love their baseball," said Byrd. "That's what I've learned. I got down here early, played a whole season of winter ball. Baseball is the No. 1 sport. It's just amazing."

In Clark's three seasons with Obregon, the team has won the Caribbean World Series twice (2011, 2013). The Yaquis have taken the Mexican Pacific League pennant in each of his seasons with the team.

Clark, who turns 37 on March 2, has played professional baseball since 1998, when he was drafted out of the University of Massachusetts by the San Francisco Giants, who took him in the seventh round. He played eight seasons in the San Francisco farm system, then one with Oakland. Over that span, he had only two brief stints in the major leagues – eight games with the Giants in 2005, six with Oakland in 2006.

He spent the next three seasons playing in Korea, before moving on to establish himself as a star performer in Mexico.

"His Caribbean World Series heroics really are so typical of Doug," said Steve McKelvey, a University of Massachusetts professor who doubles as a sports agent. He and his partner, Jim Masteralexis, run the DiaMMond Management Group, which has represented Clark since his career began.

"Doug is just a fun client to have. He's the perfect guy for this Caribbean story, because he has a way of really embracing adventure in baseball. He did it in Korea, and now he's doing it in Mexico," McKelvey said.

Mike Stone, coach of UMass baseball since 1988, said he was thrilled to see Clark's performance in the Caribbean series.

"Here's a guy who walked onto our program, started from scratch and made himself into a player. Doug is such a good athlete, and such a great person, it's good to see him have success," Stone said.

Clark went to UMass after starring at quarterback in 1993 on the first Springfield Central High School football team to win a Super Bowl. He became a wide receiver at UMass. Then, as a sophomore, he decided to give baseball a try, as well, even though he had not played the sport in high school.

In three years of varsity play at UMass, he hit .366 with 21 homers and 49 stolen bases. In the 1998 Beanpot Tournament final at Boston's Fenway Park, Clark made a dazzling running catch of a line drive to center field, saving a no-hitter for pitcher Scott Barnes.

"I was ecstatic for Doug to hear about what happened in the Caribbean Series, and even more ecstatic to hear that he will be coming home with his family," said Dan McLaughlin, Clark's Central High School football coach.

"Winning this Caribbean World Series, is the best feeling of my life," Clark told MLB.com. "My wife is here, my son is here – he was born in Mexico. This is a moment we'll never, ever forget."

Clark and his wife, Pilar, have a son, Matteo, who will be two years old in March. Until this year, Pilar had not been able to accompany Clark and Matteo to Springfield because she did not have a visa.

"The process to get a visa has been settled, and they should be visiting us by Wednesday," Clark's mother said.

Clark will have a lot of people greeting him upon his return. He's the third child in a family of seven.

Balcony for a Nightingale

As visitors to the Lyman & Merrie Wood Museum of Springfield History walk into its high-ceilinged hall on the first floor, they often ask a question:

"What's that balcony doing up there?"

Well, that balcony – tastefully set halfway up the front wall – has a very special place in the city's history. It originally was part of the Jerry Warriner mansion at 43 Howard Street, which later became the Warriner Hotel.

Jenny Lind, an operatic singer known world-wide as "The Swedish Nightingale," stayed at the Warriner for several days in the summer of 1851 while in the midst of a successful concert tour in the United States.

On July 1, she performed before a capacity crowd at Springfield's First Congregational Church in Court Square. She then stayed at the Warriner while awaiting her next concert, which was scheduled for July 7 in Northampton.

From the hotel's balcony, she reviewed Springfield's Fourth of July parade. Afterward, with a crowd still gathered below, she delivered an impromptu concert. She was especially interested in doing so, because she saw so many children of school age in the crowd. (Lind's stated motivation for doing concerts in the U.S. was to raise money on behalf of schools and charities in Sweden, her homeland).

Her "balcony concert" ranks as one of the great and impromptu moments in Springfield's cultural history.

In later years, when the Warriner Hotel was torn down, members of the Connecticut Valley Historical Society – well aware of the significance of the "Lind balcony" – saved it and had it stored in the old Pynchon Building in the Springfield quadrangle.

Guy McLain, director of the Wood Museum of Springfield History, will be forever grateful to those concerned citizens who preserved the balcony for posterity.

"The Lind balcony is one of the oldest artifacts we have," he said.

The balcony is a gift to the museum from Bertram Craig, Stedman Craig and Mrs. W.E. Perry of the Connecticut Valley Historical Society.

The only trouble was, the Pynchon Building had no place for it to be displayed, so it was consigned to the basement. When plans were set in motion for the Museum of Springfield history, McLain sought a way to make the balcony available for public view.

"I mentioned to our architect (Steve Jablonski of Springfield) that I had the balcony, with no idea what to do with it. He took one look and said, 'I think I can find a good place for this in the museum's great hall.'"

That hall has an arched ceiling from which hangs a replica of the "Gee Bee" – a Springfield-built airplane used in air races, which were a popular activity in pre-World War II America.

"Steve suggested mounting the balcony on the front wall, and he enhanced it – and the entire hall – by creating a second-floor walkway which allows visitors to get close looks at the balcony and the Gee Bee," McLain said.

On the walkway, a plaque explains the balcony's significance in connection to Jenny Lind's visit to Springfield.

Her American tour came a year after she retired – at the age of 29 – from a career as one of the most highly regarded singers of the nineteenth century. At the height of her popularity, she performed soprano roles in opera in Sweden and across Europe.

At the urging of well-known impresario P.T. Barnum, Lind agreed to come out of retirement for a tour of the U.S. With Barnum arranging her various bookings, she performed 93 concerts in 1850, then continued to tour under her own management. The Springfield and Northampton concerts came after she had completed her commitment to Barnum.

The Springfield Republican gave Lind a glowing review after her concert at the First Church.

"In no other concert on the tour has Jenny Lind sung any better, or taken more pains to please her audience," the review said. "She consented to repeat almost every song, and her Springfield audience will well remember her kindness. There is but one Jenny Lind."

Yes, and there is but one Jenny Lind Balcony. If you haven't seen it, get down to 21 Edwards Street. The balcony – and the whole wondrous Museum of Springfield History – are well worth the trip.

Skip And Snoopy, Together Again

In July, Joseph "Skip" Demerski of West Springfield went to Santa Rosa, Calif., and came home with a gold medal.

He earned it while playing with old friend Ron Checchini of Springfield in Snoopy's Senior World Hockey Tournament. This event has been going since 1975, when it was started by Charles Schulz, revered creator of the "Peanuts" comic strip.

Yes, Demerski is back on skates, playing the game he has loved since his "rink rat" days at the Eastern States Coliseum.

And, at the age of 70, he still works eight hours a day as owner of Surface Cleaning and Restoration, a West Springfield business he started 40 years ago.

For a time in August of 2011, none of the above seemed possible for him. Not after profuse bleeding from a severed femoral artery in his right leg put him near death.

It happened while he and his crew were restoring a patio area near the old Post Office building on Dwight Street in downtown Springfield. He gashed the leg from inner thigh to ankle while operating a stone grinder which suddenly went out of control. The bleeding became so profuse, he fell into a coma. He survived only because co-worker Kevin Loughman applied a tourniquet, and a Springfield police officer pinched the artery to suppress the bleeding on the way to Bay State Medical Center. There, a waiting surgeon, Dr. Neal Hadro, gave him life-saving care.

Law enforcement responders at the scene of Demerski's accident included Amy Waterman of the Massachusetts State Police, and Springfield police officers Eugene Rooke, William Smidy, William Witherspoon, David Standen, Michael Brock and James Donovan.

"As it turned out, I had a lot of good luck in a bad-luck situation. They tell me that 90 per cent of the people who suffer a severed femoral artery don't live to tell about it," Demerski said.

How, then, can he explain surviving such a life-threatening accident?

"There must have been no vacancy in hell that day," he said with a wry smile.

Once he came out of the coma and had his condition stabilized, Demerski made a quick recovery.

"I was back to work two weeks later, hobbling around with my walker," he said.

Years of playing hockey and doing physical labor undoubtedly had a lot to do with his ability to rebound from his horrific accident.

As a youngster, Demerski played for coaches Aime Levesque and Bill Vassar in Eddie Shore's junior leagues. From ages 12 to 14, he served as stick boy for the Springfield Indians on game nights.

"Working and playing at the Coliseum, I learned so much from Eddie Shore (Hockey Hall of Famer who owned the Indians franchise). He was great for teaching the value of no-non-sense discipline," he said.

At West Springfield High School, Demerski won the Berry Division scor-ing title in 1960, but that was only prelude to one of the best seasons ever put together by a Western Mass. high school player.

With long-time teammate Joe Bregoli and Mike Campofredano play-ing on his line, "The Skipper" tallied 54 goals and 75 points in a mere 20 games to lead the state in scoring. And let us remember that in those days, school hockey teams played 10-minute peri-ods.

The West Side Terriers of '61 lost in the state tournament, but Demerski made the all-state team. He and team-mates Al Runshaw, Ronnie Butterfield and Bregoli made The Republican's All-Western Mass. first team. De-merski, Butterfield and Ralph Liebro served as tri-captains of the West Side team.

Demerski went on to play four years of Division I hockey at Clarkson in Potsdam, N.Y.

Before the accident, he regularly played senior hockey and made many medal-winning trips to Santa Rosa.

After the accident? Well, it took a while.

"The leg is still pretty numb from the knee down, but it works fine for the most part. And, after two and a half years away from skating, I was able to

get back to it six months ago. That got me ready for the Snoopy Tournament," he said.

Great news for Checchini, who had been hoping his old pal would be able to skate again. He already had lost Bregoli, another long-time senior hockey teammate, to shoulder surgery.

Checchini, a former Tech High star, has played in 31 of the 38 of the Snoopy Tournaments.

"They should rename it the Snoopy and Ron Tournament," Demerski said.

"Actually, Ronnie was the reason we won it. He was the cornerstone of our defense, and we gave up only five goals in our three tournament games."

Demerski and the 75-year-old Checchini played for the Los Ange-les Silver Eagles in the tournament's "Peppermint Patty" (70 and over) divi-sion.

The Eagles grabbed the gold medal by beating the Vancouver Continentals 6–1, the Can-Am Old-Timers 3–1 (on two third-period goals by Demerski) and the Ottawa Ancient Mariners 5–3.

"We almost blew a 4–1 lead in that last game, but after they made it 4–3, our old legs lasted just long enough and we were able to score again for the win," Demerski said.

After the tourney, Jean and Monte Schulz – widow and son of the "Pea-nuts" cartoonist – presented medals to all the winners.

"It's always a special tournament, but for me, this one was really special," Demerski said.

Tech's Music Maker

In my three years at Springfield's dear old Technical High School, April meant that it was time for a traditional talent show known as "Tech Tantrums."

More specifically, it meant a chance to hear the school's jazz band. When they took over the stage, "Tantrums" reached a whole new level for the cheering audience of Tech kids.

Yes, that jazz band could play – and their talent became especially apparent in 1949, my senior year. That particular band had a terrific sax section, led by Phil Woods, a baby-faced junior with slicked-back hair parted in the middle.

When the band swung into a Harry James hit called "The Music Makers," the audience knew what was coming – a solo by Phil. He delivered, big time.

Then, for the next number, he took center stage alone and treated the audience to his rendition of "Goofus," a lively tune that had been introduced to the Hit Parade by Wayne King and his orchestra way back in 1931 – the year Phil Woods was born.

When he finished "Goofus", he rejoined the jazz band for more good music. What a night. "Tantrums" had never been better.

As the audience enjoyed the show, we had no idea that we were listening to a musician who would become one of the all-time greats in the world of jazz. Phil Woods went on to international renown, and a career that's still going.

As he traveled the world wearing his signature leather cap, he never left Springfield that far behind. Every so often, he would return to visit family and friends. And each time he came back to his hometown, he would stopped by to see Harvey LaRose, a musician's musician who had given him lessons on the saxophone when he was 12 years old.

Harvey spent his life in the background of the music world. He had a genius for repairing instruments, and made that his main occupation. Along with it, he would give lessons to players of any age. If you wanted to learn the sax, clarinet or flute, Harvey was a good place to start. He had the patience and heart of a man born to teach.

In the 1970s, one of our sons became enamored of the clarinet when he happened to turn the radio dial to WTIC for a big-bands show called "The Dean's List." The show was a labor of love for Arnold Dean, who served as the station's sports director, and also had a lifelong interest in big bands and jazz. On Arnold's show, our son heard Artie Shaw play "Begin the Beguine," and he announced – "I want to do that."

A few months later, we found out about Harvey LaRose, and our son was on his way to clarinet and sax lessons with a quiet master – and a life filled with music.

One afternoon, when we picked up our son after one of his after-school lessons, Harvey happened to mention that Phil Woods had stopped by to see him that morning.

Wow. By then, Phil was big-time in a career that included a highlight solo on Billy Joel's first hit, "Just the Way You Are" (1977). To me, as a Tech grad who had cheered Phil from my auditorium seat, he was an out-of-reach superstar. To Harvey, as celebrated as Phil might have been at the time, he still was the nice kid who listened well, worked hard and played lights out.

Oh, yes, Harvey took adult students, too. When my wife showed interest in learning the flute, she became a weekly student of his. She loved his gentle way of telling her, "Too many grace notes."

Memories of "Tech Tantrums," Arnold Dean and Harvey LaRose came flooding back to me this week, when I read that Phil Woods will be playing at Court Square on Saturday afternoon (2 p.m.) as part of the Springfield Jazz and Roots Festival. For this winner of multiple Grammys, it will be a triumphant return to a city that hasn't always realized what an international celebrity he really is.

Yes, Phil Woods has come a very long way from "Goofus" at center stage in Tech High's auditorium. He's 82 years old now...and the music plays on.

Note: Phil Woods passed away September 29, 2015. He was 83.

From Cathedral to the NFL

Bill Kingston grew up in Springfield's South End of the 1940s and '50s.

When he was 12 years old, he quarterbacked a Ruth Elizabeth playground team that would roll to the championship of the John L. Sullivan Football League.

"I'd hand off to Joe Scibelli, and he would barrel straight through the line. No deception – he just ran over people," Kingston recalled.

Although a Margaret Street kid named Nick "Skippy" Buoniconti was two years behind them in school, he became their teammate when he made the Cathedral High starting lineup in 1954 as a 14-year-old freshman. A season later, Kingston, Scibelli and Buo-

niconti would play on an undefeated championship team.

The year was 1955, when coach Billy Wise's Purple Panthers went 6-0-1 to win the AA Conference championship in its first year. Kingston quarterbacked a team which also featured George Trepanier, Paul Kononitz and Joe Mahoney in the backfield. That Cathedral powerhouse outscored its opponents 197–78 with Scibelli starting at right tackle and Buoniconti at left guard. The rest of the line included Tom Russo and Davey O'Connell at center, John Sadak at guard, Ed Slinsky at tackle and Sam Groom (later a TV star) and Barry O'Connell at ends. The team's reserves included lineman

Mike Ashe, now the sheriff of Hampden County.

"Looking back, I realize what a special team that was, especially with Nick and Joe in the lineup. I mean, how many high school teams can say they had two guys who went on to play professional football for 14 or 15 years?" Kingston asked.

Not only from one high school team, but from one neighborhood – Springfield's famed Italian-American South End.

At 5-11 and 220 pounds, Buoniconti was considered by pro scouts to be "too small." Ditto for the 6-1, 265-pound Scibelli, whom they figured to be "undersize" for a spot in a pro offensive line. Despite the naysayers, they both got drafted, and had long and illustrious careers. Buoniconti played 183 pro games, Scibelli 202.

After serving as team captain at Notre Dame in the 1961 season, Buoniconti got his chance at pro ball because Boston Patriots coach Mike Holovak liked his quickness as well as his toughness. The Patriots, then playing in the fledgling American Football League, took Buoniconti in the 13th round of the 1962 draft.

He went on to play seven seasons with the Patriots, making the All-AFL first team five times. Prior to the 1969 season, the Patriots made a bad move. They traded Buoniconti to the Miami Dolphins for backup quarterback Kim Hammond and linebacker John Bramlett – players who would have little impact on their new team. Although Buoniconti was stunned by the trade at first, he again made the most of his opportunity and became a key player on two Super Bowl championship teams. The 1972 Dolphins went 17-0 – the only perfect season in NFL history.

In 1973, Buoniconti established a Miami season record for tackles with 162. His nose for the ball led to a nickname, "Secretary of the Defense."

In his first season with the Dolphins, he earned his team's Most Valuable Player Award. He also gained that honor in 1970 and '73. When he retired after the 1975 season, he could look back on a career which included two trips to the Pro Bowl.

In 1990, the Dolphins named him to their silver anniversary team, and in '91, they made him part of the franchise's honor roll. Ten years later, Buoniconti received the ultimate honor when he was elected to the Pro Football Hall of Fame in Canton, Ohio.

In 2012, his football career came full circle when he returned to Cathedral for the unveiling of a "Hometown Heroes" plaque donated to the school by the NFL in his name.

Scibelli never had the good fortune to play on a championship team in the NFL, but he did play on five division winners with the L.A. Rams.

In April of 1960, Scibelli was drafted by the Rams and the New York Titans of the new AFL. He chose to sign with the established league, and soon made his mark as a lineman who had the quickness and power needed to block for the run and protect the passer.

Wearing No. 71 for his entire career, Scibelli became a fixture in offensive lines that also featured Charley Cowan, Ken Inman, Marlin McKeever and Tom Mack. Cowan once said that Scibelli was the kind of teammate "you'd want to go to war with."

Playing for big-name coaches

George Allen and Chuck Knox, Scibelli captained the Rams for the last 10 years of his career. In five of those seasons, he earned his team's MVP award. Other honors: The Pro Bowl in 1968, All-Pro in 1973, and the Rams' all-time team.

In 15 seasons, Scibelli missed only eight games, and seven of those came in 1969, when he missed half the season because of an injury.

He retired after the 1975 season — the same year that his friend, Buoniconti, ended his career.

Scibelli returned to his hometown and went into the produce distribution business. On Dec. 12, 1991, he died of cancer at the age of 52.

Nick and Joe. They came a long way from those Cathedral football days of the '50s, when they would practice at Emerson Wight playground, in the heart of their beloved South End.

Honoring Archie Roberts

WHEN ARCHIE ROBERTS WAS GROWING UP IN HOLYOKE, the city had no organized football program for kids.

No Pop Warner League. No uniforms. No helmets. No shoulder pads. No coaches, either.

Imagine that − no coach, even though Archie's father of the same name happened to be the head honcho of Holyoke High School's football program. Dad also happened to be a gifted athlete, an All-America backfield man and baseball star in his years at New York University.

Despite all that, Archie's father never pushed him to play sports. In his early years, he was more interested in playing cowboys and Indians, and that was OK.

The time did come, though, when Archie and his neighborhood friends decided they wanted to play some football. They would get together on Sunday mornings at whatever field they could find, for pickup games.

From that simple beginning emerged one of the all-time great athletes in the history of Western Massachusetts sports.

Once young Archie got the sports bug, it quickly became apparent that he could play anything, and play it well. He went on to lead championship high school teams as a quarterback in football and point guard in basketball (both in 1959), and from there to a starry career as the last three-sport athlete to play at Columbia University in New York.

All of that, and a brief time in the National Football League, merely served as prelude to an illustrious career as a heart surgeon.

After retiring in 1997 as an active surgeon, he founded the Living Heart Foundation, which uses mobile methods to screen patients for cardiovascular risks and raise awareness about heart disease.

The remarkable life and work of Dr. Arthur Roberts – now a 69-year-old resident of Little Silver, New Jersey – will be duly saluted on December 9, when he receives the National College Football Foundation's Distinguished American award.

The presentation will take place at the National Football Foundation's 54th annual dinner at the Waldorf-Astoria in New York City.

"Dr. Roberts stands as a living testament to the NFF's mission of building leaders through football," said Steven Hatchell, the foundation's president/CEO. "A standout student/athlete at Columbia, he has continued to excel throughout his life, becoming one of the nation's leading heart surgeons and a pioneer in the research and prevention of heart disease."

Dr. Roberts will become the fortieth recipient of the Distinguished American award. He joins a list that includes Dr. Frank L. Boyden, who was headmaster at Deerfield Academy when Roberts did one year of post-graduate study before entering Columbia.

"I was surprised when I got the call about the award, and even more surprised when I looked at the list of previous winners," Dr. Roberts said. "You wonder how a small-town boy can be part of such a robust membership that includes Dr. Boyden. It's great to be in his company, and great, too, that Western Massachusetts is represented on the list."

Roberts played at Deerfield in the fall of 1960, one season after leading Holyoke High School to a 9-0-0 record and the Class AA Conference title. With Roberts unstoppable as a passer and runner, the Purple Knights outscored their opponents 278–24.

Roberts' Holyoke teammates included two of his neighborhood pickup-game buddies, Pat Sheehan and Bob Burke.

Sheehan joined Roberts at Columbia, and became a doctor.

Burke starred at UMass as a guard, then went into teaching and coaching. In 2006, he retired as director of athletics at American International College.

"Archie was just a really good athlete when we were kids – way better than the rest of us," said Burke.

"The guys we played with went to John J. Lynch Junior High. They had a ninth-grade team, coached by Phil Hart (an AIC Little All-America in his day). We were in seventh grade, but we made the team."

When Holyoke capped its dreamy 1959 season with a 36–6 Thanksgiving morning victory over arch-rival Chicopee, the elder Archie Roberts retired after twenty seasons on the job. When Archie the younger went to Deerfield, he played for another WMass coaching legend, Jim Smith.

"What I remember most about my father as a coach was his patience in relating to me as his son and his quarterback. He somehow knew how to keep that in balance. He never pushed me too hard, yet he kept me focused on doing as well as I could. Later on, he would say that life presented choices, and it became a question of what are your priorities."

With young Archie, those priorities were clear.

"In my case, I knew by the age of twelve – although I can't imagine why I thought that way – that I wanted to be an NFL quarterback, and a heart surgeon," he said.

"It was a case of having sports as a great short-term goal, but knowing that the final goal is more important."

Roberts did achieve both goals, although he became much more successful as a surgeon than he was as an NFL quarterback.

He did spend two seasons on the Cleveland Browns taxi squad while working out an arrangement that allowed him to simultaneously attend medical school at Case Western Reserve University in Cleveland.

In 1967, he took his one fling at becoming a first-line player, leaving the Browns and getting a leave from medical school, to join the Miami Dolphins, a franchise which had entered the American Football League in 1966 as an expansion team.

"Cleveland had Frank Ryan, and he was a top quarterback. So I tried Miami, not knowing at the time of my decision that, lo and behold, they would be bringing in Bob Griese as a No. 1 draft pick," he said.

Griese, a former Purdue star, became the QB who led the Dolphins to two Super Bowl victories.

"So I played sparingly, and gave up football after that to become a full-time medical student," he said.

Roberts had gotten his chance with the Browns because of a spectacular college career in which he made All-Ivy League three times and set 17 Columbia records and 14 Ivy League marks.

As a junior in 1963, he led the nation in completion percentage (.616). For his three varsity seasons, he accounted for 3,704 yards passing. He also took his turn on defense, playing the safety position.

Roberts made the Playboy All-America team in 1964, his senior football season. He became one of three quarterbacks chosen for the Coaches All-America game alongside Roger Staubach of Navy and John Huarte of Notre Dame.

An academic standout as well, Roberts received the National Football Foundation's scholar-athlete award in 1964.

In baseball, he twice made first-team All-America as a shortstop. In his junior season of 1965 – the first year of the baseball draft – he was told that the Kansas City Athletics were thinking of making him the No. 1 pick in the nation, but they shied away because they knew he wanted to stay in school to continue football, then go to medical school.

"So they took Rick Monday as the first pick," he recalled. "Could I have been a big leaguer? That's something I'll never know."

Although he had been an All-Western Mass. basketball guard in high school, Roberts didn't play in college until one of the coaches talked him into it as a junior.

"I hadn't played since Deerfield. I could still bring the ball up, but I lost that finishing touch – pass, drive or shoot – that a point guard needs. But I did play the full season," he said.

With sports behind him after his one Miami season, Roberts finished preparation for a career in which he would perform more that 4,000 open-heart surgeries and train dozens of young doctors in cardiothoracic surgery. He has written four books on cardiac surgery.

He had held key positions at Northwestern University, the University of Nevada, University of Florida, Boston University Medical Center and Temple University. He also headed the cardiac surgery departments at the Heart Institute of Northeast Pennsylvania, and the Jersey Shore Medical Center.

In 1987, the Columbia Alumni Association presented him with the John Jay Award for distinguished achievement. In 2006, he was inducted with the Columbia Hall of Fame's first class.

Each spring, Roberts returns to his native area to present an award named in honor of his father. The Arthur Roberts Award, which goes to the outstanding high school football student/athlete in Western Massachusetts, is part of a banquet sponsored by the WMass chapter of the National Football Foundation.

"That's a great occasion – a chance to see young people starting out. An exciting and invigorating time," Dr. Roberts said. "I have great memories of Western Mass. I'll never forget the opportunities it gave to me."

Henry Clay, Hall of Famer

BACK IN THE DAY WHEN COMMERCE BASKETBALL was coached by the estimable Tom Collins, he had a backcourt of Billy Fielding and Henry Clay.

They became known as "the Commerce quickies" – undersized guards who could steal the ball and go to the hoop. When it came time for *The Springfield Republican* to pick its all-city team, Fielding and Clay both received honorable mention.

That was the best they could do as seniors in 1953–54, because the high school basketball season was dominated by a Cathedral powerhouse. The Purple Panthers of coach Billy Wise crushed all city opposition, and went 23-0 before losing 53–50 to Hillhouse of New Haven in the New England Tournament final at Boston Garden.

One of Cathedral's guards, Buzzy Connery, grew up with Henry Clay. They played sports together at Ruth Elizabeth playground, then became rivals in high school basketball and baseball.

"I remember one night at the Springfield College Field House, when Buzzy tried to make one of his no-look passes to another friend of mine, John Koljian," Clay recalled. "I wasn't big, and Buzzy figured he could throw it over my head. But I jumped up, stole the ball and made a layup. Buzzy just looked at me as if to say, 'Why you...' "

Clay also played soccer for coach Collins, and baseball for coach Bruno Rumpal.

"I competed hard, but I was by no means a Hall of Famer," he said.

Maybe so, but guess what? He will indeed be a Hall of Famer as of Saturday night, when the Springfield Public Schools Athletic Hall of Fame inducts him as part of its Class of 2012.

Clay's family and friends will be there in the audience at Central High School's gym, watching him go into the Hall of Fame as a contributor. His biggest fan is the former Dena Legon, his high school sweetheart and wife of 56 years.

Henry will become the second member of his family to be honored by the Public Schools Athletic Hall of Fame. His son, Henry III, was enshrined in 2008 in honor of his achievements as a state champion diver in 1977 and '78.

The patriarch of the family was Henry Clay Sr., who served on Springfield's Board of Aldermen in the 1940s.

Henry Clay Jr. is the kind of self-effacing solid citizen who believes that somebody else deserves such an honor more than he does.

"If you talk to Henry, he'll tell you that he doesn't know why the Hall of Fame is doing this," said his long-time friend and co-worker, Commerce boys basketball coach Gary Mindell. "That's just the way he is, but don't listen to him. He really does belong for all he has done as an athlete, coach and administrator in the Springfield school system."

What exactly has Clay done in the field of education? Well, start with the fact that over a career which began in 1962 and ended in 1994, he taught at every school in Springfield – elementary on up.

Not only that, he did just about every job there is in the field of physical education and administration – coach, athletic director, supervisor of health and in his later years, director of physical education, health and safety for the Springfield schools.

Before all of that, Clay went to Springfield College, earned a physical education degree in 1958 and went on to serve in the Navy as a pilot.

"I served until 1962 – the Cuban Missile Crisis kept me on active duty longer than I expected. Then, when I got out of the Navy, I started my teaching career at Buckingham Junior High. I worked with Dave Stratton, and we coached every sport they had at the school. I was there until 1967, when Buckingham closed."

During his early years as a teacher, Clay became an avid road racer.

"I ran a lot, including nine marathons. I ran until my knees gave out," he said.

In 1977, Clay ran into something much worse than bad knees – a life-threatening diagnosis. He developed hairy cell leukemia, an aggressive form of blood cancer which can be fatal.

"They told me I had six or seven months to live. I said, not if I can help it."

Clay underwent chemotherapy and at the same time reaffirmed his strong religious faith. Over the years, he has had to undergo more chemotherapy treatments, and he's still going at the age of 77.

He even has the energy to play golf, with Ludlow Country Club as his home course.

"I won the Super Seniors title at the club last week. That's a fancy name for the Old Goats Division," he said.

That's Henry Clay – from Commerce quickie to super senior, with a lot of stops in between. The next one comes Saturday night, when they hand him his Hall of Fame plaque.

Jack Butterfield — Hockey Icon

Jack Butterfield went straight from the University of Alberta into the Royal Canadian Air Force. It was World War II, and he wanted to do his part.

That he did, flying a Wellington torpedo bomber in combat. His wartime exploits included a crash-landing in England which left him with a broken back.

After surviving all of that, Jack spent the next 20 years working for a stern taskmaster who happened to be his uncle. Yes, Eddie Shore demanded a lot from his employees – especially Jack Butterfield and his sidekick cousin, Ted Shore.

"Name it and we did it," the younger Shore said of the long days and nights he and Butterfield spent together in one of North America's legendary rinks – the Eastern States Exposition Coliseum in West Springfield.

"We did everything in that building except sign the players' payroll checks," Ted Shore said, and he wasn't kidding.

Yours Truly can remember walking into "the old barn" one morning and seeing Butterfield up there among the Coliseum's ceiling girders, changing light bulbs.

"We swept the seats, took tickets, ran the concessions. We even got the place ready for 'Ice Capades' when the show came to town," Ted Shore said.

It was all part of working for Eddie Shore and his Springfield Indians of the American Hockey League.

"Yeah, Jack did it all – he even had time to run my dad's junior hockey program. He did the scheduling, kept the standings, and sometimes he joined me on the ice to referee the games."

Eddie Shore's career in hockey included winning Stanley Cups with the Boston Bruins, Calder Cups with the Indians and finally, election to the Hockey Hall of Fame. Perhaps more important than all of that, though, was his decision to offer the Coliseum to thousands of kids from the ages of 10 to 16 for games in his Greater Springfield Junior Hockey League.

For several hours on Saturday mornings from October to March, they would have the unforgettable opportunity to play where his Indians played on Saturday nights.

Butterfield ran the junior league the way he did everything else – full bore and with total dedication.

While he was doing every job that the rink required, he also served as general manager of the hockey club. At one point, he even served as interim coach.

Butterfield's career in hockey began in the fall of 1945. At that time, Shore was operating in New Haven because the Coliseum was still being used by the Quartermaster Corps, which took it over in World War II.

Butterfield started as New Haven's trainer, a job which happened to be open when he joined his uncle's employ. From there, he went to Fort Worth, Texas, then to Oakland, Calif., to run teams that Shore owned in the U.S. and Western hockey leagues, respectively.

West Springfield became Jack's home in 1949–50, when he started his Coliseum run.

In 1966, when the American Hockey League's presidency became vacant, the Board of Governors looked around and decided that Butterfield would be someone to consider for the job.

"His name was brought up at a meeting, and my father asked the other governors what the salary would be. When he heard the figure, he told them they should pay Jack twice that much, and they agreed."

Butterfield went on to serve the AHL, for 28 years, with the same dedication he had given all through his time at the Coliseum. He established league headquarters locally, and they remain local to this day,

When the World Hockey Association came along in the early 1970s, the new league's presence threatened the stability of the AHL. Butterfield somehow kept it together through trying times, and lived to see it grow to what it is today – a 30-team entity in which each club has an affiliation with a National Hockey League parent.

"It came down to this – if we lost Providence, we would have had only five cities and the league would fold," said Gordon Anziano, who worked with Butterfield in the AHL office for 26 years.

"Jack saved it by orchestrating a deal that brought new owners to Providence, and the league was able to keep going."

Anziano's many memories of Butterfield include his wardrobe.

"He had more cowboy boots than you could count, wore 'em every day. And he always wore a shirt and tie, winter or summer. He even mowed the lawn wearing a shirt and tie," Anziano said.

After Butterfield's retirement as AHL president in 1994, he continued to serve as chairman of its Board of Governors.

Jack Butterfield died October 16, 2010 at the age of 91. His death came only hours before a book signing event in Holyoke in honor of C. Michael Hiam's "Eddie Shore and That Old Time Hockey."

Jack Butterfield was an integral part of all that, a torpedo bomber pilot who came home to a game he always loved.

Rabbit & The Miracle Braves

ALTHOUGH THE FOURTH OF JULY does not always fall at the exact midpoint of a baseball season, it traditionally has been regarded as one of the major mileposts.

If you're in first place on the Fourth, you're in good shape. If you're in last place on the Fourth, forget about it.

Because of such conventional baseball wisdom, Boston's "Miracle Braves" of 1914 rank as one of the great teams in the history of the Grande Olde Game. They became the first to win a pennant after being in last place on July 4.

Making their story even more compelling hereabouts is that two of their key players, shortstop Walter "Rabbit" Maranville and outfielder Les Mann, played sports in Springfield before they entered professional baseball.

The Rabbit – so named because of the way he bounced around the infield – was a home-grown Springfield kid who became a big league regular at the age of 21 and stayed on the job for 23 years (the record for longevity until Pete Rose broke it by playing for 24).

In 1954, he become the first and only Springfield native to be enshrined in the Baseball Hall of Fame. He did not live to see his induction, which took place in August. He died that January 5 at the age of 62.

At its recent "Bring It Home" weekend, Springfield's baseball committee honored his memory by instituting the Rabbit Maranville Cup as top prize of a vintage baseball tournament.

Maranville played, mainly as a catcher, for Springfield High School. Although he stood a mere 5-5 and weighed 155 pounds, he caught the eye of a scout for the Boston Braves while playing for the semipro Springfield Blue Labels, and entered pro ball in 1911 with New Bedford of the New England League. He made a fast rise to the majors a year later.

Maranville relatives still live in the Connecticut Valley. One of them, Darleen Gonyer of Southwick, is a grand-niece of The Rabbit. (Gonyer's grandmother, Frances Sheehan, was his sister). Darleen wrote to *The Republican* after reading a story about the Maranville Cup game at Forest Park.

"I didn't realize there was a Maranville Cup. It was nice to see that Springfield keeps its baseball history alive," she said.

Gonyer, a former three-sport standout at Southwick High School, later coached at both Southwick and Westfield high schools. Her daughter, Kate, also excelled as a high school athlete and played on Junior Olympic softball teams that took part in national competition.

Gonyer treasures a baseball which has been in the family since 1928, when it was signed by Rabbit Maranville and his teammates with the St. Louis Cardinals.

"My father got it after Game 1, and kept it until he moved to Florida, when he handed it down to me. We absolutely are proud of Rabbit. Not many people can say they have a Hall of Famer in the family," she said.

She also has some prized photographs, one of which shows Maranville in his Cardinals uniform.

As for Les Mann, he came here from Lincoln, Neb., to become a student at Springfield College. He first made his mark as a football player on a team that gave the great Jim Thorpe and his Carlisle Indians all they could handle before losing 26–12 in a 1912 game on the gridiron at SC's old Pratt Field. In baseball, Mann's speed and quick bat made him a player sought by the pros. He went straight from SC's campus to the big leagues, just in time to be part of that 1914 miracle.

And what was so miraculous about those Braves? Well, their place in baseball lore can best be summed up by a number – 25½.

On the evening of July 4, after losing a doubleheader to Brooklyn, the Braves sat deep in last place with a 26-40 record, 15 games out of first.

By the end of that wondrous season, they not only had taken the pennant, they had done so in a headlong runaway. They finished first by 10½ games – a 25½-game turnaround from where they sat on the Fourth of July.

They ended with a 94-59 record, playing at an unbelievable .728 clip as they went 68-19 from July 5 to season's end on October 6. From September 14 until October 1, they had their hottest streak, winning 17 of 18 (plus three ties called by darkness).

Then they just kept it up, sweeping Connie Mack's favored Philadelphia A's in the World Series. Hank Gowdy, a catcher who would become the first major leaguer to enlist in the Army during World War I, hit .545 for the Braves in the World Series after batting .243 in the regular season.

Maranville regularly batted seventh in lineups made out by manager George Stallings. Yet, he somehow managed to lead the Braves with 78 RBI while hitting .246. He also led them in games played with 156 and plate appearances with 586.

One of Rabbit's teammates also had a wildlife nickname – Possum Whitted. He shared center field with Mann as manager Stallings was one of the early believers in platooning certain players.

Mann bolted the Braves in 1915 to join the Chicago Whales of the Federal League, an upstart organization that lasted only one season. He returned to the National League in 1916 with the Chicago Cubs, and two seasons later, played against the Boston Red Sox in the World Series. Altogether, Mann played 16 years in the majors.

In 1972, he was part of the first class enshrined in the Springfield College Athletic Hall of Fame.

Baseball lessons learned by Maranville from his esteemed middle infield partner, Johnny Evers, served him well in that magical season, and throughout his career. Evers came to the Braves in 1914 at the age of 32 after playing for 12 years with the Chicago Cubs. (He was part of that lyrical double-play combination, Tinker to Evers to Chance, that made the Hall of Fame as a unit in 1946).

The Rabbit, who became known for his "basket catches" of infield popups, had 1,046 fielding chances in 1914. Working with Evers and first baseman Butch Schmidt, Maranville took part in 92 double plays.

The Braves didn't hit much – outfielder Joe Connolly led the team with a .306 average – but they had the kind of blue-chip pitching that can take over a pennant race.

The 1914 "miracle" mainly was the work of Dick Rudolph, Bill James and Lefty Tyler. They never missed a start as lead work-horses on a pitching staff which posted a 2.74 earned run average.

Rudolph, a New Yorker who graduated from Fordham, went 26-10 and gave the Braves 36 starts and 336 innings. It was the best of his thirteen seasons in the majors.

James, known as "Seattle Bill," had an even better year than Rudolph, going 26-7 with 332 innings pitched over 37 starts – and an ERA of 1.90. If there ever was a one-year wonder of pitching, James would be it. His major league career totaled only three seasons, and the other two were nondescript.

Tyler came out of Derry, New Hampshire to pitch for twelve years in the big leagues. He had his best season (19-8) with the Cubs of 1918, but his 16-13 record and 271 innings made him a solid No. 3 for those '14 Braves.

The key to the Braves' comeback was a 34-9 run from July 5 to August 25. That brought them into a tie for first place with the New York Giants. From there, they flew away, going 26-5 in September.

In the American League, the A's won 99 games while featuring their "$100,000 infield" of Stuffy McInnis at first, Eddie Collins at second, Jack Barry (later the Holy Cross coach) at shortstop and Frank "Home Run" Baker at third.

In the World Series, the A's scored six runs in four games as Rudolph and James each went 2-0.

The Braves, meanwhile, scored 16 runs. Along with Gowdy's hot hitting, they got a surprising amount of offense from their middle infielders. Evers hit .438, Maranville .308.

It all added up to the making of a baseball miracle, with a lot of help from good old Springfield, Massachusetts.

Rabbit Maranville as a member of the National League champion St. Louis Cardinals of 1928 – 14 years after the "Boston miracle." (Photo from *Springfield Republican* archives)

Arresting Development

Not many people know this about Ye Olde Columnist, but I once came scarily close to spending time in a Philadelphia jail cell.

The incident in question happened 52 years ago, but memories of it always come rushing back to me – crystal clear – in the first week of December as Army and Navy prepare for their annual football showdown.

That's because my unforgettable brush with John Law occurred at the Army-Navy game of December 7, 1963. What did that service rivalry clash have to do with little old me?

Well, it so happened that Walter Graham, who ran The Sunday Republican's sports section, had decided to reward me for my work on the Western Mass. high school beat by giving me an opportunity to cover one of college football's prized matchups.

Army-Navy? Yes, that's big-time any time, but it was especially so in 1963, with Navy ranked No. 2 in the country and quarterbacked by Heisman Trophy winner Roger Staubach.

No doubt about it – the Army-Navy game was a "plum assignment" as they say in the sports journalism business. It had perks, too. For instance: To assure that I get to the Philadelphia press box on time, Walter sent me to New York City on the Friday before the game, so I could spend the night in a hotel and grab an early train to Philadelphia in the morning.

Oh, and there was one more perk – a free ticket to the game to go along with my "working press" credential for the pressbox.

The idea was that I could take my wife to the game, and she could have a seat in the stadium while I was working.

Nice idea, except for one thing – my wife didn't enjoy going to football games. I attribute that to a mistake made by me when we were still dating. I talked her into sitting in the stands at Harvard Stadium while I covered the football game against Dartmouth. It was early November – but very cold and windy. While I worked in the warmth of the pressbox. she sat outside, close to frostbite. No more football for her after that one – especially Army-Navy football in December.

So I went to Philly by way of New York alone, with an extra ticket to the game in my pocket.

As ordered by Walter Graham, I arrived at the stadium about three hours before kickoff. Even though it was early, a lot of people milled around outside the stadium, waiting for the gates to open.

I soon realized that some folks were there looking for tickets. Aha, I mused – here's a chance to do my good deed for the day.

As I surveyed the crowd around me, I noticed a well-dressed gentleman, standing alone.

I went up to him and said, "Need a ticket?"

"How much?" he asked.

"Nothing – it's a free ticket. I don't need it and I don't want it to go to waste."

He studied the ticket carefully, then opened his overcoat and showed me his badge...You guessed it. I had just offered a precious Army-Navy football ticket to a Philadelphia police detective.

"You don't know how close you came to going downtown with me." he said. "Good thing you said the ticket was free. Otherwise, you're a scalper and you're under arrest."

At that point, I somehow regained enough composure to stammer an explanation. I showed him my press credential, and he told me to put the free ticket in my pocket and stay out of trouble.

Whew...it took a while for me to get over that close call. Instead of covering the game, I could have been calling Walter Graham to bail me out of jail.

Oh, well, it all worked out. I finally settled into my pressbox seat (by the way, next to esteemed columnist Shirley Povich of the Washington Post). I proceeded to see a thriller as Navy beat Army 22–15. The game ended with Army on the Navy two-yard line and unable to get a play off.

The following   Monday, Walter Graham walked into the sports department and asked me how I liked covering Army-Navy.

"A great game, a great assignment," I said, trying to avoid eye contact.

No, I never did tell him how close I came to missing the whole darn thing.

Bruce Laird and 'Makers of the Game'

Bruce Laird twice made the Associated Press Little All-America team when he played football at American International College in Springfield.

From there, he went on to a 12-year NFL career as a strong safety and kick returner. He spent 10 seasons with the Baltimore Colts, two with the San Diego Chargers.

Laird succeeded in a violent game even though he never weighed more than 193 pounds.

"Heck, I didn't get to 190 until I was 23 years old," he said.

Now, at age 62, he's still in the football trenches, working every day on behalf of retired NFL players – "the makers of the game," as he calls them.

One of those "makers" – Hall of Fame tight end John Mackey – suffered from dementia toward the end of his life. He passed away July 6, 2011, at the age of 69.

As a rookie out of Syracuse University, Mackey became the prototype of the modern-day tight end, bringing speed and pass-catching ability to a position which previously had been used mainly for blocking.

Mackey's problems in later life illustrate the need for the NFL and all levels of sports to pay closer heed to the long-lasting effect of concussions on athletes.

In 2010, Sylvia Mackey pledged to donate her husband's brain upon his death to a Boston University School of Medicine study of brain damage in athletes. The university's Center for the Study of Traumatic Encephalopathy researches potential links between repeated concussions and CTE (chronic traumatic encephalopathy), a condition which mirrors symptoms of dementia and Alzheimer's disease.

"Here was a great player, one who served as president of the union at the time of the merger with the American Football League (1970)," Laird said.

As first president of the post-merger players' union, Mackey fought for improved salaries and benefits. As the Baltimore Sun reported, Mackey organized a strike in July of 1970 that resulted in an additional $11 million in pensions and benefits.

It was Mackey's struggle with dementia that caused Laird and other Colts alumni to rally behind him in 2005, when he was forced to move into an assisted living center, whose monthly costs exceeded his NFL pension.

"We galvanized the Baltimore chapter (of the NFL Alumni Association)," Laird said. "It wasn't on anybody's agenda until we brought it up."

As a result of the Baltimore initiative, the NFL and the NFL Players Association have adopted "the 88 plan" – named for Mackey's uniform number – which provides yearly financial assistance for nursing home care and adult day care.

"We made it happen. It wasn't even on their radar," Laird said.

The "we" Laird refers to is an organization known as Fourth & Goal, which he started. It engages in an ongoing dialog with commissioner Roger Goodell to change the pension and disability system and to gain representation for retired players. Fourth & Goal's effort have been instrumental in incremental enhancements to benefits for retired players and their widows. That includes those who suffer from Alzheimer's or dementia, Mackey did.

Laird serves on Fourth & Goal's large board of directors, whose membership includes Hall of Famers Maxie Baughan, Joe DeLamielleure, John Hannah and Sam Huff.

"Maxie Baughan was my coach in Baltimore. He's been instrumental in our efforts from the start," Laird said.

Baughan, one of the NFL's all-time great linebackers, played on the Philadelphia Eagles' championship team of 1960. He spent 12 years in the league.

After retirement, he became defensive co-ordinator for the Colts, with Laird coming under his tutelage on teams that won AFC East titles in 1975, '76 and '77.

In his work with Fourth & Goal, Laird displays the same kind of dedication that enabled him to overcome the long odds he faced as an NFL rookie from a Division II school.

However, he wasn't all that surprised when he made it in Baltimore's training camp of 1972. Not surprised, because of something his football coach at Scituate High School had said to him prior to his senior season.

"He told me I had the tools to play at a higher level. And he wasn't talking about college – he was talking about the NFL. I don't know what he saw in a skinny, 160-pound defensive back."

That coach, John "Butch" Mahoney of Quincy, played for Gayton Salvucci at AIC in the late '50s and had one season (1961) as a cornerback for the Boston Patriots, then of the American Football League.

Because of his size, Laird was ignored by Division I schools – but he had Mahoney on his side.

"He went to bat for me, called Gayton (Salvucci) and got me into AIC," Laird said.

"I cherish those years I spent up there on State Street in Springfield," he said. "It wasn't just about football. It's about the great people I met there, the great teammates I had, the wonderful professors, and the dear friends I still have."

In his AIC varsity years, Laird played on teams that generally were outnumbered.

"We didn't have depth, but our guys knew how to play a hard-nosed game. Our first 22 could play against anybody."

After his senior season, Laird had the opportunity play in the North-South Shrine game in Miami.

"I have to admit, I was intimidated, coming out of a small school. But then I began to realize it wasn't anything different, and I turned out to be the second-best running back on the team."

Laird's trip to the North-South game caught the attention of NFL scouts. He wound up being drafted in the sixth round. Chalk one up for Butch Mahoney.

Then it was on to a 164-game NFL career in which Laird had 19 interceptions as a defensive back and 3,748 yards as a kick returner.

In addition to his efforts on behalf of Fourth & Goal, Laird is involved with the Baltimore Ravens as their "uniform compliance" officer. His responsibility at each home game is to make sure jerseys are properly tucked in, socks are pulled up – and, more importantly, that there are no copyright infringements with the NFL logo.

Although he works closely now with the Ravens, Laird is still a Baltimore Colt at heart. He does not forget those years, and he especially remembers his great teammate, John Mackey – the inspiration for an advocacy program that does so much for so many NFL retirees.

Dream Time for Louie

Note: This column ran in The Springfield Republican on March 9, 1986, three days after Ludlow won the Western Mass. Division III title in high school hockey.

It was the early '70s, and one Edwin "Soupy" Tulik of Ludlow had a love affair going with the Boston Bruins. Every chance he got, he would be at Boston Garden, cheering for Bobby Orr, Kenny Hodge, Wayne Cashman and Phil Esposito.

God, how he loved those guys.

He wasn't the kind of fan to linger in the background, either. He wanted to meet those players. He wanted to get to know them. He thought of a way to work it out. He would run sports nights for his favorite club, the Polish Vets of Wilbraham. He would invite some of the Bruins to be guest speakers.

Anyone who knows Soupy knows that once he gets a plan going, there is no stopping him. Organize a sports night? Get the Bruins as speakers? In midseason, yet? Most people would quake at the thought, but Soupy just went out and made it happen. With a little help from some of his friends at the State House, he persuaded Orr, Hodge and Cashman to come to Wilbraham.

That was Feb. 17, 1971 – right in the middle of a hot NHL race. There they were, sparkling Bruins stars mingling with folks at the Polish Vets club. Only Soupy could have done it. And to this day, those Bruins players value him as a friend.

On the night of the big visit by the Bruins, Soupy decided that he would like his youngest son to meet them. So he dressed Louie Tulik, 2½, in a Bruins-type jersey and brought him along. Louie had his picture taken with the Bruins players. It was such a nice shot, it made the national wire services.

That sports night had quite an effect on little Louie. For months thereafter, when someone would ask him his name, he would shoot back, "Bobby Orr." It became a standing joke in Ludlow. Soupy's kid thinks he's Bobby Orr. Of course, Louie didn't really think so, but he could dream, couldn't he?

His dreams of being a hockey player were realized early. He lived on Haviland Pond, and by age 4, he was skating on the ice behind his house.

At age 6, he went into Ludlow's junior hockey program. People like Tony Costa and George Archibald worked with him. Later, Cy Chouinard and brothers Mike and Steve Sady helped him with his skating.

All the while, Soupy and his wife, Joan, encouraged their son. Practice at 5 a.m.? No problem. Soupy and Joan would see to it that Louie got there.

When he entered high school, he was small, and he wondered if he could make the team. Coach Rick Malek didn't wonder. He liked what he saw in Louie – a kid who loved to play, and made the most out of what he had.

By the time he reached sophomore year, the Tulik family was not as happy as it had been for so many years. Soupy and his teen-age sons, John and Louie, had to face an awful truth - Joan Tulik was very sick. For months, they nursed her at home. They put a hospital bed in the middle of the living room. They gave her all the love and attention they could muster.

On Jan. 6, 1984, Joan Tulik died of cancer at the age of 50. The family was devastated, but they carried on. Louie didn't feel like playing hockey, but he eventually decided to go back to it, and give it his best. She would want him to do that.

Because of his big heart and burning love for the game, he became a favorite of his teammates. Hey, he scored only three goals in his senior season, but so what? Louie was their kind of guy, always willing to work hard for the good of the team.

That was OK, but Louie always had been a dreamer, remember? He often fantasized about scoring the winning goal in a big game.

Now it was Thursday night, overtime in a classic duel between Ludlow and a gutsy Putnam Vocational team. Craig Falconer had the puck at center ice, but he lost control of it momentarily. At the same time, he saw a teammate breaking free, so he did the only thing he could do under the circumstances. He kicked the puck as hard as he could, well out ahead of a hard-skating Louie Tulik.

It turned out to be a perfectly-timed pass. Louie picked it up and streaked toward the goal. In one instinctive move, he pulled the goaltender out of position and lifted the puck over him and into the net.

In that shining moment, Ludlow won the Western Mass. Division III championship, and Louie Tulik lived his dream.

As he said after the game, the dream was not his alone.

"This one was for my mother," he said.

Postcript: Louis Tulik, 48, now works as a detective-sergeant in the Ludlow Police Dept. His father passed away Oct. 7, 2011, at the age of 84.

Where Are They Now – Dan Della-Giustina

IT'S 65 YEARS AND COUNTING SINCE DAN DELLA-GIUSTINA played for Springfield Tech in the Western Mass. Interscholastic Basketball Tournament.

All that time, and one name still sticks in his mind: Athol.

"Athol. Yeah, we lost to Athol in overtime. If we played 'em ten more times we would have beaten 'em ten times. But..."

Della-Giustina's Tech team featured John Jeffries –the region's No. 1 high school player and leading scorer of that 1947 season. His other teammates were outstanding, too – Bob Raymond and Alex Korbut as forwards; Al Colonna, Willie Searleman, Bob Maggi and Bob Scagliarini in the backcourt.

Yet, an unknown underdog from the north country of Western Mass. walked into the Cage at the University of Massachusetts and scored a first-round knockout against a 16-1 Tech team, coached by Johnny Kalloch, that had breezed undefeated through the Interschool League.

"Twenty-five seconds to go in overtime, and a kid named Norman Walsh hit from outside with the winning basket – and those were his only points of the game," Della-Giustina recalled.

Now, at the age of 83, Della-Giustina has another reminder of that tourney upset.

"One of my grand-daughters, Robin, got married recently, and you know what – the guy is from Athol. Can you imagine that?"

Actually, he gets a big laugh out of it. Athol, after all, is merely one of the countless memories Della-Giustina has of growing up in Springfield's South End, playing sports at Tech and American International College, coaching at the high school and college levels

– and then advancing to the chairmanship of a department at West Virginia University.

He's a senior citizen – but his career goes on.

"I was department chair for 18 years. Now I still work every day, teaching in the graduate school," he said.

Altogether, Della-Giustina has taught at WVU for 35 years.

His expertise comes in the field of safety and environmental management, in which he holds a doctorate. He has written textbooks on the subject. In the corporate sector, his writings are widely used as the foundation upon which company-wide safety programs are built.

In 2004, he was honored by the American Society of Safety Engineers with its President's Award.

He made a stop in his hometown in late May, to attend American International College's commencement. He also took part in an AIC Board of Trustees meeting, a group he has served for 20 years.

"I'd do anything for AIC," he said.

Della-Giustina graduated with the class of 1952, which was noted in the sports realm for a football team starring halfback Gayton Salvucci, a hockey team starring All-East winger Joe Buchholz – and above all, a basketball team that was the first to represent AIC in a national tournament.

AIC now plays in NCAA Division II, but in the '50s it had not yet become an NCAA member. Instead, its teams belonged the National Association of Intercollegiate Athletics.

The Yellow Jackets of 1951–52, coached by Nick Rodis, earned a spot in the NAIA's New England playoffs, with a berth in the 32-team national tournament in Kansas City at stake.

The regional was played at Colby College of Waterville, Maine. The host team stood 29-1 and rated as big favorites to win the regional, but AIC pulled two upsets, first ousting Providence College (now a Big East member), then taking down Colby.

Della-Giustina's AIC teammates included Bert Butters of Ludlow, Al Zordan, Ray Mrozack, Mickey Seisor, John Meader, Tim Matheson and Harry Collins.

Colby was coached by Lee Williams, who 14 years later would become executive-director of the Naismith Memorial Basketball Hall of Fame in Springfield.

"For years, anytime I ran into Lee, he'd talk about that NAIA game," Della-Giustina said.

Whenever he comes back to Springfield, Dan D looks up old friends, including the man who steered his college decision.

"Yes, Fred Zanetti got me to AIC. He was a real mentor to me," he said.

Zanetti captained AIC's first hockey team and also starred in baseball. He went on to an illustrious career as an educator, eventually having a South End school named in his honor.

While Della-Giustina was doing his practice teaching as an AIC junior and senior, he got his first taste of coaching when he worked with junior basketball teams sponsored by the South End's Our Lady of Mount Carmel parish.

"I had some great kids – Nick Giuggio, Jim Cardaropoli, Willie Manzi, Tom Russo, John D'Angelo and Nick Buoniconti, although he was younger than the other players," Della-Giustina said.

Long before he settled into his role at West Virginia University, Della-Giustina served in the Navy, then completed requirements for a master's degree at AIC.

From 1962 through '68, he worked as athletic director and head coach of football and basketball at Adams High School (which later became Hoosac Valley Regional).

"We had a lot of good kids. One year, we beat Pittsfield High when they had Tommy Grieve at quarterback," he said, referring to one of Berkshire County's all-time great athletes. Grieve went on to become a No. 1 draft pick in baseball, played a 12-year career, then became general manager of the Texas Rangers. He's still with the Rangers as a color broadcaster.

During Della-Giustina's Adams career, he had the opportunity to coach Tom Lamb, whom he regards as "the finest athlete and gentleman I ever coached."

Lamb became football captain at Holy Cross, then the coach of football at Natick High School, where he had a future Heisman Trophy winner, Doug Flutie.

Della-Giustina later coached at Bay City High School and Olivet College in Michigan while at the same time working toward a Ph.D. at Michigan State University.

In 1975, he was hired at West Virginia University, and has been there since.

Della-Giustina has three sons – Dan, John and David.

Dan, a Westfield State graduate, lives in Gardner and works as corporate safety director for a Milford construction company.

John and David both are graduates of the United States Military Academy and both rose to the rank of colonel in the Army. John recently was discharged and now lives in Tuscon, Arizona. He served three tours in Iraq and Afghanistan, and received the Bronze Star for valor. David, who is a medical doctor, also was discharged recently and now serves as director of emergency medicine at Yale-New Haven Hospital.

As he looks at his full life, Dr. Dan can say with conviction, "Athletics have been good to me."

Basketball is still his favorite game, and he has a rising star to follow. That's his grand-daughter, Denise Della-Giustina, who is entering her senior year at Gardner High School. She's regarded among the top talents in Central Mass.

"Denise? Let me tell you, she's a player," her grandfather said.

He should know. He's seen his share of basketball talent – going all the way back to that outside shooter for his least favorite team, Athol High.

Last Game in the Old Barn

They'll be skating at the Eastern States Coliseum this weekend.

Well, not exactly.

The skaters, taking part in a "24 Hours of Hockey" marathon sponsored by the Springfield Falcons and Big Y World Class Markets, won't be skating in the old building. Rather, they'll be playing old-fashioned "pond hockey" on an outdoor rink behind it.

Falcons executive Donnie Moorhouse sees his "24 Hours" promotion as a salute to this area's hockey history.

"By holding the event behind the Coliseum, '24-Hours of Hockey' hopes to pay tribute to the cultural and historical significance of hockey in West Springfield and the region while also introducing the sport to new fans," he said.

While the marathon games run from 2 p.m. Saturday to 2 p.m. Sunday, they stir special memories for a couple of Coliseum veterans – Ted Shore and his wife, Evelyn.

On March 17, 1991, they had the honor of taking a "Last Waltz" skate together on a Coliseum ice surface that would melt into history by the next morning.

As the son of Springfield Indians owner Eddie Shore, Ted first stepped onto the Coliseum's ice in 1939, when he was nine years old. His dad had just purchased Springfield's American Hockey League franchise – while still playing for the Boston Bruins – and

he handed Ted "a new pair of black skates" for the first of his countless times on that beautiful sheet of ice.

Except for a hitch in the armed forces during the time of the Korean War, Ted Shore worked with his dad for three decades as he oversaw the Coliseum's hockey operations.

"I did everything in that building except sign the players' checks. So did Jack Butterfield," Ted said, referring to the man who served as general manager of the Indians before starting a long term as president of the AHL.

Fifty-two years after his first Coliseum skate, Ted brought Evelyn back to the "old barn," where they had met when she was a member of the traveling ensemble for "Ice Capades," a hugely popular show that yearly sold out the Coliseum.

On the final day for the Coliseum's ice-making operation in 1991, Exposition officials opened the building for one last, nostalgia-filled public skating party.

"Later that night, Evvie and I went back. The Zamboni was going, and the ice-making equipment had been shut off. We skated for about 15 minutes," Shore said.

"It was a bittersweet time, because I knew I was saying goodbye to a rink that was my home away from home," said Evelyn, who is native of Pittsburgh.

"I had skated for five years with Ice

Capades at the Coliseum. I literally met my husband on the ice there, and I had the privilege to skate in that old building whenever it was available to me," she said.

Professional hockey left the Coliseum in 1972 when the Indians franchise moved into the new downtown Springfield Civic Center. The Indians did move back there briefly, from 1976 to 1980, and the New England Whalers of the World Hockey Association played some of their games there.

From 1980 to its closing 11 years later, the Coliseum basically served as the No. 1 venue for high school hockey in this area, often hosting state tournament play, as well.

If Ted and Evelyn had the "last waltz," who had the distinction of playing the last game on Coliseum ice?

That would be St. Joseph's of Pittsfield and Westwood High School, teams that met on March 13, 1991, for the 1991 state Division III championship. Westwood won 4–2.

In that Coliseum finale, St. Joseph's was sparked by Marc Salvi, a junior forward. For him, farewell to the Coliseum was prelude to a 1992 season in which he would score a Western Mass. record 55 goals and become the last Berkshire County player to win the Amo Bessone Award, which goes to the region's top player.

Cathedral was the last Connecticut Valley team to skate at the Coliseum. On March 9, 1991, the Purple Panthers beat St. John's of Shrewsbury 3–0 in a state Division II semifinal. Cathedral then lost to Archbishop Williams of Braintree in the state final at Boston Garden.

That 1991 season marked the first for Edgar Alejandro as Cathedral coach. He would carry the school's hockey program to the elite status it now enjoys.

It also was the season of Pat Moriarty, a Cathedral senior who scored 50 goals in 23 games and won the Bessone Award.

Moriarty, who now serves as Cathedral's baseball coach, has vivid memories of playing at the Coliseum.

"There was no better place to play – the history, the tradition, the nostalgia. You'd feel it every time you'd step onto the ice. There was something special about the Coliseum, an unforgettable aroma and atmosphere," he said.

Pat Pompei, son of a beloved hockey writer – Sam Pompei of The Daily News and Sunday Republican –well remembers his years when he virtually "lived" at the Coliseum.

"No question – it was the place to be on Saturday nights," Pat said. "And I'd love to know how many romances and marriages started for couples who had their Saturday dates at the Coliseum."

(My wife Mary and I can attest to that. We had our first Saturday date at an Indians game in January of 1952, and we're now working on our 64th year together).

Over its 65-year history as a hockey venue, the Coliseum hosted countless pro, high school, college, junior and adult league games. It also was the place for skating parties and hours of public skating.

It all began on Dec. 1, 1926, when the Springfield Indians of the Canadian-American League lost 3–1 to the Boston Cubs before a crowd of 4,400. Tex Rikard, widely known as a promoter of heavyweight title fights in New York, dropped the ceremonial first puck marking the arrival of pro hockey in this region.

The Coliseum was erected in 1916 to serve as an arena for agricultural and dairy shows.

In May of 1990, Eastern States Exposition officials, citing the prohibitive costs of maintaining the building's refrigeration equipment, announced that the 1990–91 hockey season would be its last.

Now, long after its ice melted away, skaters are at back at the Coliseum (that is, behind it) for the 24-hour marathon – a touching tribute to a region and a building, rich in hockey history.

Romeo Cyr, 23 Years Later

Forest Park Alaimos 8, Turner Cubs 3.

It happened Aug. 27, 1950 – the day I covered my first "big game" as an 18-year-old cub reporter for The Springfield Union.

Most of the Alaimos and Cubs were no more than 10 years old. Some were as young as eight. They played for the first championship of the John L. Sullivan Pee Wee League, a worthy endeavor started by an irrepressible gentleman named Romeo J. Cyr.

When Romeo wanted something done in the world of local sports, he made it happen by the sheer force of his personality. In this case, he wanted a baseball league for kids just learning to play the game.

Sandlot leagues for the 10–12, 12–14 and 14–16 age groups already were operating in the Pioneer Valley. Their pennant winners would take part in an August tournament sponsored by The Springfield Daily News. Romeo's idea was to augment the sandlot format by letting younger kids get a taste of playing on a team.

In seemingly no time at all, he had pulled together a league that included a total of 10 teams from Springfield, Longmeadow, Chicopee and Holyoke. The 8–10 year-old pee wees played mostly on Saturday mornings, and sometimes during the week. Romeo decreed that the youngsters should play on softball-size diamonds, and that their games should last only five innings.

As that first season unfolded, Romeo latched on to me as his newspaper contact. As I soon learned, no one could say no to him. So it was that Pee Wee baseball became my beat, and a fun beat it was.

As I followed that first season, I was often amazed at how well some of those little kids could play.

Come August, the Pee Wee League had its first playoffs – best-of-three series leading to the championship round. The Alaimos, coached by Russ Perkins, won the title by sweeping Dutch Klett's Turners team. In the clincher, Paul Babineau struck out six and rode to victory behind a seven-run first inning. A few years later, I would cover him again as an ace pitcher for Springfield Tech's Western Mass. champions of 1957.

The Alaimos, sponsored by a market of the same name in the Forest Park section, had a gangly shortstop named Mike Ashe. That Pee Wee season marked the start of a career that would lead him to football and baseball stardom at Cathedral High School, and in later life, to the post of Sheriff of Hampden County. He's still on the job today.

Memories of Russ Perkins, Paul Babineau, Mike Ashe and Dutch Klett came flooding back to me after I received a note from Tom Shea, a former colleague at The Springfield Republican.

"Hard to believe," his note said, "but Romeo has been gone for 23 years."

Hard to believe, indeed. Romeo Cyr passed away May 21, 1993, at the age of 84.

Whoa. That meant Romeo was only 41 years old when he organized the Pee Wee League. Somehow, to a cub reporter, he seemed much older and wiser. Maybe it was because of his special demeanor – the one that let the world know he was in charge, and would get done whatever needed to be done.

Romeo loved hockey as much as he loved baseball. In 1952, he put together an all-star team from Eddie Shore's Saturday morning 12–14 junior league, and won the New England Pee Wee Hockey Tournament at the old New Haven Arena. I remember it well, because I was assigned to cover the championship game. I rode to New Haven on the bus with Romeo and his team, and later found myself stranded in the press box, writing my story while the team bus was long gone back to Springfield. I had to take a train, and missed the victory party.

Even such an event could not dim the admiration I had for the man who liked to be known as "R.J. Cyr." He was probably the most positive person I have ever known.

Often, he would call my office phone and say, "Garry P. Brown, this is R.J. Cyr, and have I got a story for you…"

He did all that work for kids as a volunteer, while maintaining his regular job as a salesman for Nabisco. By the way, I can't imagine a better guy in a sales job.

After his successful Pee Wee experiment, Romeo expanded his vision of kid baseball. Because of him, Mitey Mite, Small Fry and Midget League teams came to Springfield, some of them for kids as young as six years old.

In all of his work on behalf of youngsters, Romeo followed the example set by John L. Sullivan, a long-time benefactor of youth sports in Springfield.

In the fall of 1950, Romeo turned to football, organizing a John L. Sullivan Football League for players 10 to 16. His championship games would be played in an impressive setting – Pynchon Park. In the first football final that I covered, a Ruth Elizabeth team rolled to victory with quarterback Billy Kingston and fullback Joe Scibelli (later of the NFL's Los Angeles Rams) as its unstoppable stars.

Romeo did not forget basketball, either. With the help of Rev. John McNamara at Springfield's Holy Name parish, he started the Catholic Junior

League in 1951. It proved to be the forerunner of Catholic Youth Organization basketball in this area.

In March of 1973, the skating rink in Forest Park was named for Romeo. A fitting gesture, since he had coached youth teams for many years at the Eastern States Coliseum. He also served as general manager of the Springfield Flyers, an amateur team that played in the Atlantic Coast Hockey League of the '40s and '50s.

Yes, Romeo has been gone for 20 years, but those whose lives he touched will never forget. I certainly won't. After all, he's the man who got me my first "big-time" writing assignment – Forest Park Alaimos 8, Turner Cubs 3.

Your Word for Today Is...

It all started with Lady Mary, the eldest and haughtiest of the three Crawley daughters in Masterpiece Theater's television blockbuster, "Downton Abbey."

Somewhat taken aback by the fact that the middle sister showed an affinity for helping out on one of the estate's small farms, Lady Mary said, "It would appear that Lady Edith has found her métier – farm labor."

Wow! I already had become entranced with Lady Mary and her insufferable, aristocratic attitude. Now, she was taking my interest to a new level by showing me the proper usage of "métier," and doing so with an elegant touch of sarcasm.

To appreciate her remark fully, one must note her exquisite and precise pronunciation of the word – that is, "meh-tyA."

Oh, that Lady Mary.

As sometimes happens to people when they try to cope with the mysterious English language, I have had a tendency to confuse certain words – "métier" and "milieu" among them.

Well, Lady Mary certainly cleared that up. Her use of "metier" proved to be just right, because its definition is "vocation, trade; an area of activity in which one excels."

As for "milieu," it actually means "the physical or social setting in which something occurs or develops." No real relation there to "métier," other than the fact that both words come from the French and have a high-falutin' tone about them.

Anyway, I was so impressed by that little scene from "Downton Abbey," I felt compelled to call our daughter Melissa. I knew that she must have seen the same episode, because it was at her suggestion that we began watching "Downton" in the first place. As a Christmas gift, she had given us videos of the first two seasons, and we raced through them to catch up.

As we chatted about Lady Mary and her "métier," Melissa gave me another welcome suggestion.

"Dad, you should sign up for Merriam-Webster's 'word of the day.'"

Of course, she was referring to the venerable Springfield publishing company which specializes in dictionaries and reference books.

So I took her good advice, found the Merriam-Webster website, and now receive daily emails with that precious "word of the day."

Was it blind luck, or fate?

No sooner did I sign up, than the first daily word to reach my mailbox proved to be – you guessed it: "métier." Of all the words in the English language, what were the odds of it coming up at that particular time?

Anyway, I am hooked now, and not just on "Downton Abbey" (Can't wait for next season). I look forward to that daily wordfest with Merriam-Webster, complete with all kinds of additional goodies like quick quizzes, true-false challenges and a test-your-memory segment, in which you're supposed to remember recent words of the day and what they mean.

Sure I do.

What's a quick quiz, M-W style? Well, try this little gem: Add a letter to the word "fast" that will give it a completely opposite meaning.

If you answered "feast," you're a wordmeister of the first rank.

Or, you might be asked for the significance of this sentence: "The public was amazed to view the quickness and dexterity of the juggler."

What's that all about? Well, it happens to be a pangram – a sentence that uses all 26 letters of the alphabet.

Egad.

Can there possibly be a word that has six consonants in a row? Yes, indeed. M-W will tell you that it's "catchphrase."

Well, I never.

Working in the – ahem – 70 and older age group, I scored 2,330 points in a 10-question true-false test in which you are judged not only on correctness, but on speed of answer. Turns out I got three wrong, but my score was about the average (2,310) for the "senior citizen" category.

What did I get wrong? No need to dwell on all three. Let it go with this: It's true that red grapes can be used to make white wine. Hey, who knew?

Now, as I check my email, I see that my latest word of the day is "nascent." Definition: Coming, or having recently come into existence."

This daily language lesson also provides background information, which points out the word's roots and some of the changes which spring from it over time. Nascent, good old M-W tells me, comes from the Latin "nasci," meaning to be born. Over the centuries, it has led to such offshoots as "nee," which came along in the 1700s to identify the maiden or family name of a married woman; and "renaissance," which came along in the 1800s to signify a revival of classical art and literature.

Gotta love those Latin and French roots, eh? I especially love the French influence, probably because my father's family came from Quebec, "la belle province."

All of which might help to explain my fascination with Lady Mary and her wondrous vocabulary. And, in turn, my fascination with the Merriam-Webster website as it helps me become immersed in my métier. Or, is it milieu?

A Farewell To Venus

In my years traveling around ball-parks, hockey rinks, basketball courts and supermarkets, the question would always be the same.

"How's Venus?"

Quite often, that query would come from people I didn't know. They knew me because of Venus the Labrador retriever, a beautiful family dog whose escapades and foibles became standard fare in my weekly "Hitting to All Fields" columns in The Republican's sports section.

A typical reference to her behavior would go like this: "Venus the Labrador retriever will steal your breakfast sandwich." (Yes, she did that, when a half-asleep family member made the mistake of leaving his food on the counter while turning his back on her).

The "How's Venus?" question often came from elderly ladies, who would freely admit that they neither knew nor cared about sports. As one said, "I just turn to the sports page every Wednesday to see how Venus is doing."

Hey, no wonder. We could always count on her to do something down-right cute, downright wacky or down-right likely to land her in the doghouse, so to speak.

One day, our son rushed her to the vet after she had devoured almost a whole roasted chicken. Another time, she got caught napping on a new sweater belonging to the lady of the house. Then there was the day she nearly electrocuted herself by chomping on a lamp cord. Luckily, my wife came upon that scary scene – and turned off the power just in time.

So it would go, day after day, week after week... Venus making mischief – or worse – and giving Ye Olde Columnist something to write about.

Altogether, Labrador retrievers have provided me with column material for decades. We had two of them – a black named Sparky and a chocolate named Koko – back-to-back for a total of 23 years. Then, in 2003, Venus came into our lives when our son rescued her from a shelter. She took up residence in Amherst and became a much-loved companion to three of our grandchildren, who were ages 11, 8 and 6 when she moved into their house.

She was theirs throughout their growing-up years. Her antics made them laugh every day, and her warm body gave them comfort whenever they needed a hug.

To us, she was a precious "grand-dog," always ready to greet us with tail wildly wagging when we'd visit.

Throughout all her Amherst days, and during each of her "vacations" at our house, Venus most enjoyed her morning walks. Along the way, she sometimes would come upon delicacies like half-eaten pizza slices and bagels (all the better if they came with cream cheese).

One day, she found an entire frozen baguette, half-buried in snow. She picked it up and made a U-turn for home, carrying it between her teeth. Another time, she became fascinated by a milk carton, which had been flattened by traffic. She insisted on carrying that home, too.

Quite often, she would meet mail-carriers, who came to be her good friends. She could always count on them for dog biscuits, kind words and scratches behind the ears.

Ah, those velvety soft ears. Whenever we would visit her, my wife would stroke them, and Venus would stay still so she could have more.

All of that behavior would provide material for my column, but the Labrador retriever references stopped as of Nov. 4. For the first time in 12 years, Venus was not mentioned.

That morning, I received a phone call and three e-mails, each asking, "Where's Venus?" Each expressed hope that she would be back in print soon.

Sad to say, she will not be back. She became quite ill midway through October. Her veterinarian diagnosed her with an inoperable tumor, and there was little to do except keep her as comfortable as possible, with hope that medication might stabilize her condition.

It was not to be. On Nov. 2, Venus had to be put to sleep.

Now, as we store away precious memories of her as a beloved member of the family, we all can take solace in the fact that Venus had so many faithful readers - along with 1,096 Facebook friends from faraway places. (Yes, she had her own Facebook page).

"Where's Venus?"

In our hearts, to stay.

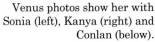

Venus photos show her with Sonia (left), Kanya (right) and Conlan (below).

From the Family Scrapbook

Photographs on this page, and the next one, come from the Brown family scrapbook. Just a way of saying thanks for the memories.

Acknowledgments

THIS BOOK COULD NOT HAVE HAPPENED without the advice and expertise offered to me by Richard Andersen – Springfield College professor, author and family friend.

Many thanks also go to executives of *The Springfield Republican* – publisher George Arwady, executive editor Wayne Phaneuf, managing editor Cynthia Simison and production editor Vernon Hill. Because of their encouragement and guidance, I'm still writing long after my retirement from full-time newspaper work. I'm also forever grateful to Angela Carbone, whose American International College adult-education class in memoir writing inspired me to try many of the columns that appear in this book.

– Garry Brown

Epilogue

I'VE BEEN A FAN OF GARRY BROWN'S SINCE CHILDHOOD; growing up in Northampton and being a Boston Red Sox fan, I read his stories and columns first in *The Morning Union* as a child and teenager. I became a co-worker when I joined the staff of the Springfield Newspapers in the late 1970s and continued an avid reader. In 2002, I was fortunate enough to be asked by Garry to team up with him for a series looking at the future of Fenway Park; in short, it wound up being a dream come true to both work side-by-side with Garry and get an inside look at Fenway and the Red Sox. I learned firsthand how well respected he is among his sports-writing peers and the leadership of the Red Sox (to say nothing of many players from back in the day.) These days, I get to edit his columns, but, in truth, he rarely needs editing. It's now a great joy and privilege to be able share his writing from retirement. To say that Garry is a legend is no overstatement of how he's viewed by readers of *The Republican* – and me.

Cynthia G. Simison
Managing Editor
The Republican
January 2016

Author Biography

GARRY BROWN joined *The Spring-field Union*'s sports department in May of 1950, and went on to a 59-year sportswriting career, all of it as an employee of The Springfield Newspapers.

He began by covering Pee Wee League baseball, then moved on to become the paper's high school beat writer. In 1969, he was named sports editor of *The Union and Sunday Republican*, a role he served for twelve years. When the Springfield morning and evening papers merged into *The Union-News*, he moved back to writing and became the paper's Boston Red Sox beat writer in 1986. He covered the Red Sox until May 10, 2009, when he worked his last day in the Fenway Park press box.

He retired from full-time work in June of 2009, but he continues to contribute columns and feature articles to *The Springfield Republican* as a free-lance writer.

In November of 1973, he started writing a weekly "Hitting to All Fields" column, which has become his signature work, still going 43 years later.

He grew up in the Indian Orchard section of Springfield, and graduated from Technical High School. He graduated from American International College in 1955, completing his studies while working nights full time. In 2014, he received an honorary doctorate from American International College.

Garry and his wife, the former Mary Helen Bukowski. have been married for 63-plus years, and live in Wilbraham. They have three children and four grandchildren.